The Boy Who Felt No Pain

Also by Robert Marion, M.D.

The Intern Blues: The Private Ordeals of Three Young Doctors

Born Too Soon (a novel)

The Boy Who Felt No Pain

• • •

Robert Marion, M.D.

Addison-Wesley Publishing Company, Inc.
Reading, Massachusetts   Menlo Park, California   New York
Don Mills, Ontario   Wokingham, England   Amsterdam   Bonn
Sydney   Singapore   Tokyo   Madrid   San Juan

Library of Congress Cataloging-in-Publication Data

Marion, Robert.
   The boy who felt no pain / Robert Marion.
      p.   cm.
   ISBN 0-201-55049-0
   1. Pediatrics—Case studies.   2. Sick children—Biography.
   I. Title.
   RJ58.M38   1990
   618.92'009—dc20   90-31289
                                                        CIP

Jacket design by Paul Bacon
Text design by Sherry Streeter
Set in 11-point Bauer Bodoni by DEKR Corp., Woburn MA

ABCDEFGHIJ-MW-93210
First printing, July 1990

Contents

Once you start studying medicine,
you never get through with it.
—Charles H. Mayo

Preface

• • •

AS A PEDIATRIC GENETICIST, I've spent most of my professional life caring for children with congenital malformations. In most cases, the disorders that afflict my patients are rare and, as such, each child I see is pretty much a "textbook unto himself."

Making a diagnosis in a patient with a group of congenital disorders is like putting together the pieces of a jigsaw puzzle. The task of taking a series of seemingly unconnected signs and symptoms with which a patient presents, and assembling those signs and symptoms into a single entity, an established syndrome that's caused by a known etiologic agent, is always a challenge.

But making the diagnosis is truly only the beginning. Following many of my patients over a long period of time, watching them grow and develop, seeing them persevere and thrive against all odds, has been, to say the least, awe-inspiring. What makes the people who I've written about here so distinctive, what has made these patients and their families stand out so in my memory, is the fact that in every case, from every involvement, I have continued to learn important lessons.

The lessons have been very different and have been taught under rather unusual circumstances. Some patients, such as James Stone Jr. ("The Boy Who Felt No Pain"), Alex Hernandez ("Alex Goes For a Walk"), and Denise Sanderson ("Denise Gets Discharged"), taught me, through their lives, about the resiliency of children, and how, in spite of what we physicians may believe about their poor chances for recovery or survival, they can, and often do, bounce back.

Working in clinical genetics, I rapidly came to recognize that, very often, the patients who need the most attention are not the child with the disease, but rather their parents, or in some cases, others who aren't even relatives. There are those children for whom the situation is so dire, the disorder so utterly hopeless, that there is little we as physicans can do. In these cases, as occurred in the stories of Meghan McGuinness ("The Most Unselfish Thing") and Tanya ("Angela's Eyes"), attention had to be focused on the survivors, people whose lives had been torn apart by the impending deaths of these children.

But mostly, from my patients, I've learned, as one of my former students said, "how to be a Doctor with a capital D." For instance, from Cassandra Giovanni ("Galactosemia"), I have learned never to take anything, no matter how seemingly reliable, for granted. From working with the families of both Sarah Hamilton ("Teaching Rounds") and Molly Richmond ("Two Videotapes"), I had the chance to recognize that the people who come to my office—parents often undergoing the most serious crisis of their lives—are not the same people they were prior to that crisis; each has led other, separate lives during simpler times, lives I've only rarely had the opportunity to glimpse. And, from experiences with my own daughter ("Jaundice"), and with Theo Papadapoulas ("Theo and the Octopus"), I have learned that it's occasionally okay to let go and relax, and not worry as much as I usually do.

Although they are not arranged in chronological order, these stories span my career, from my earliest days of medical school, when I first laid eyes on Denise Sanderson ("Denise Gets Discharged") in the hallway of Jonas Bronck Hospital, to just a few weeks ago when I last checked Molly Richmond ("Two Videotapes"). There are stories from my third and fourth years of medical school ("The Boy Who Felt No Pain" and "Galactosemia"), my internship in Boston (part of "Jaundice"), my pediatric residency in the Bronx ("Alex Goes for a Walk"), my fellowship in human genetics ("Angela's Eyes"), and my life after training, as director of the Center for Congenital Disorders at a major teaching hospital in the Bronx, New York ("Peter and Paul" and "The Most Unselfish Thing").

All of the stories that follow are based on real cases. To provide the children and their families with as much anonymity as possible, a number of details have been altered. Additionally, the names of the hospitals, physicians, and staff members have all be changed. In spite of these alterations, however, this is a work of nonfiction; the basic facts in each story remain true to life.

This book was written with the help and cooperation of a large group of people. First, there are the people who form the basis of my stories, my patients; without mentioning their names, I'd like to thank each of them, as well as their parents and family members, for allowing me to enter their lives.

Next, this book would not have been possible without the help of my teachers who led me toward, and prepared me for, my life in academic medicine. Specifically, I'd like to thank some of my mentors at the Albert Einstein College of Medicine: Lewis Fraad, Andrew P. Mezey, Steven P. Shelov, Celia Henerofsky, and Michael I. Cohen.

Finally, I want to thank my wife, Beth, for her love and encouragement; my children, Isadora, Davida, and Jonah, for allowing me the time to write; my agent, Diana Finch, for once again leading me down the right path; and my editor, Nancy Miller, her husband, Stephen Kling, and their children, Benno and Sam, who, over the years, have been a lot more than just friends.

To my children,
Isadora, Davida, and Jonah,
who have taught me how to be their father.

And to the children I've cared for
during my career, who have taught me, and
continue to teach me, how to be their physician.

The Boy Who Felt No Pain

The Boy Who
Felt No Pain

● ● ●

I FIRST MET JAMES STONE, JR., in the pediatric emergency room
at Jonas Bronck Hospital, a municipal facility in the Bronx, New
York. The boy, eight months of age, had been brought to the hospital
by ambulance after suffering what was thought to be a prolonged
and serious convulsion. According to his mother, Jimmy had been
sick for a few days with intermittent bouts of high fever. Mrs. Stone
hadn't been very concerned about her son until that morning, when
Jimmy hadn't wanted to get out of his crib; he cried whenever his
mother approached him, preferring instead to just lie there alone,
whimpering softly to himself. He had refused to eat breakfast, something he'd never done before. The mother, who had been alone in
the apartment at the time, had given her son some liquid Tylenol
drops, and after a few minutes, Jimmy had fallen off to sleep. An
hour later, however, when she went to check on him, she found the
boy "burning up" with fever. It was at that point that she decided
to wake him and give him a cool bath in an attempt to bring his
temperature down. He had been in the bathtub for only two or three
minutes when the seizure began.

The next few minutes were a blur to Mrs. Stone. She was able
to remember that Jimmy's eyes had rolled back in his head, that his
arms and legs had begun to jerk rhythmically, uncontrollably, and
that, from the sitting position into which he had settled at the begin-

ning of the bath, he had begun to swoon. At about that point Mrs. Stone had grabbed her son and pulled him out of the tub before his head had had a chance to submerge. She had carried him to her bed and, after laying him down, had thrust a pencil into his mouth, in an attempt to prevent him from swallowing his tongue, something she had once heard you were supposed to do when someone was having a seizure. That was all she could think of doing; this was the first time anything like this had happened to her. Jimmy was her only child, and up until that week, he had been in perfect health.

Jimmy's seizure had lasted about fifteen minutes; when the tonic, clonic jerking of his arms and legs had finally stopped, the boy had immediately fallen into a deep, sound sleep. This sleep, a phenomenon that typically characterizes the period following an epileptic seizure, had continued during the entire ambulance ride to the hospital.

Jimmy awoke about twenty minutes after being placed in the trauma area at the back of the pediatric ER. When he regained consciousness, he didn't look terribly ill. But he still had a high fever, and when he was examined by one of the residents, no obvious cause for that fever could be determined. The examining resident believed that while Jimmy had probably experienced nothing more than a simple febrile seizure, a fairly benign condition that's thought to be caused by a rapid alteration in body temperature, he needed to be admitted to the hospital for observation and to rule out the possibility of meningitis, a serious infection of the central nervous system. It was at this point that the resident decided to call me down to the emergency room to pick up my new patient. I was a senior medical student at that time, working the two-month rotation known as subinternship, a requirement for graduation from medical school.

To most physicians, Jimmy Stone's case would have seemed straightforward enough; but to me, with my nearly complete lack of experience and knowledge, everything, including the workup of a child with a simple febrile seizure, was a real adventure. I was hopeless: almost immediately, I realized that blood needed to be drawn and a spinal tap had to be performed, and to say the least, I was not yet technically expert at either of these tasks. To make matters worse, Jimmy was on the plump side, and by that point had pretty much recovered from his post-ictal lethargy; his fever had come down into the normal range, he was awake and alert, and he had become very active. This was not a terrific combination for an inexperienced blood drawer and spinal tapper such as myself. And so, upon arriving with Jimmy at the pediatric ward, I immediately called the senior resident who was covering me that afternoon and begged him for help. After taunting me about my inexperience and, therefore, my total worthlessness as a human being, the resident finally agreed to "hold my hand" while I attempted to perform the required invasive procedures. Accompanied by the resident and a nurse, I left Mrs. Stone behind in the baby's assigned room and carried Jimmy into the ward's treatment room to get the dirty work out of the way.

The nurse prepared to hold the boy down while I nervously set up the equipment to draw the blood. With her just about lying on top of him in order to keep him pinned down on the examining table, I tied a rubber tourniquet around the upper part of Jimmy's right arm. Luckily for both Jimmy and me, a large vein was visible through the skin covering the antecubital fossa of the elbow. "A pipeline!" the resident announced. "You can't miss! A gorilla could get blood out of a vein like that."

I thanked him for his confidence in me as I swabbed the skin over the vein with three coats of an antiseptic solution, and then I braced myself. Concentrating all my attention on the needle and the vein, I plunged the sharp metal tip under the boy's skin, and relaxed as blood immediately began to fill the tubing connected to the needle. I felt a rush of tremendous relief and pride; I had successfully completed half of the required workup.

The resident and nurse did not congratulate me, however; instead, I found them staring at the baby with puzzled looks on their faces. "That's strange," the nurse said as I pulled back on the syringe's plunger. Blood began bubbling up.

"He didn't budge," the resident agreed. "Not an inch. And he didn't scream. I've never seen that happen before."

He was right. Instead of letting loose the bloodcurdling shriek that would be expected from a baby whenever an invasive procedure was being performed, Jimmy was smiling at the nurse and cooing something that sounded like "Da da ba ba."

I squirted samples of the blood into all the specimen tubes I had gathered before starting, and then turned my attention to preparing for the spinal tap. "I don't understand it," the resident added. "That was unnatural. Let's see what happens when you stick a needle into his back."

I didn't reply; I was concentrating on my work. While I had drawn blood a few times before, I had never successfully performed a spinal tap on anyone, child or adult. So with the nurse loosely holding Jimmy on his left side, and with the resident standing directly behind me, I nervously prepared the skin on Jimmy's lower back for the procedure. When all was ready, I said, "Okay. Here goes nothing."

The long, sharp needle passed through the skin of the baby's back. But again, rather than shrieking, the boy continued on with his monologue: "Da da ba ba." And then he actually began to laugh at the nurse.

"This is strange," she said again. "I'm not really holding him at all. He seems to like lying on his side like this. It's as if he doesn't feel a thing."

"He definitely doesn't feel a thing," the resident responded. "I've never seen anything like it."

I was distracted by their discussion, but even had there been utter silence, I would have been completely lost. I didn't know what the hell I was doing or whether the needle was anywhere near the spinal canal, the cavity that houses the all-important spinal fluid. "Need help?" the resident asked, pulling on a pair of sterile gloves.

I didn't answer; I simply moved out of the way and let him take over. "At least you didn't hurt the kid," the resident said as he directed the needle into the spinal canal. As soon as he removed the trocar from the spinal needle, crystal-clear fluid began to fill its hub, without any trace of the cloudiness that usually indicates a serious infection.

The resident drained off just enough fluid to do all the tests required to rule out meningitis. "If this kid's got meningitis, I'll eat my beeper," he said to me as he pulled the needle out of Jimmy's back. "He does have something, though, and I have no idea what it is. Let's go talk to his mother."

After the nurse and I had made some attempt at dressing the child, I carried him out to his room. Mrs. Stone, greatly relieved to see us, and more relieved to see her happy son, rose as we came closer. "Is everything okay?" she asked.

"Everything seems to be fine," the resident responded. "We did all the tests we needed and it looks as though the baby's going to be all right. But we did notice something unusual about Jimmy. Have you ever noticed anything strange about him?"

"Strange?" Mrs. Stone asked. "What do you mean?"

"Well, he didn't complain or cry when we were taking his blood and spinal fluid. Have you ever noticed whether things seem to hurt him?" the resident asked.

"Oh, no, nothing ever hurts Jimmy," the woman answered, taking the baby from my arms. Back with his mother, Jimmy was saying "Da da ba ba" again, and smiling broadly. "He's a good boy. He never cries at all. Does that mean there's something wrong with him?"

"No . . . well, I'm not exactly sure what it means," the resident answered. "It isn't something that we usually see in babies of this age, though."

"My husband says not feeling pain should give Jimmy a special edge in the world," she responded. "He says Jimmy could grow up to be a football player or something like that, because a football player who doesn't feel pain would probably be really great. Do you think that's possible?"

"I guess it's possible," the resident answered. "I think we'll need to do some tests to figure out exactly why Jimmy doesn't feel pain, though. We're going to ask another doctor, a neurologist, to come around and see the baby, if that's all right with you." She nodded.

"Call neurology, stat!" the resident ordered after we had left the baby's room. "I'm dying to hear what Myklos has to say about this."

•   •   •

As ordered, I immediately went to the nurses' station, called Abe Myklos, the pediatric neurologist, and told him we needed a stat consult on a patient who had just been admitted. He said he'd get over to the ward as soon as he could. While I waited, I daydreamed about what life might be like for someone who felt no pain: no headaches, no backaches, no sore throats, no nagging muscle sprains, nothing to interfere with the enjoyment of life. Pain, after all, is one of the most debilitating conditions to afflict us. Much of what medical students are taught during their training, and the majority of time spent by many physicians in their practices, is directed toward the eradication of this single symptom. So to be born with a condition that would allow you to be unable to perceive pain, to be permitted to never have to suffer the agony, frustration, feelings of dependency, and vulnerability that accompany chronic, unremitting pain, to be born the way Jimmy Stone apparently had been born, would appear, at least to an untrained fourth-year medical student, to be a singular, distinctive advantage. For all I knew, Jimmy's father could be right: Jimmy's inability to perceive pain just might allow him to grow up to be a champion football player.

My thoughts were interrupted by the sudden appearance of Abe Myklos. The neurologist was obviously in a hurry; he ran into the nurses' station, shouting, "I got here as soon as I could. Where's the patient? What is it? A seizure?"

Rising from the chair in which I was sitting, I called "Follow me," and led the way out of the nurses' station and down the hall toward the room in which Jimmy had been placed a few minutes before.

Jimmy was alone in the room when we got there. When we reached the crib, the neurologist stopped and looked down at the baby, who was happily sucking on a bottle. When Myklos looked up, he startled me with his anger. "What are you, crazy? There's nothing wrong with this kid. How dare you call me for a stat consult on a baby who's as happy as this?"

A little unsure of myself now, I answered, "I wasn't the one who wanted a stat consult; it was the resident." Then I spoke the sentence that I was sure would stop him cold: "This baby doesn't seem to feel pain."

"You called me stat to see a baby who doesn't feel pain?" he yelled angrily. I had obviously miscalculated his response. "I rushed over here because I thought there was something critically wrong with one of the patients, something like a seizure that couldn't be controlled, and I get here and what do I find? Nothing. Just a patient who doesn't, in the great opinion of . . . what are you, anyway, a subintern?" I nodded my head sheepishly. ". . . In the great opinion of a subintern, a patient who doesn't seem to feel pain." Then he stopped and thought about this for a minute. "What do you mean, he doesn't seem to feel pain?" Relieved, I suspected I finally had his attention.

"This is James Stone," I said. "He's an eight-month-old who was admitted earlier today with a febrile seizure. We couldn't find a source so we did a spinal tap and some blood work. He absolutely didn't mind having either of the needles stuck into him."

"Didn't mind having needles stuck into him?" Myklos repeated, at last eyeing the cooing baby with interest.

"No," I continued. "In fact, he seemed to like it. He even laughed at one point."

"No, that can't be," Myklos said, as he unzipped the pouch he always wore strapped to his belt. The neurologist removed various pieces of equipment from that pouch and began using them to examine the baby. He took out a tape measure and measured Jimmy's head circumference; he produced a ball of red yarn and tested Jimmy's eye movements; somewhere in the pouch he found a vial and removed the top, releasing the smell of peppermint into the air. When Myklos placed the vial under the boy's nose, we both watched as Jimmy immediately pulled away. Myklos brought out a packet of salt, tore it open, and dropped a few grains on the boy's tongue; Jimmy immediately made a face and rolled his tongue around in his mouth. Myklos directed the nipple of the baby's bottle back into his mouth and let him take a few sucks. The neurologist's anger had all but abated by that point, and a peaceful, serene expression had appeared on his face. He was performing his exam in a matter-of-fact way, not speaking to me or to the patient, just observantly going about his work.

Myklos finished testing the function of Jimmy's cranial nerves and began on his trunk and extremities. He tested Jimmy's muscle strength and tone; the exam appeared normal. He tickled the boy's chest, and Jimmy responded with a laugh. He took a reflex hammer out of his pouch and began lightly tapping the muscles over Jimmy's joints; each tap elicited a slight jerk of the underlying muscle. He scratched the soles of Jimmy's feet; the boy's toes, in response to the scratching, flexed and curled downward. Then Myklos replaced the reflex hammer in the pouch and calmly addressed me directly for the first time since starting the examination: "Well, I can't say I'm very impressed," he said. "Everything seems to be completely normal. This patient hears, sees, smells, and tastes; his cranial nerves work normally, his muscles and reflexes are completely fine. He's ticklish, so his sense of touch must be intact. There seems to be nothing wrong with him."

"You haven't tested pain yet," I responded.

"I know," the neurologist replied as he reached back into his pouch and produced a safety pin. "I've been saving that for last." Opening the pin, he held the boy's left foot in his left hand and barely touched the skin of that foot with the sharp, exposed tip. Jimmy looked at Myklos, made serious, direct eye contact with the neurologist, and then, as I expected, his face broke into a broad smile.

Myklos looked back at the boy quizzically. Still holding the baby's foot in his hand, the neurologist jabbed the needle a little deeper into the skin. This time Jimmy added his "Da da ba ba" to the full-faced smile. "That's bizarre," was all the neurologist said. "That's really bizarre." He repeated the test on the boy's right foot, but when the sharp tip of the needle reached the skin, Jimmy's expression remained basically the same.

Then Myklos quickly and methodically began stabbing the baby everywhere. Both arms, both legs, from the end of each extremity to its junction with the trunk, and then over the front and back of that trunk, Abe Myklos stuck that baby again and again with the tip of his safety pin. He stuck him lightly, never once drawing blood, but he stuck him repeatedly, a deed that, done to almost any other child, would have been an act of reportable child abuse; in Jimmy Stone, however, it represented nothing more than a friendly attempt at infant stimulation.

When he was finished, Myklos dropped the pin and told me to stay put. He ran out of the room, returning seconds later, carefully carrying a dripping wad of paper towels. Without a word, he applied the wad to the back of my hand, and I let out a yelp. The towels were boiling hot. "Hot water," he said. "I got it from the coffeepot in the nurses' station." Without hesitation or another word, he applied the wad of towels to the boy's right forearm. Jimmy again made eye contact with the neurologist and began to babble. "What a nice baby," Abe Myklos said. "He doesn't feel a damned thing, but he really is very good-natured. Let's go to my office."

We put up the crib's guardrail, and I followed the neurologist down the hall to the cubicle that served as his office. Myklos sat down at the desk, immediately pulling a copy of a textbook of pediatric neurology from its place on the shelf. He shuffled through some pages, and while he browsed, he told me a little about the neurological aspects of pain.

I learned from Myklos that pain is a fairly complicated sensation. When the skin receives a noxious stimulation like a pinprick, something happens within the skin that stimulates a group of specialized nerve endings. It's not known exactly what happens, but once the stimulation has occurred, a message is transmitted up the nerve to the spinal cord through a small bundle of nerve fibers called the posterolateral fasciculus.

After the nerves enter the spinal cord, they split and meet with neurons in the lateral spinothalamic tracts. These tracts travel up and down the spinal cord and bring the message into the brain. Pain is perceived when the message is received in the somesthetic area of the thalamus.

Myklos explained that Jimmy's problem could be due to a defect anywhere along this pathway; in the skin, the nerve, the spinal cord, or the brain. He concluded his discussion by saying, "All we have to do now is figure out exactly where the lesion is."

"How are we going to do that?" I asked.

"I have absolutely no idea," Myklos replied. "That's why we're here, so I can look it up in the book."

I sat silently while he read the entire chapter on the evaluation of the patient with congenital insensitivity to pain. After a few minutes, he jumped up, startling me, and said, "We've got to get some histamine. I'll go to the pharmacy. You head back to the ward and see if you can round up the kid's mother."

•   •   •

Complete inability to sense pain is, as Myklos explained, a symptom of a number of disorders that share two things in common: all are hereditary, illustrating either an autosomal dominant (meaning transmitted from affected parent to affected child) or autosomal recessive (in which both parents, though normal, are carriers of an aberrant gene that, when present in two copies, leads to the abnormal features) mode of inheritance; and all are very rare, occurring in less than one in ten thousand individuals. Many of these disorders are associated with other unusual abnormalities, but Jimmy's examination revealed only isolated defects in pain and temperature perception. Therefore, we quickly narrowed down the number of disorders possible in his case to only a handful. The histamine test, as I learned later, would narrow the possibilities down even further.

The histamine test is a simple, safe, and specific screen for dysfunction of the peripheral nervous system. The test is performed by injecting a small amount of histamine, the naturally occurring substance that mediates allergic reactions, under the skin. Initially, a red patch appears at the site of the injection. This patch, called a wheal, represents a local reaction and doesn't require any neurological input. If the sensory nerves are functioning normally, the stimulation caused by the histamine will be carried to the spinal cord, and a reflex reaction will occur: the wheal will blossom into what's called a flare, producing streaks of redness up and down the arm. The flare will develop if the nerves are intact even if the central nervous system is impaired. If the nerve is damaged or abnormal, however, no flare will result; only the wheal will persist.

Following Myklos's orders, I walked back to the room in which we had placed Jimmy a little over an hour before. The boy's mother was sitting by the baby's crib with a very large and somewhat disheveled man wearing a shabby flannel shirt and dirty jeans. "Dr. Marion," Mrs. Stone said, "this is my husband, James Sr."

I shook hands with Mr. Stone and brought him up-to-date on his son's medical condition. I told him we thought Jimmy was going to be fine, but that we were trying to figure out why he didn't feel pain. Mr. Stone nodded silently. At that moment, Abe Myklos breezed into the room carrying a small vial and a handful of syringes and alcohol swabs. "Are you Jimmy's parents?" he asked, and when they nodded, he continued. "I'm Dr. Myklos, the neurologist. I'm going to do a simple test on the baby. I promise it won't hurt him. . . ."

"Nothing hurts him," Mr. Stone interrupted. "That's why you're doing the test in the first place, isn't it?"

"Right," Myklos answered. "What I mean is, it won't do him any harm. It's a test to see if the nerves that carry the sensation of pain from his skin to his brain are working properly. If it's all right with you, I'd like to also do the test on both of you. Dr. Marion here will serve as the control."

The Stones nodded, and since I hadn't been offered a choice, we all rolled up our sleeves. Myklos injected Mrs. Stone first. He drew a tiny amount of histamine from the vial into one of the syringes, swabbed a one-inch circle of skin on the back of the woman's left forearm with alcohol, stuck the thin needle attached to the syringe just under the precleaned skin, and pushed the plunger. Mrs. Stone winced when the histamine entered her skin, and a small bleb was present when Myklos removed the needle. The area instantly turned red.

Working silently, the neurologist repeated this procedure on Mr. Stone, and then on me. When he stuck the needle under the skin of my forearm, I felt a short, sharp prick. The histamine was discharged, and I immediately experienced a burning sensation. Then Myklos removed the needle and got ready to inject Jimmy. He grabbed the infant's left arm and swabbed it with the alcohol. When he jabbed the needle under Jimmy's skin, the boy showed absolutely no change in his happy demeanor.

My arm was itching unbearably at the site of the injection, and Mr. and Mrs. Stone were also scratching furiously. All four of us had developed large, red blotches on our forearms. "It shouldn't take long," the neurologist assured us. "Just a few minutes."

Mrs. Stone's flare was the first to appear. Streaks of red shot up and down her arm like rays of light from the sun. While Myklos was measuring the lengths of the streaks, a flare showed up on my arm as well. "Well, now we know two things," Myklos said. "We know you two have intact nerves. We also know the histamine works. Mr. Stone, I don't see a flare on your arm. Do you have any problem feeling pain?"

He answered by pulling up the cuff of his jeans, exposing a large scar on the lower part of his left leg. "See this?" he asked. "My mother dropped a cup of tea on my leg when I was a kid. I never felt a thing. Jimmy must have gotten it from me."

The neurologist nodded his head, as if that statement had clarified the entire case for him. And then we turned to Jimmy.

He was sitting up now, playing with a couple of rattles his mother had given him soon after we'd finished the spinal tap, having a long baby-talk conversation with them. The wheal on his arm remained intact, but there were absolutely no streaks coming out of it. We stood by and watched silently, those of us who had received histamine injections occasionally scratching our arms, for a good ten minutes. Myklos broke the silence: "Well, that was easy: he's obviously got hereditary sensory neuropathy, which he inherited from his father. Amazing."

The neurologist and I soon left the room to figure out what we were going to tell Jimmy's parents. "What a lucky kid," I said. "Imagine never having any pain!"

"Lucky?" the neurologist repeated. "You think this boy's lucky? Would you call someone who's deaf or blind lucky? This kid may even be worse off than someone who doesn't have vision or hearing. He's going to be a disaster. Pain's an essential sensation. I'll grant you it isn't terrific if it becomes intractible or chronic, but can you imagine a toddler who doesn't feel pain? Children that age need to feel pain in order to learn what's safe to do and what's not safe. This kid's never going to learn anything about safety. He's going to bite off his fingers, stick his hands into open flames, cut his arms and legs with knives, play with hot irons, all sorts of horrible things, and never think twice about it. We're going to have to go back into that room and tell those people that unless they watch that kid like a hawk twenty-four hours a day, he's going to destroy himself before he turns three."

"I hadn't thought about that," I said. "But what you're saying doesn't make sense: Mr. Stone has the same condition and he seems fine. If not feeling pain is so bad, why hasn't he destroyed himself?"

"I haven't tested him yet, but I'll bet the father's sensory loss is much less severe. It probably involves only his hands and his feet," the neurologist replied. "That's the usual pattern in this disorder. Jimmy's problem is much more unusual: his whole body's involved, and because of that, he's much worse off. I bet even his internal pain receptors are abnormal. Do you know what that means? He's going to get appendicitis and not know about it. He's going to wind up rupturing his appendix and getting peritonitis. There are all sorts of things like that to consider. Pain's a sense, and it's as important as all the other senses."

"Isn't there anything we can do to help him?" I asked.

"Nothing," Myklos replied. "Outside of making the diagnosis and telling his parents to make sure he's carefully supervised twenty-four hours a day, there's not a thing that can be done for him. I'll tell you one thing: I'm sure as hell glad this isn't my kid!"

●　　●　　●

Two years passed. After graduating from medical school, I had become a resident in pediatrics and was now doing a rotation in

Jonas Bronck's outpatient department. As part of that rotation, I had been assigned, one afternoon a week, to Outreach, a service that provides home-based health care to children with chronic, debilitating medical problems. On that Thursday afternoon, Janet Gibbs, one of the Outreach nurse practitioners, and I were going out on home visits.

Our rounds began in a bleak neighborhood in the South Bronx. As the cab inched along the street, we passed building after devastated building. "I think you'll find our first patient very interesting," Janet said as the cabdriver pulled the car to the curb in front of one of these abandoned-looking buildings. "He's a two-year-old with hereditary sensory neuropathy. He doesn't feel pain. . . ."

"Jimmy Stone?" I interrupted.

Janet had opened the cab's door, and we were standing on the sidewalk in front of the imposing damaged hulk of what had once been a fashionable apartment building. "Oh, you know Jimmy?" the nurse asked.

"Yeah," I replied softly. We were now walking into the building's lobby. It was dark and filthy, and it smelled of urine. The only light came from the doors and some broken windows that looked out on an open courtyard. The place scared me to death. "I took care of him once when he was in the hospital."

I hadn't seen or heard about Jimmy since his discharge. We finally concluded at that time that his seizure had been due to fever caused by nothing more serious than an underlying viral infection. Following his admission, no recurrence of the fever or of the convulsion had occurred, and he had gone home after a three-day stay. Before discharge, we had carefully examined the boy's father and found exactly what Myklos had predicted: Mr. Stone's sensory deficit was distributed in what the neurologist described as a "stocking-glove" pattern, involving only the most distal parts of his arms and legs. I was eager to see what had happened to Jimmy, but being in that lobby was quickly tempering my enthusiasm.

Janet walked over to the stairs, saying, "I stop off to see him about once a month, just to make sure he hasn't developed any horrible infections. Their apartment's only three flights up. The elevator doesn't work. For some reason, it stopped the day the city turned off the building's electricity. Can you imagine living in a place like this?"

I couldn't possibly imagine it. The light was dimmer on the stairs than it had been in the lobby, and up ahead in the darkness, it seemed as if something were moving. Janet and I pushed on, and pretty soon we were standing in the hall in front of the door of the Stones' apartment.

Our knock was answered by Mr. Stone, who was dressed in clothes reminiscent of the ones he had worn the day I had met him in the hospital two years before. He greeted Janet with a smile and, after the nurse reintroduced us, offered me his hand. "Come on in," he said. "We've been waiting for you."

Through the door, we entered directly into one of the apartment's two rooms. The place was a wreck: The floor was a mosaic of peeling, battered, and missing linoleum tiles. The walls were bare, except for an old, faded photograph of John F. Kennedy that had obviously been torn from some magazine article years before. Large chunks of plaster had peeled off the walls and off of the frame of the room's only window. Adjacent to the window was the kitchen area, comprised of a battered aluminum card table and a couple of folding chairs, a sink that may or may not have been working, and a camp-style cookstove complete with cans of Sterno. The apartment was damp and smelled of mildew.

I was trying to take this all in when Jimmy's mother appeared in the doorway of the apartment's second room. After flashing a smile toward us, she turned and said, "Jimmy, come see who's here."

The boy appeared shortly thereafter. He was small, and he walked with a strange gait: his feet were spread widely apart, he waddled, and he slammed his shoes down on the floor with every step, as if he were trying to clean mud off their soles. I later realized that he walked this way because, without sensation, he had no way of judging when his feet had come into contact with the ground. He had to slam his shoes down in order to be sure his feet weren't still suspended in air. As he came closer I noticed the scars: he had deep, thick ones around his lips and up and down his arms. He ran up to Janet and gave her a big hug. When he released his grip, the nurse pointed toward me and asked, "Do you know who this guy is?"

"Don't you remember me, Jimmy?" I asked as he looked at me quizzically. "I took care of you once when you were in the hospital." When he just stared back at me, I continued: "You were only eight months old, so I guess it must be hard for you to remember. How are you doing?"

I put out my hand with the palm turned upward, in hopes that the nearly three-year-old would "give me five," and he slapped his right palm down hard onto mine. That's when I got a good look at his fingers: they each lacked the distal tip. None of the fingers had nails, and the stumps appeared raw and inflamed. Abe Myklos's words resounded in my mind. He had predicted this; Jimmy Stone's congenital insensitivity to pain had turned him into a walking disaster.

It was staggering: Among the boy's millions of genes, the complex genetic blueprints that had come together at the time of his conception to form him, there had been a single, tiny error, a simple alteration in the sequence of DNA, an aberration that had been a legacy from his father, who, because of the genetic phenomenon called variability of expression, had suffered a much milder problem. And that single programming error, that minuscule defect that had led to the failure of development of every sensory nerve, had apparently turned Jimmy into this, a scarred, abnormal boy, who, I thought, could not possibly have any chance of living a normal life.

"How's Jimmy been doing?" the nurse asked. "Any new problems?"

"No," Mrs. Stone answered. "No problems. He seems to be doing fine." Then, looking toward me, she said, "He's a very nice little boy."

"Is he taking his medication?" the nurse asked.

"Three times a day," the mother replied.

Because of chronic infections of the bones of his fingers that had occurred due to the boy's habit of biting their tips, Jimmy had been treated with antibiotics for months. After explaining this to me, Janet said, "Well, let's check him out." From her bag, the nurse began removing her instruments as Mrs. Stone took off the boy's shirt and pants. His little body was a wreck. He had scars everywhere.

During Janet's exam, I watched Jimmy closely. He seemed to be an excellent patient, cheerfully doing everything the nurse asked him to do—from following her finger when she examined his eyes, to bending over and touching his toes when she checked his spine for curvature—with a smile on his face. When Janet gently palpated his abdomen, the boy broke into uncontrollable laughter. Turning toward me while Jimmy's laughter continued, Janet said, "We seem to have discovered his problem; the poor kid has terminal ticklishness.

"Well, you're right, Fiona," Janet concluded, more serious now that she had carefully inspected every part of the boy's body. "He does seem to be doing fine. His fingertip infections are healing nicely. And you're getting so handsome, Jimmy."

The boy smiled broadly. "Jimmy, would you like to show Dr. Marion your crib?" the nurse asked. "I'd like him to see how your mom and dad fixed it up so you won't accidentally hurt yourself when you go to sleep."

Jimmy said, "Sure," and, still undressed, he clumsily led us toward the other room.

Passing through the door, we entered the bedroom. This room was gloomier than the first; its lone window faced onto an airshaft, and most of the sunlight was blocked. Through the dark, I could make out a double bed pushed against one of the walls. Against the opposite wall was the crib, but it looked like no crib I had ever seen before: its wooden slats were heavily padded with foam rubber, and each of the crib's four legs was suspended in a steel bucket. On closer inspection, I found that the buckets were half filled with water. "Jimmy's crib," the nurse said, pointing at the thing. "Mr. Stone's own invention."

Soon we were standing by the door, saying good-bye. Jimmy gave Janet another hug before we departed. On our way down the stairs, the nurse asked, "Well, what did you think of that crib?"

"The foam rubber's a clever idea," I replied.

"Mr. Stone thought of it himself. We've always been after them to watch Jimmy, so he doesn't hurt himself. For a while, they used to take turns staying awake at night so someone was always with him. Then Mr. Stone got the bright idea that if every surface was padded, there'd be no way Jimmy could cause himself harm. Pretty sound thinking, huh? The buckets of water were Fiona's idea. You have any idea what they're for?"

I shook my head. We had reached the lobby and were walking briskly toward the front door. "They're to keep the rats away," Janet said. "Fiona read about it somewhere in an article about leprosy. One explanation for why people with leprosy lose their fingers and toes is that rats come along during the night and eat them off. Since they don't have sensation in their hands and feet, they can't defend themselves when they're asleep. So to prevent the rats from getting at them, they put buckets of water under the legs of their beds. Fiona figured that if it would work for lepers, it should work for Jimmy. Pretty smart, huh."

"I don't know about smart," I replied, "but it definitely is horrible. Isn't there anything that can be done to get them out of that apartment? Isn't there an agency or something that can help them?"

Janet shook her head. We were now standing in the court-yard, heading toward the comfort and reassurance of our waiting cab. "It wasn't this bad until a few months ago, when the city condemned the building and shut off all the utilities," she replied. "The Stones are very proud people. They won't take charity from anybody. Mr. Stone's a musician; he plays the trumpet, but he hasn't worked in over a year. We've tried everything; they just refuse to leave that apartment until they can afford to move themselves."

"But what about Jimmy?" I asked. "Wouldn't he be better off somewhere else?"

"Does he look like he's doing so badly?" she answered. We were both back in the cab now, and the driver pulled away from the curb. "It's really amazing when you think about it. Here's a kid who seems to have nothing going for him; he lives in horrible squalor, in a condemned building that's overrun with rats and God knows what else and that doesn't have heat or water or electricity. On top of all that, he's got this bizarre neurologic problem that allows him to get burned and scarred and mutilated without even knowing it. And yet, in spite of all this, he's a fairly well-adjusted, cheerful three-year-old. It's as if his hereditary sensory neuropathy prevents him from feeling the emotional pain of his situation as well as the physical. It doesn't make sense."

Janet was right; it didn't make sense. Jimmy Stone was still very young, and he still had a long way to go before we could assume that he would grow into a reasonably normal adult; but on that afternoon, he showed me that even though the presence of a genetic defect might seem overwhelming, even though the coexistence of a brutally hostile environment might make that defect seem insurmountable, there can be something in the human spirit that simply will not be overlooked or taken for granted, some intangible drive to survive that can emerge and flourish and even cut these obstacles down to size. That's the lesson I learned from Jimmy Stone, a lesson that's stayed with me through the rest of my career in medicine.

Two Videotapes

• ● •

*T*HERE'S AN ODD SENSATION I get sometimes when I'm examining a patient. It occurs only a couple of times a year, a queasy feeling deep in the pit of my stomach that starts at the moment I realize that there's something terribly wrong with the patient lying on the examining table in front of me, something potentially life-threatening, something that hadn't previously been suspected. The first time it occurred was during my residency. I was doing a routine admission physical on a six-month-old who had been born with aniridia, or congenital absence of the irises of the eyes; he was coming into the hospital at that time for elective ophthalmologic surgery, and while palpating that boy's abdomen, I unexpectedly discovered a huge mass. The queasy feeling occurred just then, because I knew immediately that that mass had to be a Wilms' tumor, a malignancy of the kidney that occasionally is associated with this particular eye malformation. And that feeling came on me once again the first time I met Molly Richmond.

Molly was a little over a month old at the time of that first visit; she'd been referred by her pediatrician for evaluation and genetic counseling. Born at one of the small community hospitals in Westchester County, her arms and legs had been noted immediately after birth to be covered with what looked like waxy pimples. The pediatrician had never before seen anything like the warty bumps that covered the girl's limbs, and, alarmed, he'd immediately called one of the dermatologists on staff at the hospital, asking him to have a look at the infant. After a brief examination, the dermatologist had performed a biopsy, removing some of the material from one of the bumps, and had sent the sample to the pathology lab. It took three weeks to get the results of that biopsy, but when they were available, they confirmed the skin expert's initial impression: the specimens showed the characteristic changes that occur in an extremely rare and unusual disorder called incontinentia pigmenti, or IP, which, because of its unusual X-linked dominant pattern of inheritance, occurs nearly exclusively in girls.

By the time of Molly's visit to my office, I had painfully learned the lesson that in many individuals with IP, the skin lesions that herald the diagnosis are about the least of the problems the girls are likely to encounter during their lifetimes. During my career as a clinical geneticist, I'd cared for two other patients with IP. Although one of them, Diane, was doing reasonably well, getting by with only minor problems, the other had turned out to be a disaster. Samantha was eight years old at the time of Molly Richmond's birth, and during her life, she had suffered nearly all the major complications associated with the disorder. Like Molly, she'd been born with warts on her arms and legs; as is usually the case in patients with IP, Samantha's warts had vanished by the time the girl had been three months of age, giving way to a spidery pattern of light and dark pigmented whorls distributed along the skin of her legs and trunk. By six months of age, Samantha had developed a serious seizure disorder that proved to be almost impossible to control with conventional anticonvulsant medications; developmental delay had first been diagnosed at eight months, and, following a battery of sophisticated tests, the girl had been classified as severely retarded. At a little over nine months of age, teeth had begun to appear in the girl's lower jaw, but were markedly abnormal; sharp and cone-shaped, they looked more like the teeth of a young dog or cat than of a human child.

Over the course of the next few years, Samantha had become microcephalic and spastic, her muscle tone markedly increased. Her parents, who loved the child, took exceptionally good care of her for as long as they could manage, but by the time the girl turned six and weighed enough that it was nearly impossible for her mother to carry her around anymore, they had decided to place her in an institution for children with incurable diseases, a hospice where she'll live out the rest of her life. So when I read the diagnosis on the cover sheet of Molly Richmond's chart, I began to prepare myself for the worst.

Usually when I'm dealing with a child whose diagnosis carries a not-very-good prognosis, I try very hard to keep some distance from the family; it's a defense mechanism, I guess, one I've evolved to protect myself from getting hurt when the inevitable finally happens. But after spending no more than five minutes with the Richmonds, I was sure that keeping my distance was not going to be easy.

I liked them immediately. They were about my age, and Molly was their first child. I sensed quickly that, had we met at a party, or anywhere other than my office at the medical center, the Richmonds and I would probably have become fast friends. But I knew that becoming friends with these people would be very difficult now. They'd come to see me because their only child had a serious disease, and it was going to be up to me to tell them all about it. And after they'd heard what I was going to have to tell them, I didn't believe they'd want to ever have anything more to do with me.

Susan Richmond did most of the talking, while her husband, Jerry, cradled the infant in his arms, occasionally shaking a rattle to get her attention when she let out a cry. The history Ms. Richmond gave was typically benign: The pregnancy had been completely normal; in fact, during the nine months of Molly's gestation, Susan had felt healthier than she had in a long time. Nobody in either her or her husband's family had been born with any kind of birth defects; she'd had no pregnancies before Molly, and no one in her family had had an undue number of miscarriages.

Next, I performed a cursory examination of the infant; again, there was nothing too impressive to note. Other than the warty growths on her limbs, and what I thought might be the beginning of a couple of areas of increased pigmentation on her trunk, Molly appeared completely healthy and developmentally appropriate. As Ms. Richmond got her daughter dressed, I found myself hoping that Molly would turn out to be one of the lucky ones, a child with IP who would escape most of the terrible problems my patient Samantha had suffered.

"Well, I have to agree with the diagnosis," I told the couple after they had settled back on chairs in my office, "but it's important to point out that, right now, Molly looks fine. We should talk a little about her disorder, though. How much do you know about IP?"

"Not much," Jerry Richmond replied. "The dermatologist told us about what we can expect to happen to her skin, but that's all we know."

Ms. Richmond, who'd begun nursing the baby, added, "From the way our pediatrician treated us when he found out the results of the biopsy, we know there's got to be something other than the skin problems."

I nodded and paused. I was going to have to tell them now. Even though I'd done this many times before, even though it was an integral part of my job, I hated it. Over the course of the next five minutes, I was going to provide this couple with information about their child that was going to devastate them, and possibly change the course of the rest of their lives. But it had to be done; so I took a breath and launched into it.

First, I covered the easiest part: I told them about the genetics of the disorder. I explained that, since Ms. Richmond herself had none of the characteristic features of IP, the abnormality in the gene on one of Molly's X chromosomes that caused all her problems must have resulted from an accidental change in her genetic material, a phenomenon known as a new mutation. I told them that this mutation might have occurred in either Mr. Richmond's sperm or in Ms. Richmond's egg, that there was no way to be sure which was the case, and that the problem had to be present before Molly was even conceived; I emphasized the fact that nothing Ms. Richmond had or had not done during her pregnancy could have in any way altered the outcome.

Next, I explained how IP affected parts of the body that were derived from two primitive cell types: ectoderm and mesoderm, the embryonic germ layers that formed Molly's skin, teeth, hair, eyes, bone, and, most important, her brain. Then, trying not to make eye contact, staring off at a blank spot on the wall behind the Richmonds' chairs, I went on into the "danger zone," briefly outlining the spectrum of abnormalities that had been reported in children with the disorder, how at least a third of the patients had been affected with serious developmental retardation and seizure disorders. The picture I painted wasn't pretty, but it was representative. I pulled no punches, and by the time I finished talking, there were tears not only in the eyes of both of Molly's parents, but in my eyes as well.

Often at this point in the informing interview, the parents will become angry at me for saying such bad things about their child, or they'll try to belittle or deny that there really is anything at all actually wrong with their baby, but the Richmonds didn't say a word; they just sat on their chairs, looking down at the infant Ms. Richmond was now cradling in her arms, and cried. Because the mood was becoming too much for me to bear at that point, I did something I don't often do; I apologized. "I'm sorry I had to be the one to tell you about this," I said, my voice breaking a little.

"No, don't be sorry," Mr. Richmond said through his tears. "You did what you had to do."

"We appreciate your being so honest," his wife added, wiping her eyes with a tissue.

"You understand that none of this may actually happen to Molly," I said, trying now to soften the blow I had just laid on them. "In fact, she seems to be doing so well right now, I wouldn't be surprised if she continues to do well in the future."

Within another few minutes, all of us were back in control of ourselves. I knew we were nearing the end of this difficult session, and personally, I was feeling greatly relieved that the worst was now behind us. I assured the couple that I'd be around for them and for Molly in the future, and urged them to call me at any time if they had any questions about IP, no matter how picayune or inappropriate the question might seem. And then, to conclude, I said, "Do you have anything you want to ask about now?"

There was silence for a few seconds, and I was getting ready to rise from my chair to walk them to the door, when Mr. Richmond said, "There is one thing. It's probably nothing, I probably shouldn't even mention it, but we've been noticing that Molly's been having these funny movements. . . ."

"Funny movements?" I interrupted, snapping to attention. "What do you mean by that?"

"Well, it doesn't happen all the time," Ms. Richmond replied. "But occasionally, she jerks her arms like this." She imitated the kind of motion made by one of those wind-up monkeys that bang cymbals together over and over again. "She'll do that for maybe fifteen or twenty seconds and then it'll stop."

Becoming more concerned now, I asked, "How often does this happen? Every day?"

"It started about a week ago," Mr. Richmond answered, "and since then, I'd say I've noticed her doing it once or twice a day."

Just then, the baby started to do it. Right in front of me, while she was being held in her mother's lap, Molly started to move her hands back and forth rhythmically, over and over again. That's when I felt it: that terrible queasy sensation in the pit of my stomach.

• • •

Seizure disorders are not uncommon in childhood. Approximately 5 percent of all children will, at some point between birth and adulthood, experience one or more convulsions. Often the manifestation of an injury or insult to the brain that was suffered in either prenatal or postnatal life, seizures or convulsions are nothing more than the body's response to abnormal electrical activity in the brain. Generally speaking, the more severe the aberration found in the brain's pattern of electrical activity, the worse the prognosis. The majority of seizures suffered by children are found in association with fever, and are of no long-term significance. Of all the types of seizures that occur in infants and children, though, none has a worse prognosis than the category known as infantile spasms.

Children with infantile spasms frequently present very much the way Molly Richmond did. The spasms are generally first detected between the ages of one and four months of age, because the parents have noticed some unusual movements that have occurred over and over again in the child. Dismissing these movements as normal infant development the first few times they happen, the parents generally become more concerned when the frequency with which the spasms occur increases. Seeking medical attention at that point, the parents get the diagnosis confirmed during an electroencephalogram, or EEG, a record of the brain-wave activity over a long period of time. What's seen on the EEG in patients with infantile spasms is so striking, so abnormal, that even someone without formal training in neurology can make the diagnosis: the brain-wave activity, which under normal circumstances is ordered, symmetric, and rhythmic, shows a completely and continuously abnormal pattern, a pattern known as hypsarrythmia.

My suspicion that Molly had infantile spasms was more than a hunch; I knew that these seizures were found much more frequently in children with IP, as well as in patients with a number of other genetic syndromes. But it wasn't just this realization that caused that queasy sensation to start up deep in my gut. Rather, the feeling came on because at that moment, I realized that if Molly had infantile spasms, then the IP had definitely affected her brain, and this meant that, rather than being one of the lucky ones, rather than getting off easy, Molly was doomed to suffer all of the problems my patient Samantha had suffered. Seeing those subtle, repetitive shaking movements of the girl's arms had screamed out to me that Molly would wind up severely or profoundly retarded, able to do nearly nothing for herself, depending fully on others to dress her and wash her and feed her and change her diapers; she would undoubtedly become an increasing burden to her parents, these nice people who had walked into my office only an hour or so before, not having even a clue that their lives would be forever changed by the information that would be given to them over the next few hours. It was this realization that had come on me in the blink of an eye as I watched Molly Richmond shake her arms, that had caused that terrible feeling in me.

My suspicion had to be confirmed, and it had to be done immediately, because treatment to control the seizures needed to be instituted as soon as possible. Within minutes of seeing the girl's arms shaking, after briefly informing the parents that yes, these might represent seizures, I was on the phone with the EEG lab. I told the technician I had an emergency; she told me that, luckily, they'd just had a cancellation and if I sent the patient up immediately, they could fit her right in.

After sending the Richmonds off to the EEG lab, I went back to work; I had a full schedule of patients for that afternoon. But really, going on with my day as if nothing had happened was pointless; I couldn't concentrate at all. My heart and my mind were with Molly and her parents, up on the seventh floor of our hospital, in a place called the Closed-Circuit Television Electroencephalographic Laboratory, a small room with an enormously long name and a huge amount of expensive and high-tech equipment. In that room, electrodes were glued to Molly's scalp and a video camera was pointed at her. A tape recorded the child's movements and a simultaneous tracing of her EEG.

A little over two hours later, after finishing with most of my scheduled patients, I broke away from the office and went upstairs to review the videotape with Samuel Scheinfeld, a pediatric neurologist. As the taped image was projected on a television screen, I saw it all: flashed across the upper two-thirds of that screen was a picture of tiny Molly Richmond lying uncomfortably on a cot, with different-colored wires, like technicolor spaghetti, emanating wildly from the leads that had been glued to her small head. I watched as the little girl's arms jerked rhythmically, as if she were a marionette being manipulated by an invisible puppeteer, while her frightened and overwhelmed parents kneeled on the floor on either side of the cot, as if in prayer, trying desperately to comfort and protect their daughter. Meanwhile, on the lower third of the television screen flashed the simultaneous readout from the electroencephalogram. "Look at that," Scheinfeld said, pointing with the tip of his pen at the scattered, asynchronous lines that were appearing at the bottom. "It's classic. Notice that there's absolutely no relationship between the hypsarrhythmia and the movements. Whether she has a spasm or not, the brain is firing off like this. It's a textbook case of infantile spasms."

"She has to be admitted," I said, more as a statement than as a question.

"Right away," Scheinfeld responded. "I'll try to get a CAT scan done this afternoon. Then we'll start the treatment. You want to tell the parents?"

No, not really, I thought to myself; telling these parents what we've found and where we go from here was about the last thing on earth I wanted to do. But I had to; so I went back down to my office, where I had left the Richmond family a few minutes before, and took the same seat I'd been in when I'd spoken with them earlier in the day.

Molly, who had been very quiet through most of this, was crying now; she was obviously tired out from the tests and becoming very cranky. Looking at Ms. Richmond, who was trying to get the infant to take her breast, and at Mr. Richmond, I realized that they already knew what I was about to say; the looks on their faces conveyed that. But I told them anyway: "The EEG showed that the baby has a condition called infantile spasms," I began, again focusing not on either of their faces, but on the spot on the wall behind them. "It's a kind of seizure disorder that needs to be treated very aggressively.

I've spoken with the neurologist, and he feels that Molly should come into the hospital to begin a course of medication immediately."

"This means her brain's abnormal, doesn't it?" Ms. Richmond said. She had finally managed to get Molly to latch on to her breast, and the infant seemed to be falling asleep.

"Yes." I answered flatly, trying not to show any emotion, because I knew I'd start to cry.

"And that means that she'll be retarded," Mr. Richmond said. It was not a question.

"We can't be sure," I continued. "But certainly, she's at greater risk now that these seizures have been discovered than we knew she was before we did the EEG."

Over the next fifteen minutes we talked on like that, the Richmonds working hard to reevaluate the situation they were in now that the circumstances had so drastically changed, with me trying desperately hard to get them to understand that, although things looked bad, nothing was set in stone. Then I got a call from Scheinfeld: he had arranged the CAT scan and had reserved a bed for Molly on the infants' ward. The wheels were turning rapidly now, and things had moved out of my hands; I sent the family off down the hall toward the CAT scanner, and told them I'd see them later in the day up on the ward. After they were gone, emotionally exhausted by the afternoon's activities, I settled down to finish some paperwork.

• • •

Molly Richmond spent a total of fifteen days in the hospital. The CAT scan of her head done just before her admission had revealed no obvious structural abnormalities of the girl's brain, and immediately upon reaching her crib on the infants' ward, she had been started on the drug of choice for the treatment of infantile spasms, the hormone ACTH. The medication needed to be administered intramuscularly, so twice a day the girl was given a painful injection into the soft tissue of her arms, thighs, or buttocks. The drug, which was started at a very low dose and gradually increased, caused severe behavioral changes in the little girl. By the fifth day of her hospital stay, when the dose of ACTH had been more than doubled over the dose she'd initially received, Molly was miserable. The child, who had, according to her mother, been an "easy baby" prior to the start of the medication, had turned into a monster: she cried perpetually, as if she were in constant pain; she slept poorly and fitfully, always awakening after a half hour or so, screaming at the top of her lungs, as if she were having night terrors; and because of the medication's effect on her appetite, she'd become ravenously hungry, wanting to nurse at least once every hour. As a result, Susan Richmond had to spend almost every minute with her daughter, and within days, she herself had become chronically overtired; even worse, Ms. Richmond picked up one of the many viral illnesses that are always floating around pediatric wards and developed a terrible head cold. But still, she stayed with her daughter, allowing the infant to nurse on demand, learning how to give the injections that seemed to be causing the child so many ill effects.

During the course of Molly's hospitalization, I visited the Richmonds twice a day, spending at least fifteen minutes with them every morning and every afternoon. Entering the room Molly had been assigned, I would sit on one of the chairs as if I were an old friend come to visit the family in their living room, and we'd talk, usually while Ms. Richmond was nursing her daughter. We discussed all sorts of things: their work, their past experiences, why they decided to wait so long to have a child.

I got to know them well during those visits. Susan Richmond was thirty-nine years old at the time of her daughter's birth. An artist, she designed and created enormous, brightly colored tapestries in a studio in New Rochelle. Although she'd been working at her art for nearly two decades, it had begun to receive serious attention only over the past four or five years. "The turning point for Susan was *The Red Anemone,*" Mr. Richmond told me, proudly. "When she did *The Red Anemone,* everybody began to take notice."

The Red Anemone, it turned out, was a two-story-high tapestry of a single, brilliant crimson flower on a light-blue background, which Susan Richmond had begun to create seven years before I met her and her husband. After three long years of constant work, she succeeded in getting the tapestry exhibited as part of a show at the Museum of Modern Art in New York in 1984; it hung from the top of the museum's immense main lobby and extended nearly to its floor. *The Red Anemone* had drawn large crowds, and a great deal of media attention. And the tapestry's success was apparently the reason they'd put off having a baby for so long. "After that, my work was suddenly in real demand. It was like I'd become an overnight sensation. We'd always planned on having at least one baby, but when everything I'd been working toward for so long started happening all at once, I found I couldn't just drop everything. And then, suddenly, we looked up and I was thirty-eight, and Jerry and I both realized that we didn't have a whole lot of time left. It was either have a baby now, or not have one at all. So we decided to put everything on hold, and go ahead with this pregnancy."

"During the pregnancy, Susan was approached about the possibility of a traveling exhibition of her works," Mr. Richmond said. "It sounded like a great opportunity. We decided I'd take a leave of absence from my job [Mr. Richmond was an assistant district attorney in the Bronx], and we figured the three of us would travel around the country with the show for six months or a year. Now, I just don't know. . . ." He was silent after that. It was the only time in all our talks when we spoke of the future. That was the only topic that seemed to be taboo, the only area in which our discussions could not wander. The Richmonds were hurting so badly: it was one thing for them to deal with a child who might possibly suffer some sort of neurological or developmental deficit in the future; it was quite another to come to grips with the fact that those problems were already present, that there was no way now that Molly would ever be normal, and, as a result, no way that their lives could possibly continue along the path they'd been heading along prior to the birth of their daughter.

But at least there seemed to be something about which they could be optimistic; by the end of the first week of ACTH therapy, Molly's episodes of abnormal movements seemed to vanish. Before the first dose of medication had been given, Sam Scheinfeld had informed the couple that only about two-thirds of patients with infantile spasms who are begun on ACTH respond to the drug, and that it could never be predicted before treatment who would do well and who wouldn't. Although the EEG still showed some residual abnormal brain-wave activity, Sam had told the Richmonds he wasn't too concerned about it. "It's going to take time," he told them, "but she's definitely responding. Take my word for it: she's going to be one of the lucky ones."

But it was hard for the Richmonds to take the neurologist's word for it. Prior to the start of the ACTH, their daughter had been an easy-to-manage, lovable infant; now she was a screaming wretch. Were these changes permanent? Had they sacrificed the child's pleasant disposition for a cure for what appeared on the surface to be a minor seizure disorder? Although both Sam and I reassured them that the girl's personality would revert to its former state after the medication was stopped, they didn't fully believe it.

Our daily conversations continued; I began to share with them bits and pieces of my personal life, something I rarely did with the parents of patients. I talked to them about my wife and our children, and about my medical school experiences; on one of my visits to Molly's room, I even brought them a copy of my first book, a novel about my internship. Gratefully accepting it, they reciprocated by lending me a copy of a videotape that had been made during the period Ms. Richmond was creating *The Red Anemone*. "It's kind of a documentary," Mr. Richmond told me as he handed me the box. "It's been shown on some of the public broadcasting stations around the country. We'd love to hear what you think about it."

•   •   •

That evening, I popped the tape into our VCR and settled back on the couch. I expected . . . I'm not sure what I expected. I guess I thought the documentary would be lacking in humor and imagination, a dry look at an artist at work. But as I watched the story unfold over the next forty-five minutes, I became pleasantly surprised. Because what I was watching was not simply the tale of the creation of *The Red Anemone*; the tape also gave me a clear look at what life had been like for the Richmonds prior to the birth of Molly.

Interspersed between views of the tapestry as it grew longer and longer in the studio, and later, as it was carefully hung at the museum, were portraits of the Richmonds as they looked and acted back then. The woman appearing on the television screen looked a little younger than the Susan Richmond I had come to know, and she appeared far less tired and frazzled. In an interview near the beginning of the documentary, she talked about what had drawn her to art in the first place: "I've always felt a need to create things," she told the interviewer. "One of the first things I remember is a night when my parents were entertaining some of their friends at our house; I couldn't have been more than three. I made up a play and acted it out, all by myself; I played three or four different parts. Then, when

I got a little older, I realized that what I really wanted to do was make things with my hands."

Later in the tape, there were sections showing Jerry, Susan, and Susan's assistants clowning around the studio during various phases of the work. One memorable sequence near the end focused on the "wrap party," the celebration that occurred following completion of the tapestry; the camera followed the couple, who had dressed in formal attire for the occasion—Susan in a floor-length, white sequined gown and Jerry in a tuxedo—as they joyfully danced round and round the messy studio to tape-recorded waltz music. Their exuberance and unfettered joy were nearly palpable right through the television set.

I was held spellbound by that documentary. It drove home to me the fact that the people who come to my office, the parents of children who have been born with some congenital malformation or syndrome, are not the same people they were prior to the birth of that child. Like the Richmonds, they have lived lives full of plans and hopes and dreams, plans that were predicated upon their having a baby who would be born normal and healthy and happy, dreams that have been shattered by the birth of a child like Molly, who would never be normal or healthy. Seeing Susan Richmond on that TV screen, looking healthy and vibrant and excited about life, and contrasting that image with the overtired, concerned woman who had taken up residence in a room on the infants' ward, made me realize that I could never really know the parents of my patients, never really understand what the birth of their baby has meant to them: how it has changed their lives in the present or destroyed their plans for the future. That videotape gave me something precious, a rare insight into a family I truly thought I'd come to know and understand. Seeing them on that screen made me realize how little I really knew about the Richmonds.

So Molly Richmond's history was related to me through the use of two videotapes. In the first, the closed-circuit TV EEG, I had learned about the extent of the girl's disease; I had discovered, while watching her seize as her worried parents looked on helplessly, that her incontinentia pigmenti had not confined itself to her skin, but had silently invaded her central nervous system, where it would undoubtedly cause her countless difficulties throughout the remainder of her life. In the second videotape, the documentary called *The*

Making of The Red Anemone, I came for the first time to truly understand what this disease would mean to Molly's family: how it had already affected, and would continue to affect, Susan and Jerry Richmond. Medical technology and art had combined to offer me a rare glimpse into the life of one of my patients.

• • •

On the fourteenth day of treatment with ACTH, a repeat closed-circuit TV EEG revealed that Molly Richmond's brain waves had reverted to a normal pattern. Sam Scheinfeld had been correct. The drug had worked; she had been cured of her hypsarrhythmia.

Molly was discharged the next day, and Ms. Richmond continued to give the girl her intramuscular injections twice a day at home for another three weeks. All during this period, Molly continued to be as irritable and as difficult to manage as she'd been during the hospitalization. Then, following another normal EEG, Sam Scheinfeld began to gradually taper the girl's dose of medication.

Over the next two weeks, as predicted, Molly's behavior started to change. She became less fussy, less restless; she began to smile again. On their next visit to my office, the Richmonds were obviously very relieved; Molly seemed like a completely different child from the one who had been discharged from the hospital the month before.

The little girl has been out of the hospital for over a year now. The seizures have not recurred. Molly is given an EEG every few months; she's had a total of five since her discharge from the infants' ward, and thus far, every one of them has shown normal brain-wave activity. But the disease has definitely affected her central nervous system: her muscle tone is abnormally low, and she's behind in all her motor milestones; at her last visit, when she was sixteen months of age, Molly could not yet sit without assistance. However, she was bright and alert, able to say three or four words, to clap her hands on command, and to play some interactive games like peekaboo. And she seemed happy.

As expected, life has become pretty complicated for the Richmonds. They've enrolled Molly in an infant stimulation program, which she attends five days a week, working with the physical therapists to build up her muscle tone and strength. Mr. Richmond's work schedule doesn't allow him to accompany his daughter on many of her visits to the program, so this duty has fallen almost exclusively to his wife. At the beginning, she tried to combine her responsibilities to her daughter with her work in the studio, but these two full-time jobs wound up taking too much of a toll on her. So when Molly was nine months old, her mother sadly decided to pack up her supplies and equipment, put all the stuff in storage, and relinquish her lease on the studio in New Rochelle. But as Molly has gotten older and her care has settled into a regular routine, Ms. Richmond has begun to have more free time. When, during Molly's last visit to my office, I asked Ms. Richmond how things were going for her, she happily informed me that she had just begun to look for a new site to set up a studio.

Theo and the Octopus

• • •

*T*HE ATTENDING UROLOGIST, who preceded the stretcher into the recovery room, seemed jubilant as he explained to us that the operation had been a complete and absolute success. As soon as the new kidney had been laid into place, he said, and he'd had a chance to connect its ureter, artery, and vein to the appropriate stumps inside Theo's body, clear, clean, golden urine had begun to form and, for the first time in over a year, slowly trickle down into the boy's bladder. It was a little after two o'clock in the afternoon when the urologist spoke with us, and in spite of his enthusiasm, I have to admit I felt somewhat less than thrilled. "Terrific," I whispered to Scott Anderson, the intern who was scheduled to be on call with me that night. "The man performed a major surgical tour de force. You better get ready for the worst night of your life."

I was being a little overly cynical, but I was almost positive it was going to be a terrible night. I knew that when Theo Papadopoulos arrived in the recovery room, he was going to be sick as a dog, so overloaded with excess fluid he'd been given intravenously during the operation that he'd probably be in respiratory distress due to pulmonary edema ("water on the lungs"); his body's electrolyte balance would also probably be so out of whack from the surgery that it might very well take a computer analysis to figure out exactly what needed to be done to get it straightened out again. I estimated that we'd probably have to put in at least twenty-four hours of close observation and manipulation to get this poor kid stable enough so that we'd be able to safely ship him out of the cold, sterile confines of this recovery room and back to the more hospitable environment of the suite he was sharing with his mother on University Hospital's pediatric floor. I was cynical, but I was sure I had the right to be, because I had been through this before: during my residency, I'd been on call the night three other patients had received renal transplants, and I'd learned the hard way that the surgery itself, no matter how skillfully executed, was usually a piece of cake, the easiest part of the entire process. The key to any kidney transplant's success or failure was dependent almost exclusively on two elements: luck, and the quality of post-op management the patient received.

Theo was fourteen years old, and so far, luck hadn't been on his side. He was from Greece, and had come to New York specifically for this operation. In reading through the medical reports that had accompanied him to America, I learned that he'd been in perfect health until about three years before, when, during a routine physical examination, his pediatrician had found a mass in the boy's abdomen. A workup had been done, which revealed that the mass was, in fact, the boy's right kidney, a kidney that had become massively enlarged due to the formation of mammoth cystic structures. The workup also revealed that similar cysts had begun to form in the boy's left kidney, which still appeared normal in size, and, even worse, that the function of both of these kidneys was way below what it should have been. On the basis of these findings, a diagnosis of polycystic kidney disease was tentatively made.

The nephrologist to whom Theo was referred following this evaluation immediately doubted the diagnosis, for two reasons: first, the type of polycystic kidney disease (or PKD, as it's usually called) from which Theo seemed to be suffering is a disorder that's almost never diagnosed in children. It's a disease of adulthood, a syndrome that doesn't usually begin to take its toll until after the affected individual's fortieth birthday. Second, PKD is an inherited disorder, an autosomal dominant trait that's passed along from affected parent to affected child, and no other member of Theo's family on either his mother's or his father's side had ever been known to suffer from any kidney disease.

The nephrologist's doubt deepened a few months later, when a third unusual fact came to light: although PKD is usually a very slowly progressing entity, leading ultimately to renal failure after years and years of milder symptomatology, Theo's renal function had deteriorated with alarming rapidity: at this point, a little more than half a year after the pediatrician had first discovered the boy's mass, hemodialysis had become necessary, and an arteriovenous fistula, a device that would allow the boy to be hooked up to a hemodialysis machine, was implanted in Theo's left wrist. By the time another year had passed, the boy's renal function had become nonexistent; he'd developed anuria, producing no urine at all. Theo now depended completely upon the hemodialysis machine to clear his blood of the toxic waste products that, if left circulating, would eventually build up to levels high enough to cause his heart to stop beating. Even though the nephrologist still doubted the diagnosis of PKD, he knew that the boy's only chance of ever escaping the grasp of the artificial kidney machine, from which he was now requiring treatments three times a week, was through a renal transplant. So, after discussing it with Theo's parents and receiving their enthusiastic approval, the nephrologist had placed a long-distance phone call to his old friend Arthur Weldon, the director of our pediatric renal service, and had made an appointment for Theo to be admitted to University Hospital, or, as it was known among pediatric nephrologists throughout the world at that time, "Mecca."

During the time preceding Theo's trip to New York, a fact came to light that allayed all of the Greek nephrologist's doubts concerning his patient's diagnosis. After the boy's parents were told that Theo's chances for a successful transplant would increase astronomically if the donated kidney were to come from a member of the family rather than from an anonymous, recently deceased body, they both volunteered and underwent complete physical exams and full evaluations of their renal function. Although Mrs. Papadopoulos received a clean bill of health, her husband's renal ultrasound showed, surprisingly, that the parenchyma of both of his kidneys was studded with tiny cysts. This finding did not explain why the child had become so sick at such a young age, or why his disease had progressed so rapidly, but it did solve one major piece of the puzzle: it proved that Theo definitely did have PKD; he had inherited the gene from his father, who, at age forty-two, still hadn't manifested any symptoms. The finding also answered the question of who would provide Theo's new kidney; it was clear that Mrs. Papadopoulos would have to donate one of her kidneys to her son.

Getting Theo and his mother to the United States was not easy. The Papadopouloses were shopkeepers in Athens, and, although financially comfortable, they didn't have a great deal of excess money available for major emergencies such as this. And because the boy was not an American citizen and had no health insurance, University Hospital administrators had demanded that a cash deposit of $10,000 be made before they'd even consider admitting Theo. It seemed as if it would be impossible to raise such a large sum of money, but Mr. Papadopoulos, driven by love and possibly by guilt, managed to do it: borrowing money from every friend and relative he could contact, the boy's father somehow got together every last penny. Of course, it would be impossible for him to accompany his son to America; he'd have to stay home and work two jobs, attempting to raise the money necessary to repay some of the debt. And so, on the day before their scheduled admission, Theo and his mother flew into Kennedy Airport, and, after spending the night at a motel in the Bronx, settled into the two-bedded private room on the pediatric ward at University Hospital in which many transplant patients and their parent-or sibling-donors spent most of their hospital stay, the part of the ward known to us house officers as the "Honeymoon Suite."

It was in that suite that I met Theo and his mother for the first time. It was about three o'clock on the afternoon before surgery; I walked in to introduce myself as the senior resident on the ward, and within a very short time I realized we were going to be in serious trouble. The boy looked horrible; he was lying in bed, and seemed too weak to even lift his head off the pillow. His body was bloated with excess fluid, but at the same time he appeared wasted. His skin was pasty and pale, and I knew right then that this kid was sick, very sick, and that he'd been very sick for a long, long time; he'd used up most of his body's reserves, both physically and emotionally, just keeping himself alive long enough to reach this point in time, and I knew there couldn't be much left inside him that would help heal his wounds after the operation was over. I knew just by looking at him that Theo was going to be a major postoperative problem, and perhaps worse, I knew that he knew it. Deep in his eyes I could see a look of fear, a look of terror; this boy had watched himself fade away over the past three years, and those eyes knew that without this transplant, he would soon be dead, but that even with the transplant, there was a good chance he'd die anyway. That look held my attention for a few very uncomfortable seconds. And then I broke away and tried to make some small talk with him: "So Theo, I hear this is your first trip to America. What do you think of the beautiful Bronx?"

He didn't answer. He just stared back at me with that same look in his eyes.

"They don't speak a word of English," replied a heavyset woman who was sitting in a chair at the boy's bedside. She introduced herself as Anita, a hospital administrator who'd been asked by Dr. Weldon to act as official translator for the family.

I smiled weakly. "Tell them I'm Dr. Marion," I said, "and that I'm the senior resident on this ward. Some other doctors and I will be taking care of Theo while he's here in the hospital."

Anita spoke to the family in rapid-fire Greek. The translator's words brought a smile to the lips of Mrs. Papadopoulos, a thin, middle-aged woman who was sitting next to Anita at her son's bedside, and then a brief response in Greek. When the mother fell silent again, the administrator turned back toward me and said, "Mrs. Papadopoulos says she's happy to meet you, and that she and Theo are very happy to be here. She wants to know if you're the one who'll be performing the operations."

I smiled and explained that no, the transplant would be performed by the attending urologic surgeon, and that we members of the pediatric housestaff would be around mainly to help Dr. Weldon's nephrology group manage Theo's fluid and electrolyte balance following the surgery. After another exchange in Greek, I saw the mother's smile fade, and after she nodded, I excused myself and said I'd see them later.

"Terrific," I sighed, as I headed out of the room, realizing how much more difficult our jobs were going to be without the ability to communicate directly with the patient and his mother. "Another University Hospital Special!"

•   •   •

University Hospital had achieved its reputation as an international leader in pediatric nephrology in the late 1960s, after it had been the site of the world's first pediatric kidney transplant. Since that time, Dr. Weldon, who had been there from the very beginning, and his handpicked and trained staff of urologic surgeons, nephrologists, and nurses, had had more experience in managing children prior to, during, and following this operation than any other group of physicians in the world. As a result, Dr. Weldon's team was internationally renowned, and the pediatric ward always seemed to be home to at least one celebrity or foreign national child, who was either waiting for, or had just received, a transplanted kidney. This situation made life extremely difficult for us house officers. Weldon and his staff treated us as little more than scut puppies for these patients; we were called on to do the legwork for the Big Shots, running down apparently lost lab results, delivering "precious" specimens of blood or urine, ordering tests the purpose of which would never be explained to us. We learned almost nothing from our involvement with Dr. Weldon's private patients and were never invited to offer input when important decisions concerning their management were being made; we were there, it seemed, simply to carry out the wishes of the attendings and fellows. So I suspected that, following Theo Papadopoulos's appearance in the recovery room that afternoon, Larry Hawkins, Dr. Weldon's nephrology fellow on call that day, was going to run Scott Anderson and me completely ragged.

Larry didn't let me down. As expected, Theo's fluid and electrolyte balance was about as screwed up as any human's could possibly get. The boy was wheeled into the recovery room in a light coma induced by the anesthesia; he was attached to a ventilator, and gallons of urine were pouring out of the catheter that had been passed into his bladder at the start of the operation. This prodigious outpouring was completely normal; it represented the body's attempt, through the use of its newly restored renal function, to mobilize and regulate the immense overload of fluid with which Theo had come out of the operating room. Theo was losing literally entire pounds of weight before our eyes, and this was causing major shifts in the balance of the electrolytes sodium, potassium, and chloride in virtually every compartment of the boy's body.

As soon as Theo was handed over by the anesthesiologist, Larry Hawkins put us to work. His first act was to order Scott Anderson to draw and send off a whole batch of blood tests. "And make sure that stuff gets done stat!" he yelled as the intern, tubes of blood and lab slips balanced precariously in his hands, ran out of the recovery room in the direction of the lab. The renal fellow ordered me to do an immediate urinalysis, so that he could judge how the new kidney was functioning. He ordered that the recovery room nurses make up three different IV solutions, so that we'd be ready to make an immediate change just as soon as results were available from the laboratory. The man was certainly organized, but he made all of our lives miserable.

The activity continued at this level throughout the rest of the afternoon and night. Neither Scott nor I got any sleep; we spent all of our time running around the hospital. It wasn't just the work Larry lined up for us that made that night crazy: in addition to our jobs as scut runners for the renal fellow, we had the responsibility of caring for all the other patients who were up on the pediatric ward. So when we weren't being ordered around by Larry Hawkins, we were off attempting to prevent some other disaster. And the worst part of all this was that we never had any idea of what exactly was going on with Theo; we were doing all this scut work, but we didn't know whether he was getting better or becoming more unstable. The boy was still anesthetized, so even when we had a chance to look at him during one of our brief sweeps through the recovery room to either pick up the next blood sample or drop off the results from the last, we weren't able to monitor his condition by seeing how he responded to our presence. He did continue to put out huge quantities of urine throughout the night, though; we had no trouble seeing that. He appeared to be shriveling up like a prune.

Although Scott and I were exhausted the next day, Theo, at least on paper, was much better; in the afternoon, Larry authorized the boy's discharge from the recovery room, and Theo was moved back to the pediatric ward, to the bed next to his mother, who herself was making a rapid recovery from the surgical removal of her right kidney. But even though the boy's output of urine had slowed to a more normal range, and his electrolytes were pretty much back to levels considered at least within the range of normal for a human, Theo was still very sick. Again, that information was obvious not from any single blood test or X-ray study, but from the frightened look that persisted deep within the boy's eyes.

Over the next few days, Theo made slow, but steady, progress. I had to admit he was doing pretty damned well postoperatively; in fact, he'd had fewer complications than any of the other transplant patients with whom I'd been involved. He seemed to be cheering up, too; on rounds one morning, we caught him watching a rerun of "I Love Lucy" on television, and even though he didn't understand a single word the characters were saying, there was an actual smile on his face and occasional peals of laughter emanating from his mouth. "Amazing," I told my team as they reminded me of the dire predictions I had made when the boy was admitted. "Just shows you how much you can trust me." I was beginning to believe Theo was going to make it through this transplant without a single disaster.

But then, just when he seemed to be coming out of the woods, a problem appeared: the blood work we were sending off every day showed that the new kidney's function was worsening. An extensive workup was undertaken, and the nephrologists diagnosed acute rejection crisis, a serious complication in which Theo's immune system, beginning to recognize his mother's kidney as foreign, was producing antibodies designed to destroy this newly discovered invader. Immediate action was needed.

After a conference with Dr. Weldon, Larry Hawkins came back to us with the nephrology group's plan: they were going to start Theo on anti-lymphocyte globulin, or ALG, an experimental drug that had recently been developed for rejection crisis. ALG was designed to destroy the patient's B-lymphocytes, the white blood cells that produce anitbodies, before those cells have a chance to respond to the challenge of the "foreign invader." Scott Anderson and I were, to say the least, somewhat reluctant to carry out the nephrologists' wishes; we knew ALG had been tested on rats and mice, but the drug had never been used on humans. "You're going to treat a kid who's this sick with a drug that's never been used on humans before?" Scott asked Larry when the fellow informed us of the plan. "Why don't you just take a gun and blow the kid's brains out?"

But Larry didn't offer us an answer. The nephrologists did what they wanted to do: Theo was immediately begun on the treatments. This translated into more headaches for Scott and me. Because the use of ALG was experimental, we were going to have to be extra careful in monitoring the boy. Larry told us that we needed to check the boy's pulse, blood pressure, and urine output every hour, test his blood electrolyte levels and renal function every eight hours, and do an ultrasound test of his kidneys and X rays of his chest each day.

"But the most important thing you've got to do," Larry added, "is always make sure you check out any complaint the kid might have. We don't know what side effects this stuff might have on him; we have no idea what problems, if any, we can expect. So if he complains of an ache or a pain, no matter how minor it might seem, make sure you take it seriously."

"Yeah, Larry, that sounds great," Scott responded when the fellow had finished. "We'll be sure to take anything he says seriously. Only problem is, the kid speaks nothing but Greek. How are we supposed to take his complaints seriously if we don't know what the hell he's talking about?"

"Well, ask the translator," the fellow responded.

"Terrific solution, Larry," I replied. "Anita's wonderful as long as she's around. But she only works eight hours a day, five days a week, and she's got a lot of responsibilities of her own. The fact of the matter is, most of the time, we have absolutely no way to communicate with this kid or his mother."

Larry thought about it for a minute. "Well, just do your best," he concluded as he began walking away.

Fine. We did just what the fellow told us to do; we did our best, but sometimes our best just didn't seem good enough. Scott was now spending almost all his time with Theo and the boy's mother. Because the ALG was not approved for use in children, or even in adults, for that matter, the entire nursing staff had refused to administer it. We house officers were the ones who had to give Theo every single dose. So Scott stayed in there, just about moving into the Honeymoon Suite with Theo and his mother; he watched the boy's eyes, and he listened to him scream and complain in Greek every time the medication was squirted into his veins. "He says it burns his arm," Scott explained to me as I watched the process one day. "The translator told me that."

"Anything we can do?" I asked.

"Nope," Scott replied. "Just listen to him scream, I guess."

Scott was the first to bring to my attention the fact that Theo, who was thin and wasted, was beginning to dwindle away to nothing. "He doesn't eat a thing," the intern told me. "His tray comes into the room, sits on his bedside table for a couple of hours, and then leaves completely untouched by human hands."

"Is it a problem with his appetite?" I asked.

The intern nodded, and I asked, "Is that something we need to worry about?"

"Larry Hawkins says no," Scott answered. "He says it's just because the kid's renal function is still not too terrific. He says we'll know Theo's doing better when he starts wanting to eat again."

Within another few days, we were all beginning to get pretty discouraged. Theo's renal function was slowly getting worse. Other than burning his veins every time it was given to him, the ALG didn't seem to be having any effect. We all knew that if this episode of rejection crisis continued for much longer, the boy would lose his mother's kidney; he'd have to go back on the dialysis machine, and when that happened, his chances of survival would drop dramatically.

I don't think anyone told Theo any of this, but I was pretty sure he knew it. That look I'd seen in his eyes the night before the surgery, which had disappeared in the days following the transplant, gradually began to reappear. I got the feeling that Theo was also beginning to give up hope. He knew he was reaching the end of the line.

•   •   •

Days passed. Theo held on, enduring the painful injections of ALG, his mother's kidney piddling along inside him, its function apparently stabilizing, not getting appreciably better, but at the same time becoming no worse. He managed to learn a few words of medical English, like _blood pressure_ and _IV_, but still not nearly enough to communicate his needs, or complaints, or feelings, or thoughts to those of us who were caring for him.

On rounds one morning, we reached the Honeymoon Suite and found Theo angrily yelling something at us in Greek. The look of fear was no longer in his eyes, but the boy had a very serious, almost grave expression on his face. It had been exactly ten days since the experimental medication had been started, and the fact that Theo was so obviously unhappy about something made me more than a little panicked. "What's wrong with him?" I asked Scott Anderson, who knew Theo better than any of us. "Do you have any idea what he's saying?"

The intern shook his head while Theo once again shouted the phrase at us. "Where's the translator?" I asked. "How come that Anita's never around when we need her?"

"Today's her day off," Scott replied. And then, again, the boy said the words, very angrily and seriously.

"Is he sick?" I asked, becoming more rattled. "Has there been any change in his vital signs?"

"Nope," Scott replied, looking over the boy's bedside chart. "His pulse and blood pressure are all normal. His urine output is about the same as it's been. He doesn't have a fever. . . ." Scott was interrupted by Theo's voice. The boy seemed to be getting angrier.

"Well, there must be something wrong," I went on. "What are the latest results of his 'lytes and function tests?"

Scott flipped a page on the bedside clipboard and scanned the sheet in front of him. "No change," he said after a few seconds. And then, Mrs. Papadopoulos also said the phrase. She seemed to be getting angry with us, too.

Just then the renal team arrived. The room became crowded as Weldon—the essence of the cool, calm clinician, wearing a heavily starched, knee-length, ultrawhite doctor's coat—sauntered into the room, followed by the attendings, nurses, and fellows who made up the rest of his entourage. "Well, how's our little Greek god doing today?" the Big Man asked, directing his pearly-white smile in the direction of Mrs. Papadopoulos. The boy and his mother took this opportunity to, in unison, hit the group with their loudest, angriest, most dramatic repetition of the phrase yet.

"What's wrong with them?" Weldon asked, his fixed smile diminishing slightly.

"We don't know, Dr. Weldon," I replied. "None of us can understand what he's saying."

"Where's Anita?" he asked.

"She's off today," Scott said again.

"Surely there must be someone else within the confines of this major teaching hospital who understands Greek and can act as a translator," the attending said.

"I've tried on a number of occasions," Scott answered. "There's no one here except Anita. And, like I said, she's off today."

"Well, how are his clinical signs?" Weldon asked, turning his attention to Larry Hawkins. "Certainly if there's anything wrong with the boy, our tests would have uncovered the problem."

Larry Hawkins then launched into a soliloquy on where Theo

had been over the past day and where, apparently, he would be heading over the next twenty-four hours. Standing at attention, without relying on notes of any kind, Larry flawlessly recited ranges of vital signs, as well as the results of every blood and urine test that had been performed over the past day; he produced and interpreted X rays and ultrasound pictures. And when he was done, Weldon looked back at the boy and said, "Well, there seems to be no perceptibly significant change in any single parameter. These people apparently want us to know something, but what that something is, I haven't the foggiest idea." The man thought for a minute or two more, and then, without another word, turned and walked out of the room. The entourage briskly followed after him, no one making a sound. As they reached the hall, the boy angrily yelled out the phrase once again.

"Well, that was enlightening," Scott said after they were gone. "What should we do?"

"Nothing, I guess," I replied after some hesitation. "If those guys weren't able to come up with a single thing for us to do, there must not be anything for us to do. I guess we'll just observe him."

So we spent most of the rest of that day observing him. What we mainly observed was that Theo and his mother were getting angrier and more exasperated as the hours passed. Whenever the boy would see any of us, he'd yell out his phrase. A few times, his mother walked out into the nurses' station exclusively to yell the same thing at some member of the staff.

But, at the same time this was happening, we were noticing some positive things. That day, for the first time, the boy's kidney function tests showed some improvement; his urine output, which had gradually dropped down to very low levels over the past few days, began to pick up again. It seemed, at last, that the ALG was having some effect on the rejection crisis. But at the same time, we were all concerned; if he was getting better, why was he complaining so much?

Somehow we all made it through that night without any of us going completely batty. And the next morning, we all knew, Anita was scheduled to be back at her desk in the administrative office on the hospital's first floor. As soon as eight o'clock rolled around, I called her number. She picked up on the second ring. "You've got to get up here right away," I told her. "We've got an emergency with

Theo. He's been trying to tell us something since yesterday morning, and we haven't been able to understand him. We're really getting worried."

She assured me she'd be up right away, and emerged from the elevator onto the pediatric ward in slightly less than five minutes. I hustled her into the Honeymoon Suite, followed close behind by Scott Anderson, as well as the rest of the ward's staff of nurses, interns, and medical students.

Upon seeing her, Theo's eyes opened wide. His face retained that solemn, serious look that had been there since the morning before, and he repeated the phrase he'd been trying to get us to understand, without a shred of satisfaction, for over twenty-four hours now: *"Thelo ohtapothi, do thelo tiyanito, ke do thelo tora."*

I watched Anita's face carefully, trying to read from it the significance of the boy's words. The translator, initially concentrating deeply while the boy spoke, broke into a brief smile when the message was complete; then suddenly, uncontrollably, that smile was replaced with hysterical laughter. "That's it?" she managed to get out between laughs. "That's the big emergency? You've been worried about this for how long?"

"Since yesterday morning," I answered. "What's he saying?"

"This is what he wants you to know," Anita replied, trying to sound as solemn as the boy had sounded:

"'I want an octopus, I want it fried, and I want it now!'"

"That's it?" I asked as the entire team began to laugh.

"That's it," she responded. "Can I get back to my desk now?"

I told her that she certainly could, and, apologetically, thanked her for all her help. "I guess this means he's really getting better," Anita said as she headed for the door.

"I guess so," I replied. "It looks like he's finally getting his appetite back."

A little while later, after rounds were finished, I sent one of the medical students on our team on what had to be the most crucial task of his career so far. His pockets heavy with donations made by every member of the staff who'd cared for Theo during the three weeks he'd been in the hospital, that student set off to purchase as many fried octopuses as he could get at one of the many seafood restaurants on City Island. He returned a little over two hours later, loaded down with three whole fried octopuses and all the trimmings.

Within minutes, we watched as Theo, a broad smile on his face and delight in his eyes, wolfed down each and every one of those cephalopods.

That was indeed the first sign we had that Theo was on his way to recovery. A few days after his octopus feast, the boy's rejection crisis was officially declared to be at an end. The ALG, a drug that became widely used in the years following Theo's transplant, had saved the kidney. By the end of my one-month rotation at University Hospital, Theo was ready for discharge. He and his mother returned to Athens, to be reunited with his father and the rest of his family. As far as I know, he's still there today, leading a productive and fruitful adult life, his mother's kidney still toiling away, cleansing his blood of toxic impurities.

Sometimes, performing all the sophisticated and fancy tests in the world just doesn't provide enough essential information; sometimes, you have to feed a kid an octopus to find out whether or not he's getting better.

Angela's Eyes

• • •

ANGELA'S EYES LED ME down a path that occupied my professional life for nearly two full years. The appearance of her face led me into a world I'd never have otherwise been able to enter; it allowed me to view, from the inside, the events that occurred in the lives of fifty-five extraordinary infants and children. It would not be incorrect to say that this little girl's eyes changed the course of my academic career.

I first saw those eyes in 1981, when Angela was less than a month old. She had been brought to the pediatric emergency room at Jonas Bronck Hospital by her aunt, who, during a visit to the girl's mother's apartment, had become alarmed because her niece looked terrible—thin and wasted. The girl's mother, who had been using drugs since early adolescence and had been shooting heroin for the past five years, explained to the aunt that Angela had been having diarrhea for the past two weeks, and that she hadn't yet managed to get around to taking the child to a doctor for a checkup. The physicians who saw Angela in the emergency room at Jonas Bronck, after documenting that she weighed six pounds, seven ounces, a full pound and a half less than she'd weighed at birth, assessed her to be between 5 and 10 percent dehydrated and, after sticking an IV into her arm and giving her an infusion of normal saline, admitted the infant to the pediatric ward for further evaluation and treatment.

The girl was managed in the way most infants with the diagnosis of gastroenteritis (an infection of the lining of the stomach and intestine) usually are: she was begun on a drip of intravenous fluids that was carefully calculated to provide all the electrolytes necessary to keep her system in balance, and was made NPO ("nothing per oral"; NPO patients are given nothing to eat or drink by mouth), in an attempt to allow time for her gastrointestinal tract to heal itself. To identify a possible infectious agent, samples of her stool were sent to the lab and cultured for the presence of abnormal bacteria and parasites. But in spite of all this, the child's diarrhea persisted. After two days, a gastroenterology consult was requested; the GI service's attending physician offered a long list of possible diagnoses, and made some helpful suggestions regarding the girl's management. But even after these suggestions were put into effect, Angela's diarrhea continued. Although the lab reported growth of only normal intestinal bacteria in the stool samples, an infectious disease consultation was obtained. Again, in spite of the changes suggested by this team of doctors, Angela's diarrhea simply would not stop.

The baby was having between ten and twelve large, watery bowel movements each day. Her weight continued to plummet; seven days after admission, for the first time in her life, it dropped below six pounds. The infant's clinical status was growing more serious with each passing day, and the senior resident running the pediatric ward, after talking the situation over with the chief residents, decided it was time to embark on a "million dollar workup."

That's how I first came to meet Angela. I was a resident at that time, doing a one-month elective in human genetics, and as part of the infant's planned workup, our group had been asked to offer its opinion. We had been called because, when she had been admitted to the hospital, Angela had been noted to have some slightly unusual facial characteristics. The questions the house staff wanted us genet-icists to answer was, Could Angela's unusual facial features and her chronic diarrhea be in any way connected? Did the infant have some rare, previously undiagnosed syndrome?

So I went up to the ward to see her. She'd been placed in an isolation room, down toward the end of the hall on 8 West. When I first saw her from the doorway of her room, I was struck by how pathetic she looked: thin, cachectic, and chronically ill, her arms and legs seemed like toothpicks stretching out from her wasted body. But as I got closer, I realized she was actually quite cute; her face looked doll-like and familiar, and I thought for sure I'd seen this little girl someplace before. After gazing at her for a few seconds, it finally came to me: Angela looked just like one of the small, wide-eyed waifs painted by Walter Keane, whose portraits were popular for a time in the early seventies.

The longer I gazed at her, the more I realized it definitely was her eyes that gave her this unusual appearance. Big and beautiful, slightly widely spaced and upward-slanting, Angela's eyes were made more striking by the fact that the scleras, the parts that usually are white, were sky blue in color. There was something majestic about those eyes, a quality that immediately drew one's thoughts away from her cachexia and her pathetic, unremitting intestinal disease.

The rest of her exam was basically normal. Having no idea what disease or syndrome, if any, would explain those eyes and that diarrhea, I told the resident on the ward I'd be back later in the day with my attending, the director of the genetics service, in tow. When we returned that afternoon, he too was struck by the appearance of the girl's eyes, or her "palpebral fissures," as he called them; like me, though, he could come up with the name of no syndrome or disease that would explain her symptoms and signs. He suggested that we perform cytogenetic studies, a blood test to examine the child's chromosomal makeup. When the results came back, showing that Angela had a normal 46,XX karyotype, the director concluded that Angela's problem was not of a genetic nature; thus, my official involvement with the girl came to an end.

Angela's workup continued, however. Physicians from the metabolism, renal, and endocrine services came by to offer their opinions. Diets and medications were recommended, none of which had any significant positive effect. The child's diarrhea persisted, essentially unchanged. In an attempt to prevent her weight from dropping any further, the decision was made to start Angela on total parenteral nutrition, an IV solution containing everything needed for growth, including protein, fats, and carbohydrates. Although the solution was calculated to provide enough calories to keep the girl in metabolic balance, her weight finally bottomed out at slightly above five pounds. And then, in desperation, having exhausted every logical step in the workup that might shed some light on the etiology of Angela's disease, the chief resident suggested that the immunology team see the child.

It was illogical, he thought, but perhaps the girl's intestinal problems were in some way related to one of the rare, inherited immune system deficiency states. He knew this was a long shot, but there was nothing left to consider.

It took the director of the immunology service less than five minutes to make the diagnosis. For the past two years, he and the other members of his division had consulted on the cases of at least five other children at hospitals around the Bronx who, like Angela, had been afflicted with severe, chronic diarrhea during the first year or two of life; all had eventually gone on to develop serious, recurrent bacterial infections, and four of the five had died of overwhelming pneumonia. In the laboratory, each child had been found to have abnormally functioning T-lymphocytes, the white blood cells that fight off infection. Finally, like Angela, all had been born to women who had been long-term intravenous drug users. The immunologist was sure that Angela had this disorder, a disease that simply over-whelmed the immune system. This illness closely resembled an entity that had only recently been found in adult gay men, which, since the publication of a series of articles in the _New England Journal of Medicine,_ was being called acquired immune deficiency syndrome, or AIDS.

The immunologist's diagnosis, and its verification through the series of lab tests he performed, stunned most of us house officers. By that time, every one of us had at least heard of this mysterious AIDS; we had all read the continual reports of mortality and mor-bidity, devastation and destruction that the disorder seemed to be wreaking in New York City and San Francisco, but none of us had, up to that point, ever actually seen a person with AIDS. We never imagined that we'd end up caring for a patient with the disorder; after all, we were pediatricians, and AIDS was not a disease of children. It was a disorder that afflicted only adults who belonged to one of four apparently sharply defined groups: gays, hemophiliacs, intravenous drug users, or Haitians. That Angela had AIDS, the fact that this disease could and did occur in small children who had none of the risk factors usually associated with the adult disorder, made us pause and think of the consequences. House officers and staff members of Jonas Bronck's pediatric service who had not yet been directly involved with Angela's care flocked to her bedside. Some believed Angela to be something of a freak, a child with a rare disease that they hadn't seen before and weren't likely to see again. Others, such as the immunologist who had first made the diagnosis, knew differently; they understood that Angela most likely represented the sad face of the future.

Of course the immunologist was right; our amazement was all too short-lived. Just a little over a month after Angela's diagnosis had been confirmed, after the girl's diarrhea had finally, thankfully, slowed up and ultimately ceased, after she had been restarted on oral feedings and was beginning to gain some weight, a sixteen-month-old boy was admitted to 8 West through the emergency room, with symptoms that were identical to Angela's. Also the child of an IV heroin user, Jesus had had continuous diarrhea for the past two months, and he'd lost a total of just over three pounds. Jesus was the second patient with AIDS on the pediatric service, but he was far from the last. His admission signaled the beginning of the onslaught, the start of an epidemic that has continued unabated ever since, an epidemic that has changed the face of pediatrics and pediatric residency training in New York and throughout the rest of the United States.

I didn't have much to do with Jesus when he first appeared at Jonas Bronck. I was away from the hospital at the time, doing rotations at facilities affiliated with our program; during those months, I lost touch with life on the pediatric wards back in the Bronx. But when I returned four months later for my next rotation at Jonas Bronck Hospital, I was astonished at what I found: fully 10 percent of the hospital's pediatric beds were filled with children who had AIDS.

That was in July, the first month of my senior residency. Walking around with my team of three interns on the first day of that new month, I found it almost too much to believe. In the short time I'd been away, everything had changed; the entire back area of 8 West, three rooms that had previously been used for isolating patients with acute infections, had been turned into housing for five children with AIDS. Angela, then eight months old, her eyes still as large and wide and regal as they'd been the first day I'd seen her, now shared her space with Jesus, Martin, Nora, and Eduordo. Together these five unrelated kids formed a new kind of family. These children, having been rendered pariahs because of a disease over which there was absolutely no control, having been abandoned by their mothers who themselves were growing sick and weak with the disease, and by their grandparents and other relatives who feared the repercussions— both the very real social ones, and the imagined medical ones—of caring for a child diagnosed as having AIDS, had already come to depend on each other for entertainment. They had also come to depend on us—the ward staff—for the love, attention, and nourishment every child needs. As the senior resident, I knew that it would be up to me to hold all of this together. I would be the one who had to make sure that the necessary treatments were provided, that all the goods, both medical and emotional, that these children required were delivered; at the same time, I would have to assure that my interns and I were protected from the trauma and the pain of caring for a group of children who, sometime in the near future, were almost certain to die.

And then, one night when I was on call, it happened. An infant was admitted from the emergency room in severe respiratory distress. Jeffrey was a four-week-old baby who was breathing eighty times a minute, much faster than normal. The child had a fever of 103.6, and his chest was retracting violently with every breath. He had a hoarse, rattling cough, and on X ray, infiltrates were seen throughout both of his lung fields. All of these findings were compatible with pneumonia caused by *Pneumocystis carynii,* a deadly parasite that is one of the hallmarks of the immunodeficiency found in AIDS. And, like the children in the back rooms on 8 West, this baby was the child of a woman who used IV drugs.

Because of his severe respiratory distress, the infant was intubated in the emergency room; a plastic tube was passed down into his windpipe via his mouth and through his vocal cords. Immediately after the tube was in place, the boy was put on a ventilator and transferred to the pediatric intensive care unit, where an intern and I were waiting for him. When I saw Jeffrey for the first time, I did a double take.

He had the eyes. He was deathly ill, critically sick, but there could be no denying it: big and beautiful, with a slight upward slant to them, widely spaced, with scleras as blue as the sky, his eyes looked just like Angela's. In fact, the resemblance between the two children was startling: even though they were not related and weren't even of the same ethnic group, even though one was a boy and the other a girl, the Jeffrey I saw that night in the pediatric ICU and the

Angela I'd seen months before as a genetic consultant on 8 West could have passed for twins.

Unfortunately, Jeffrey did not survive. He died of respiratory failure in the ICU three days after he was admitted; he was never able to make it off the ventilator. As expected, he was found on autopsy to have been suffering from an overwhelming *Pneumocystis carynii* pneumonia, and the immunologic tests that had been done right before he died confirmed that Jeffrey had been suffering from the effects of AIDS. I saw him only briefly before his death, but Jeffrey's eyes, like those of Angela, stayed with me. And because both had those eyes and that diagnosis, I began to consider the possibility that these two things might somehow be related; this couldn't, I figured, just be a coincidence.

I had no way of really explaining it. Maybe, I figured during brief spare moments, there was something about this disease, something as yet unknown about its pathogenesis, that caused affected children to have those big, Walter Keane–like eyes. Maybe somewhere within those eyes there was a clue to the way in which this horrible disease did its dirty work. I guessed it was possible; at that time, anything seemed possible. But as of then, it was nothing but speculation, and although I knew that sitting back and trying to imagine some connection between children's eyes and pediatric AIDS wasn't bad, it was little more than an idle pastime, a luxury that a house officer simply could not afford. There were just too many other things that had to be done: admitting, caring for, and discharging patients; starting IVs and doing spinal taps; tracking down lab results; discussing problems with subspecialists, surgeons, and social workers; scheduling tests and tracking down results; going to conferences; teaching medical students and interns; and, if time permitted, getting a couple of hours of sleep. There was just no time left for a senior resident to lazily contemplate the origins of AIDS. So my thoughts about the link were put on a back burner. I had to survive my residency before I could even consider solving this puzzle.

I did survive, and after beginning a fellowship in our medical school's human genetics program the following July, I stopped in to discuss Angela and Jeffrey with the staff of University Hospital's Pediatric Immunodeficiency Clinic. By that point, I'd begun to doubt the link myself; if there really was something there, I'd been thinking for the past few months, why hadn't someone else figured it out yet? But, in speaking with the immunologists, I found that not only did they not think my idea was crazy, they seemed to agree with it. In fact, the director of the immunology program, the man who had diagnosed Angela's condition within minutes of seeing her, said that, over the course of the past year, he himself had noticed that a number of the patients seemed to resemble each other, and that he'd tried to figure out what significance this phenomenon might have.

That's how I became a member of the pediatric AIDS team at University Hospital. Over the next two years, working with Alan Werner, a friend and former co-resident at Jonas Bronck who had gone on to become an immunology fellow when I'd entered the genetics program, I traveled the Bronx, examining children with AIDS in hospitals and outpatient clinics, searching for physical similarities. But inevitably, my involvement with these children didn't end with the completion of those brief physical examinations. Rather, our initial contacts were more often than not the beginning of what became long-standing relationships with these patients and their families. And many times, the stories that unfolded as a result of these relationships were nothing short of extraordinary.

•   •   •

On our first trip to Bronx Episcopal Medical Center, a hospital in the South Bronx, Alan Werner and I met Emilio Diaz, a five-month-old who had been living on the pediatric ward for over three months. Emilio had been brought to the hospital by his mother at seven weeks of age because of a bad cough and rapid breathing. A diagnosis of pneumonia had been made, Emilio had been admitted to the ward and treated with IV antibiotics, and after two weeks had passed and the boy seemed healthy again, the doctors, in an attempt to discharge him, had tried to contact the mother. When multiple attempts to call the number listed on the boy's chart ended with no answer, a telegram had been sent, asking the mother to contact the pediatric ward as soon as possible. But the telegram also had gone unanswered. Finally, after nearly two more weeks had passed and the social worker assigned to the pediatric ward had reported the case to the Bureau of Child Welfare, the state agency charged with protecting minors, Emilio's father had finally telephoned the ward.

He was sorry no one had been by to visit the boy, he told the social worker, but things were in an uproar in their family: just after Emilio had been hospitalized at Bronx Episcopal, the boy's mother had been admitted to Jefferson Hospital, also in the South Bronx, with bacterial meningitis. She had been in a coma ever since, and just a few days before, the doctors there had told the man that his wife had AIDS and was dying of the disease; they didn't expect her to survive for more than a week or so.

The father, who'd been devastated by this news, admitted that although he'd like to take the boy home with him, there was no way he could care for Emilio by himself. He was addicted to heroin, and in addition to everything else, feared that he, too, would soon become sick with the disease that was quickly claiming his wife. So there was no choice: even though Emilio was now in excellent health, even though no diagnosis of AIDS had yet been made in him, the boy had no place to go. And so, like Angela and the growing list of others, he simply stayed on at the hospital as a boarder. The boy became attached to the nurses and the house officers who worked on the Bronx Episcopal's pediatric ward, quickly coming to consider them his adoptive family.

When I first saw Emilio, I was struck again by those eyes and by his resemblance to Angela and Jeffrey. By that time, our number of similar-appearing children was unfortunately growing, and both Alan Werner and I were becoming fairly proficient at predicting which children would turn out to be affected with AIDS and which would not. In looking over Emilio's hospital chart that first afternoon, Alan noticed that the level of total protein in the boy's blood was extremely high, an early laboratory sign, he knew, of AIDS. He requested that blood be sent to the immunology lab for further testing, but looking at those eyes, we both knew what the test results would be before the blood was even out of Emilio's vein.

We were right; so Emilio was added to our study. He stayed on at the pediatric ward at Bronx Episcopal, the only home he'd really known. Alan and I visited him there every Wednesday during our weekly trips to the South Bronx, and watched him gradually grow and develop. During our rounds, we picked him up and carried him along with us when he grew tired of sitting in his crib; we were there the day he took his first step in the corridor outside the pediatric ward's run-down playroom at fifteen months of age. We became attached to him, this cute little kid with the great big eyes. And then, one Wednesday, when we showed up for our regular weekly visit, Emilio was gone.

Death doesn't usually come quietly or gradually to children with AIDS; it comes rapidly, and with a roar. One day a child can be perfectly healthy and happy; the next day, he might be attached to a ventilator in an ICU, fighting with all his might for his every breath. So when Alan and I realized Emilio was gone, we both cringed for an instant. But thank God, no, he hadn't died. When we were told by the chief resident what had actually happened to the boy, we both agreed that it sounded a lot more like fiction than like real life.

It turned out that, while most of the Bronx Episcopal pediatric staff had, like Alan and me, grown attached to Emilio, one nurse had literally fallen in love with the boy. She had been his primary nurse, caring for him every day during his stay in the hospital; it was she who'd spent the most time with him, working on his development, getting him to stand and to walk and to speak, first in single words and then in sentences; it was she who'd changed his diapers and wiped his constantly runny nose, apparently not concerned, or simply ignoring the possibility, that such close contact with Emilio, as with any other patient with AIDS, might put her life in jeopardy. And it was she who, after investigating and finding out from the ward's social worker that adopting Emilio outright would be impossible as long as the boy's father was still in the picture, approached that father with an extremely unorthodox proposition: she would marry Mr. Diaz, and after taking Emilio home, they would live together in her apartment as a family. Mr. Diaz, who loved his son very much and had always regretted the fact that the child was wasting away in a steel crib on a hospital ward, jumped at the opportunity.

They were married in a civil ceremony at the Bronx County Courthouse, and that afternoon, they took Emilio home. Over the next two years, that nurse did everything she could to give the boy as full a life as possible. She understood from the very beginning that they wouldn't have a great deal of time. After taking a leave of absence from her job, using the money she'd saved over the years for her own retirement, the three of them began to travel. They flew to Puerto Rico, to visit relatives of the boy's father and deceased mother whom Emilio never even knew existed; they spent three weeks there, seeing everything tourists were supposed to see, as well as visiting family and friends. They spent a month the next winter driving through the southern United States to Florida, where they visited every attraction, from Disney World to the EPCOT Center, that a nearly three-year-old could possibly understand and appreciate. Emilio was loved and cared for in the way all children need to be, and every one of his days was packed with as much activity as the boy, who, as time passed, was gradually becoming thinner and weaker, could handle.

When Emilio was nearly three-and-a-half years old, he developed what appeared to be an upper respiratory infection. His adoptive mother, retaining the instincts of a top-notch pediatric nurse, immediately brought him to the emergency room at Bronx Episcopal. A chest X ray revealed diffuse pneumonia, most likely caused by *Pneumocystis carynii.* The boy was immediately intubated and placed on a ventilator, and then transferred to the pediatric ICU at Jonas Bronck. It was in that ICU that Emilio, unconscious and unstable, spent his last week on earth.

When the end came, Emilio's father and adoptive mother had absolutely no regrets. They knew the score, and, without prompting, had requested that a Do Not Resuscitate order be written on the boy's chart. They told the staff that they didn't want Emilio to suffer; he had lived a good life, and they wanted his end to come comfortably and with dignity.

These two people had at first been joined together not because there was any real love or even attraction between them, but for convenience. It was a marriage that had occurred in order to fulfill a simple, practical purpose: to facilitate getting the little boy, about whom they both cared greatly, out of the hospital-prison in which he'd been condemned to live out the rest of his short life. But as time passed, something changed in the relationship between this man and woman: even a casual observer could see that something real had grown up between them, a respect and caring for each other that transcended their common love for Emilio. I never saw Emilio's father or his adoptive mother again after the boy's death, but I've often wondered whether they're still together out there, fending off the death and destruction that surrounds them on the streets of the South

Bronx, an odd couple now held together by something more than their memories of a very special little boy.

•   •   •

I was more intimately involved with Tanya; I knew her at three different stages in her short life. We first met during one of her regular visits to the Pediatric Immunodeficiency Clinic when the girl was a little over a year old. It was the first day I had attended the clinic, and she was the third patient I saw that morning. She had the facial features I was becoming more confident existed as part of the disease, and we entered her into our study. Her story was similar to so many I'd heard before, and so many I've heard since: The daughter of a woman who'd been shooting heroin for years, Tanya, at the age of two weeks, had developed thrush, a yeast infection of the mouth, that just wouldn't go away. At two months of age, she developed that terrible, debilitating diarrhea that now seems so much a part of pediatric AIDS; she lost over a pound in weight, and was hospitalized at Jonas Bronck for nearly two weeks, receiving IV fluids and a course of antibiotics. By the age of six months, during her second admission to the hospital for pneumonia, the diagnosis of AIDS was confirmed. But Tanya's story from then on was slightly different from all the others'. After recovering from that bout of pneumonia, the infant was sent home to her grandmother's apartment, where she actually thrived, coming to the Immunodeficiency Clinic every two or three weeks for treatments of intravenous gamma globulin, a therapy that seemed to be doing some good for her, as well as for many of the other clinic children.

Tanya was like many of the children I met in the clinic, kids who were still in the early stages of the disease, in whom the virus still hadn't had much effect on their central nervous systems. Tanya, on that first day, was a plump, outgoing toddler, who had only recently learned how to play peekaboo. I made the mistake of playing the game with her once, and from that point on, I was trapped. She demanded that I repeat it over and over again; she cried every time I tried to walk away. And so, a sucker for a child in tears, I did the only thing I possibly could: I covered my face with a hospital towel and pulled that towel away for nearly three hours, to the delighted squeals of this one-year-old.

The second time I met Tanya was over a year later, after I'd

completed my work in the immunodeficiency clinic. I was moonlight-
ing in the emergency room at Jonas Bronck, working as the attending
in charge one Sunday afternoon in November, when the girl's grandmother brought her in. Late that morning, Tanya had had a seizure
that affected only the left side of her body. Seizures in general are a
bad sign in children with AIDS; they usually indicate that something
is terribly wrong with one part of the brain. So we took Tanya's
seizure very seriously. Her chart was put at the top of the triage pile,
and I saw her as soon as the nurses had finished taking her vital
signs.

I couldn't believe this was the same child I'd met two years
before. That child had been playful, full of life. This child was
lethargic and wasted, too weak to do anything more than smile
slightly toward her grandmother. And yet, those eyes had survived
the years of devastation. Those big, beautiful, mesmerizing eyes still
had the power I'd seen in them on the day we first met.

As expected, there was something wrong with her brain. An
emergency CAT scan done that afternoon revealed that a large mass
was taking up much of the right side of the girl's head. The neurologist whom we had called to evaluate Tanya thought the mass represented either an infected abscess or a malignant lymphoma. In
either case, the prognosis was horrible.

It turned out to be a lymphoma. During the hospitalization that
followed that ER visit, the neurosurgeons biopsied the lesion and
made the diagnosis. The immunology team, in consultation with the
neurologists and an oncologist, came to the conclusion that the tumor
was incurable. After a discussion with the girl's grandmother, the
physicians opted for no further treatment. Tanya would be kept as
comfortable as possible; everybody hoped that the end would come
swiftly.

It took nearly two months for that end to come. By chance, I'd
been assigned to be the official attending on the pediatric ward at
University Hospital that January. Tanya had been transferred to that
ward following her brain biopsy, and during the second week of the
month, Sylvia Ruiz, the intern who was the girl's primary caretaker,
had noticed that Tanya's vital signs had become unstable. During
the last month or so, the girl had been drifting in and out of consciousness, but recently, the periods of coma had been lasting longer
and longer. Sylvia, who had been spending a lot of time in the girl's

room, and the rest of us knew the end was near; it couldn't possibly be more than a few more days. And then, one morning during attending rounds, we had just started discussing the patients who had been admitted the night before when Joanne, Tanya's nurse, poked her head into the conference room. "I'm sorry to interrupt," she said, "but I think Tanya's dying." She told us that the girl's blood pressure had dropped precipitously. Slowly, we rose from our chairs and began walking toward Tanya's room.

She was breathing in a terminal pattern, inhaling once or twice, then stopping for a minute, then taking one or two more inspirations. The monitor reading out her heart rate was beeping only forty times a minute. We huddled around her bed, standing at her side as if to guard the dying child from an intruder. I was at the girl's right; Joanne stood next to me; Sylvia stood across from me, cradling the girl's hand in hers. And we stayed like that, frozen, unable to do anything to help this helpless little girl, for the fifteen minutes it took for the cardiac monitor to finally stop beeping.

We declared her at 11:48 A.M. Sylvia Ruiz, with tears in her eyes, ran from the room. The other team members slowly filed out, going sadly back to their duties. Attending rounds were over for the day, that was clear. There was not much left for me to do but gather up my stuff and get ready to head back to my office.

Before leaving the ward that morning, I went to find Sylvia. I was worried about her; patients had died when I had been an intern, and I knew what it felt like. I figured that by talking with her, I might be able to ease her mind.

She was lying on the cot in the interns' on-call room, crying. "Is there anything I can do?" I asked as I entered the tiny room.

She didn't answer; she simply pointed to the room's only chair, and I sat down. "It's a horrible feeling," I sighed.

"She was just a baby," Sylvia said through her tears. "She's been sick all her life. She didn't have a childhood. She never even had a chance to live. . . ." The tears took control of her again.

I took Sylvia's hand and gave it a squeeze. I felt so bad for her. This horrible disease was changing things so fast. In seemingly no time at all, a whole flock of innocent babies, an entire generation of inner-city kids, like Tanya, and Emilio, and Jeffrey, and Angela, was dying right in front of our eyes, dying for no good reason at all, and it was destroying us, all of us who care for children and adults;

virtually every physician in New York was being torn apart by AIDS. I could see the strain of all of this on Sylvia's face, could hear it in Sylvia's sobs.

"All the time she's been here, all I've been able to think about is my girls." Sylvia, who was in her mid-thirties then, had two adolescent daughters. "When they were Tanya's age, I was so proud of them; they were so active and bright. Seeing her like that . . ." Again, the intern was consumed by her tears, and I felt the tears coming to my own eyes.

There was nothing I could say, so I just sat there with her, listening to her cry, trying to hold back my own tears. After a few minutes, she was able to compose herself again. "I'm sorry, Bob. I'm a little tired. I was on last night and I didn't get much sleep. I'd like to try to get some rest. I don't want to cry, but . . ." And with that, she started to cry again.

I nodded, understanding that she wanted me to leave. I released my grip from her hand and rose from the chair. "Are you going to be all right?" I asked. She nodded, and I turned to go.

"Thanks, Bob," I heard her say as the door was closing behind me.

After asking the senior resident to check on Sylvia through the afternoon, I grabbed my briefcase, took the stairs down to the lobby, and, leaving the hospital, headed back to my office.

• • •

Everyone who's worked with patients who are dying of AIDS has had experiences like the two above; every one of us, whether working with children or with adults, has been touched by the patients we've cared for, in ways completely different from those in which most patients touch physicians' lives. That's because AIDS is so different from virtually every other disease that afflicts humanity in large number. There are three reasons for this. First, it attacks people not at the end of long and fruitful lives, as most terminal diseases do, but in the prime of their lives, at a time when they're just starting to live. Children and young adults are not supposed to die; those of us who work in medicine take such deaths almost as a personal affront.

Second, physicians very often identify with patients with AIDS. In 1990, nearly every physician in residency, and those of us who have recently completed our training, knows of at least one contemporary, a friend from high school or college or medical school, who has died or is dying of the disease. We empathize with the patients who are filling our beds, who are slowly but steadily deteriorating. We all know that those patients could be us, and we know there's nothing we can do to stop or even retard their inevitable downhill course.

And finally, AIDS scares us to death. Since the viral etiology of the disease was first discovered, it has become clear that the human immunodeficiency virus can be transmitted through certain types of contact; one of those is the sharing of needles. Every house officer, every physician, at one time or another, during training or while in practice, has inadvertently stabbed himself or herself with a needle that had been used to draw blood from a patient. There have been clearly documented instances of physicians contracting the disease through such accidents. Therefore, in the back of every doctor's mind, as he or she makes the morning rounds and draws the blood work necessary for that day, is the thought that today might be the day, that this might be the hour when I draw that blood and stab myself with that needle, and in a few years, I'll be dead. A whole generation of doctors is being trained to think this way.

In all, Alan Werner and I examined fifty-five patients during our study. We concluded that a significant number of infants and children with AIDS have a characteristic facial appearance. The unusual eyes, along with a few other major characteristics, such as a very prominent forehead and a flattened tip of the nose, were seen most commonly in children such as Angela, Jeffrey, Emilio, and Tanya, children who became sick and were diagnosed as having AIDS within the first four months of life. We reported these findings and conclusions in a series of papers published in the _American Journal of Diseases of Children._

Although there has been a fair amount of controversy surrounding our findings, Alan and I believe that these facial features are present in these affected children because the human immunodeficiency virus has infected them during the first few weeks after conception, at the time the primitive face is beginning to form. This, we believe, is the reason these children become sick so soon after birth. If infection were to occur later in gestation—say, in the second or third trimesters, after the face has already formed—no striking facial features would be seen, and the disease, which presents months or years after infection has occurred, would not be diagnosed until after six months of age. Therefore, the facial features we've described represent a marker, a sign that a child may become sick very early in life.

I have photographs of all the children who were enrolled in our study. Almost all are dead now, and those crude black-and-white mug shots taken for research purposes represent the only tangible memories Alan and I will carry with us of this study. But there is one exception: Angela is still alive. Ironically, the very first patient admitted to Jonas Bronck Hospital with AIDS, the infant who introduced so many of us to the disease, has somehow managed to survive for eight-and-a-half years.

Angela spent nearly the entire first three years of her existence living in a steel crib in one of those converted isolation rooms at the end of 8 West. And then, as if by a miracle, she was placed in a foster home. For the past five-and-a-half years, Angela has lived with Shirley Richardson, a remarkable woman who, thus far, has provided a loving and caring environment for four children with AIDS. Mrs. Richardson is one of the unsung heroes of the AIDS epidemic; if there is a heaven, she will definitely be in it after she dies.

Angela has thrived in Mrs. Richardson's home. Her foster mother's love, coupled with the gamma globulin treatments she receives on a biweekly basis at the immunodeficiency clinic, has kept the girl healthy and happy. At the age of five, amid only a small amount of controversy, Angela entered kindergarten within the New York public school system. Since then, she's continued attending school, and when I last talked with her, she seemed to be doing fairly well.

Angela demonstrates the fact that we really don't know that much about this disease. How she could have been so sick so early in life, and then gone on to thrive, while others have gotten sick much later in life, and died a rapid and horrible death, remains a complete mystery.

Denise Gets Discharged

• ● •

*I*N ORDER TO HAVE THE PLACE READY by the time Denise got back from her last day of school, Kathy Jones, the hospital's child-life worker, spent most of the afternoon decorating the playroom on 8 East. She locked the doors at a little after noon and got down to the serious business at hand; after about two hours of blowing up balloons, stretching crepe paper streamers across the ceiling, and setting up the tables of refreshments, the room was transformed, no longer looking like the plain, toy-littered, converted office that had been set aside years before as a place where hospitalized children could play. Dr. Franklin, the chairman emeritus of the Department of Pediatrics, helped Kathy finish up by nailing to the wall the huge poster-board sign the older children had helped make during the morning. It was that sign that I noticed first when I entered the room at a little before three o'clock. It read Good-bye Denise, in big, bold letters, and it forced me to finally accept the rumor I'd been hearing over the last couple of days: that Denise Sanderson, age eighteen, was actually being discharged from Jonas Bronck Hospital.

Up until that day, Denise had spent her entire life as an inpatient on one of the wards at our hospital. Although she'd been leaving the hospital building almost every day, at first to visit friends and to go on short trips, and then for the past few years to attend a public high school in the Bronx, she had spent virtually every night sleeping in a bed in a room at the far end of 8 East, having her vital signs checked and plotted every eight hours by nurses whom she had come to view more as family members than as hospital workers.

Denise had been born at Jonas Bronck, and it was during her initial neonatal physical exam that a pediatric resident had first noticed the abnormalities in her lower extremities: there appeared to be bowing of the upper parts of both of Denise's legs, and the lower portions were obviously shorter than they should have been. The resident, not having a clue as to what might have caused such deformities, ordered a "babygram," a single X ray of the infant's entire body, in hopes that something would be seen that might explain these findings. That one X ray revealed some startling abnormalities: all of Denise's bones showed osteoporosis, a condition, often seen in postmenopausal women, that is caused by lack of deposition of calcium; this condition leaves the skeleton weak and flimsy, and subject to easy breakage. And that was the other striking abnormality noticed on that initial X ray: there was widespread evidence of fractures; numerous bones in the girl's arms and legs were shattered, some showing breaks in two or three places. It was as if the simple act of being born had been too much for Denise's weak bones to bear. On the basis of this single radiograph, a diagnosis was made that would affect the rest of the girl's life: Denise had osteogenesis imperfecta, or brittle bone disease.

The form of osteogenesis imperfecta, or OI as it's usually called, that was present in Denise was caused by an error in the way her body made Type I collagen, a protein essential for the formation of the bone's matrix, the part of the bone on which calcium is deposited. Because of a tiny defect in her ability to make this single protein, Denise's bones were rendered permanently and irreparably weakened. The girl was, from birth, destined to suffer repeated, painful fractures after what would otherwise be considered trivial trauma; she would develop progressive deformities of her legs and her arms, which would cease to grow and appear to become smaller as she got older; and her disease would restrict her ability to get around, ultimately causing her to require the use of a wheelchair, because her bones would simply be too weak to ever bear the stress that walking would place on them.

Denise was admitted to the neonatal intensive care unit, and her legs were placed in traction. During those first few days, the neonatologist carefully explained Denise's condition to her parents. The Sandersons were told that, although all of their daughter's vital organs appeared healthy and well formed, her bones were extremely fragile and that, very possibly, any of the simple, day-to-day activities that are necessary parts of the care of an infant could result in the fracture of one or more of Denise's bones. These activities were spelled out for them: everything, including grabbing her leg a little too vigorously while changing a diaper, carrying her to the tub for a bath, even picking her up to give her a hug, had the potential to cause major harm. Mr. and Mrs. Sanderson, who had spent a great deal of time gazing down at their baby lying uncomfortably in the bulky traction apparatus that had been set up in her crib, knowing that there was nothing they could do to comfort her, knowing that the simple act of holding her in their arms could result in a painful, debilitating fracture, thought all this over very carefully, and ultimately came to the only decision they could reach: that they couldn't possibly care for this infant at home, and that she'd be far better off staying in the hospital where she'd get the protective care she needed, including prompt treatment for her fractures when they occurred. And so, after a short stay in the intensive care nursery, the infant was transferred to a room toward the back of 8 East, one of the general pediatric wards, and it was in this room, sometimes alone and sometimes in the company of a roommate, one or another of a small group of long-term patients, that Denise thrived and developed into first a child, then an adolescent, and finally, into the nearly adult young woman who was finishing her senior year of high school the day of the party. In all, during these eighteen years, she had suffered more than 150 separate fractures.

But this was all past history, part of a childhood that apparently now was coming to an end. Denise had decided that it was time to set off on the next phase of her life. After her last day at school, she would be moving to a home for "orthopedically challenged" adults in upstate New York. With her discharge, it was as if a piece of the hospital were vanishing.

*   *   *

Denise was seven years old when I met her. I was a first-year medical student, doing a clinical elective that required me to spend a few hours every week at Jonas Bronck. It was only the third or fourth session of the semester, and the sights and sounds of the hospital were still very new to me; I was a spectator of medicine, a gawker who walked down the corridor on the hospital's main floor with my jaw dropping open every time I saw something out of the ordinary. It was in that main corridor, coming at me in her motorized wheelchair, that I initially saw her, an event that caused my jaw to fall straight toward the floor.

Denise looked much younger than seven, like a baby almost, except that her face was much more mature than that of any baby I'd ever seen. She appeared to be all out of proportion, and as her wheelchair came closer, I was struck by the fact that she looked just like a seal, all trunk and head, with small, withered arms and legs; the hands and feet that came off those wasted limbs looked like flippers. As she drew closer, I tried hard to control myself, to get my mouth closed, and to take my eyes off this sight, but I guess I didn't succeed, because at the point where we were opposite each other in the hallway, I heard her say, "What the hell are you staring at?" in a gruff, harsh, high-pitched voice—another feature, I was to learn much later, of her disease. My face immediately flushed, and I found myself unable to come up with any response. I felt, for the first time, a mixture of emotions that's occurred again and again during my medical career, a combination of embarrassment, fascination, and curiosity, the basic mix that I still feel every time I encounter a patient with a new or unique combination of unusual physical characteristics.

Although I felt the need to know who this little girl was and what it was that was wrong with her, I had no way of finding out. I certainly wasn't going to run down the hall and ask her. And, being a novice in the hospital, I had no idea whom to ask or even what to say. So I waited, thinking about that little girl in the wheelchair occasionally, always keeping a picture of her in the back of my mind. And two years later, on the very first day of clinical rotations at the start of my third year of medical school, I finally got the answer.

Pediatrics was my first rotation, and I had been assigned to work with an intern on 8 East at Jonas Bronck Hospital. We started work rounds that first morning, and about halfway down the ward's main corridor, I saw her again. She was two years older now, but almost no bigger; she sat in the same motorized wheelchair, and, pointing one of her flipper-hands toward me and the two other new medical students on the team, she asked, "Who are those guys?" with that Munchkin-like voice.

"New students," Peter Uris, the senior resident, answered.

"Oh yeah?" she asked. "What rotations have they done so far?"

"None," the resident responded. "This is the first time they've been on the wards."

"Well, do me a favor. Don't let any of them near me with a needle. I don't need any brand-new medical student practicing on me." Without waiting for a response from the resident, she turned, using her right hand to maneuver the chair's specially designed control lever, and steered her chair down toward her room.

"That's Denise," Peter said for the benefit of us students after she was gone. "Don't mess with her; she's tough."

"What's her problem?" I asked.

That's when the question I had been asking myself for the past two years was finally answered. "She's got osteogenesis imperfecta," the resident replied.

I spent most of that afternoon in the medical school's library, reading everything I could find about OI. For some reason I couldn't then explain, the whole topic fascinated me; for the first time, I felt compelled to learn as much as I could about a disease. And during the next seven weeks, the length of time that rotation lasted, I also tried desperately to make friends with Denise. This wasn't as easy as I thought it would be.

I guess I was a little naive in the manner in which I went about doing this. After all, I figured, here was a nine-year-old who spent all her time sitting in a wheelchair on the pediatric ward of a hospital. Sure, she got to go to the playroom for a few hours every day, and frittered away another couple of hours in the special classroom that had been set up for inpatients by New York's Board of Education, but that left her with apparently little or nothing to occupy the vast bulk of most of her days. I figured that a girl like this must've been dying for some companionship, even if it were to come from a medical student on his first clinical rotation. I soon found out I was very much mistaken.

Every day during work rounds, our team stopped in Denise's room to check her vital sign sheet. Her room was a mess; there was junk piled all over the place. But among the television and the ghetto blaster, the toys and the stuffed animals and clothes, there was one island of order: it was the table that stood next to her bed. On this table was a chessboard, all set up for play. Chess, it turned out, was the only game Denise enjoyed. I wasn't very good at it, but on a few occasions, when things were quiet on the ward and I didn't have anything important to do, I asked her if she'd like to play with me. Each time I asked, she had an excuse ready and waiting. Once, she told me she was waiting for a friend who said she was going to stop by that evening, a visitor who never actually materialized; another time, she told me that she was too tired and wanted to go to sleep (a little while later I found her sitting up in bed, watching her TV). A third time she gave me the ultimate brush-off: she told me that this was the night that she washed her hair. I eventually got the hint; I figured she simply didn't like me. But then, one night when my intern and I were on call, one of the residents explained Denise's behavior to me. "Don't take it personally. It's not just you she doesn't like; she doesn't like anybody."

He was close, but he wasn't exactly right. As time passed, I learned that it wasn't that Denise didn't like any of us; it was just that she had learned that she couldn't trust us. Living in the hospital for nine years had made her tough. She had essentially been abandoned by her parents and by the rest of her natural family, who came to visit her once a year, on Christmas Eve. Over time, she had come to realize that medical students, interns, residents, and most nurses also all eventually abandoned her, that we came into her life for only a short period of time, and then, sooner or later, all undoubtedly moved on. Denise learned that forming attachments with doctors or nurses would ultimately result in nothing more than more pain. And so, except for a small group of people—including Kathy Jones in the playroom; Dr. Franklin, who came to visit her at least once a day, occasionally sitting down and playing chess with her; the teacher who ran the Board of Education's hospital classroom; and one or two of the nurses who provided her with most of her care—this girl would have nothing to do with any of us. She had built a solid, impenetrable wall around herself.

During the years I knew her, I was able to break through that wall on only two occasions, and both of them occurred during the month I was functioning as senior resident in charge of 8 East. The first time it happened was at about seven o'clock during an evening early in the month when I happened to be on call. By that time, Denise was leaving Jonas Bronck every day to attend classes at a public junior high school, located about a mile and a half away. A special van would pick her up every morning and bring her back to the hospital in the afternoon, and on that day, one of the van's other passengers had accidentally dropped a book bag on the lower part of Denise's left leg. She didn't mention anything about it at the time, but a few hours later, when she could no longer bear the pain, she told her nurse that she had definitely fractured a bone and needed some pain medication right away. The nurse immediately paged me, asking if I'd come down and check her out.

There was a look of intense pain and sadness on Denise's face. It was the most vulnerability I'd ever seen her show. "It's broken," she said as soon as she saw me. There was something different about her voice; although it still was high-pitched, it sounded less harsh than usual. "It hurts real bad," she continued. "I need something to stop the pain. Please give me something, Bob."

With the nurse perched at my side, I quickly examined her. There was no question about it: Denise had fractured the lower part of her tibia. After asking the nurse to give her 25 milligrams of the pain medication Demerol, stat, I went to page the on-call orthopedic surgery resident. The painkiller did the trick: within a half hour of getting it, Denise fell asleep. She slept like a baby throughout the orthopedic consultant's entire exam, as well as the subsequent wrapping and splinting of her lower leg.

Before rounds the next day, I came by to see how she was doing. I had been thinking about Denise for most of the night, worried about her, but also touched by the fact that she'd let me see a side of her that she rarely revealed. I figured this would signal the beginning of a new phase in our relationship, one in which the girl would finally allow me to gain entrance into her small circle of friends.

She was lying in bed when I arrived. Not knowing whether she was sleeping, I tiptoed into her room, trying not to disturb her; being quiet wasn't necessary, though. "What do you want?" I heard her say in her "old" voice, the gruff, harsh one, when I got within two feet of her bed.

"I just came to see how you were doing," I replied, a little startled by the sound of her voice. "I was worried about you. How does your leg feel?"

"It feels okay," she said, closing her eyes again and ending the conversation. From that point on, the events of that evening were never again discussed; the fracture was never mentioned, and our relationship returned to its former status. It was as if the incident had never occurred.

The second incident occurred later that month. I was awakened at three in the morning by a stat page. Pulling on my shoes, I ran down the hall from the on-call room, and made it to the ward to find one of the nurses waving her arms, gesturing for me and the intern who was following right behind me to get our asses down toward Denise's end of the hall.

When we reached her room, we found the girl in severe respiratory distress. She was in the middle of one of her asthma attacks, a condition she had developed over the past few years. According to the nurse, she had been perfectly fine and sound asleep until about ten minutes before, when the shortness of breath had awakened her. She hadn't been too bad at that point, but her lungs were getting "tighter" with each passing inspiration.

It was clear to me that she was critically ill; she was sitting up in bed, with her body leaning forward, and was gasping for air like a fish out of water. Her lips and fingertips were blue. She was so short of breath, she couldn't talk, but no words were necessary; the look on her face said it all. There was terror in Denise's eyes.

The intern and I sprang into action. We ran down the hall to the treatment room and got the ward's cardiac arrest cart. After rolling it at top speed back down the hall and into Denise's room, we pulled open all the drawers and began removing necessary equipment. I immediately gave Denise a subcutaneous injection of epinephrine, a fast-acting medication that reverses the spasm of the breathing tubes, one of the major components of asthma. Meanwhile, the intern set up the cart's emergency tank of oxygen and, after placing a mask over the girl's face, opened the valve all the way. Next, I asked the nurse to draw up a dose of aminophylline, and immediately set about starting an IV in Denise's left arm; luckily, she had enormous veins and I managed to get it in on the first try. By the time I had completed taping the IV's catheter in place, the nurse had returned with the syringe filled with medication, and we began slowly dripping the drug through the IV tubing and into the girl's vein. By working together, we had finished this initial part of the treatment in just under fifteen minutes. Then we stood back and watched.

Although she was still in a great deal of distress, I could tell Denise was already feeling a little better. When she was able to talk, her first words, uttered in that softer voice I had heard earlier in the month, were "I'm going to die. I know it."

"No, you're not," I answered, trying to sound as soothing as I could at that hour. "You're going to be all right. Do you really think we'd just stand here and let you die?"

She didn't respond to my question; instead, she managed to shake her head slowly from side to side.

Within another twenty minutes, she was clearly out of danger. Although she was still wheezing, her breaths were coming more easily now; the blue discoloration, caused by lack of oxygen in her blood, had vanished from her lips and hands. We decided to start her on a constant infusion of aminophylline and, in order to monitor her more closely, transferred her to the intensive care unit for the rest of the night. The intern and I stayed with her until about six in the morning, when Denise finally was comfortable enough to fall back to sleep. We managed to get about an hour of sleep ourselves before morning work rounds were scheduled to start.

Denise awakened again at about ten o'clock. I happened to be standing at her bedside, listening to her chest with my stethoscope, when she opened her eyes. Almost predictably, her first words were "Get that stethoscope away from me."

"I've got to listen to you," I replied, "to hear how your lungs sound. In case you don't remember, you were pretty damned sick last night. You thought you were going to die."

"Well, I may have been sick last night, but I'm fine now" was all she said, but the anger was gone from her voice. She didn't try to stop me from listening to her lungs after that. She even cooperated a little by taking a deep breath when I asked her to. Later that day, she was returned to her room on 8 East, and once again, our relationship reverted to the way it had been prior to that night.

Over the next five years, our relationship remained pretty much the same. So I had come to Denise's party for two reasons: first, to say good-bye to her; and second, to see how she'd respond to this outpouring of emotion from her small circle of friends, as well as from those of us who could only call ourselves acquaintances.

•   •   •

By three-thirty, the playroom was packed. At least fifty people had shown up for the party. Some, like me, were staff who had been around Jonas Bronck for a long time; some were nurses, ward clerks, or residents who had worked with Denise when she had been young, people who had eventually moved on and were returning now to say good-bye because this girl had in some way touched them. While we waited for the guest of honor to appear, there was only one topic of conversation: none of us could actually believe that Denise was finally going to be leaving the hospital.

The decision had been all hers; she had made it months before. School was ending, and most of the friends she'd made in the class for orthopedically impaired adolescents were moving on to college or to jobs. Denise had decided it was time for her to move on as well. "I'm not a kid anymore," she had told Kathy after returning from school one day during the winter. "I don't belong on a pediatric ward."

After that, the search began. Once Kathy Jones and Dr. Franklin, the two people who, over the years, had come to function pretty much as Denise's surrogate mother and father, became convinced that the girl was truly determined to leave Jonas Bronck Hospital, they began looking for a suitable place for her to live. They knew that finding such a home was not going to be easy; this had, after all, been Denise's problem all along, the reason that she'd never left Jonas Bronck Hospital in the past. There seemed to be no place outside of an acute care facility where a child with brittle bones could live. Her parents hadn't taken her home because they'd been convinced that doing so would do her more harm than good; foster agencies, once they understood the nature of her disorder, had refused to even consider placing her. So this task was not going to be easy.

But Denise had set her mind on it, and the search continued. At last, near the end of May, Dr. Franklin found a place that seemed perfect for the girl: a group home for orthopedically challenged adults. The house and its surroundings were completely wheelchair-accessible; there were ten private rooms, occupied by residents who were, like Denise, of normal intelligence, but were, for one reason or another, confined to wheelchairs; there was an older, married couple living in a building adjacent to the house, who acted as caretakers; the place was located in a beautiful rural area, surrounded by farms, in the Catskill mountain region of upstate New York; and, perhaps best of all, one of the rooms was expected to become available sometime in June. Dr. Franklin immediately called and inquired; he was told that, at least over the phone, Denise sounded like a perfect candidate. The next day, Dr. Franklin got Denise and her wheelchair into his car, and they drove up to visit. The girl fell in love with the place immediately, and after the complex financial arrangements were worked out, the plans were finalized: Denise would be moving on the morning following her final day of high school.

The party had been Kathy Jones's idea; she had planned the whole thing, and it came off without a hitch, because as soon as Denise entered the playroom at about a quarter of four, it was obvious that the whole thing was a complete surprise. For a second, her eyes lit up, like the flashbulbs that were popping from the two or three cameras brought to record the moment. Although she was speechless, she did manage to kiss Dr. Franklin, who had accompanied her into the room from the elevator down the hall, and Kathy, and some of her other friends who bent over her wheelchair. As far as I could tell, she didn't say a word to anybody during the entire party. She clearly was overwhelmed by this outpouring of love; she simply didn't know how to respond.

I stayed for only a few minutes. It was getting late, and I still had some work to do. But later, before leaving the hospital for the evening, after the party had ended, I stopped by Denise's room one last time to say good-bye.

She was packing, putting whatever small stuff she could manage into the boxes Dr. Franklin and Kathy had gathered up for her. She was alone when I got there, and she didn't hear me enter the room. I watched her for a few moments in silence, this small, deformed adult whose development from child to adult had closely paralleled my passage from medical student to practicing physician. "I came to say good-bye, Denise," I said, and the sudden sound of my voice startled her. I offered my hand and she took it in her right flipper. "Good luck at that new place," I continued. "Try not to break anything, okay?"

A smile flashed across her face. "I'll try not to break anything if you promise you'll go out and get a real job," she answered. She'd been telling me for years that real doctors don't work at Jonas Bronck, only residents do, and that, since I'd never left, I couldn't possibly be a real doctor.

I smiled back at her and released my grip. Without another word, I turned to go. When I'd reached the door, I looked back and waved. She gazed up at me with an expression of sadness on her face, the same expression I had seen the night she had broken her left tibia. I thought I saw a tear forming in one of her eyes. It probably wasn't a tear, it was more likely just the reflection of the room's fluorescent lights off her cornea, but it could have been a tear, I thought it was a tear, and that's the way I'll always remember her.

•　•　•

It's been a little over two years since Denise left Jonas Bronck Hospital. If this were fiction, if I were able to make up the ending of this story, I'd write about how well she was doing in her new life, how she was managing perfectly on her own. But the truth of the matter is that Denise did not do very well after leaving us. In fact, she survived in the group home for less than a year.

Following the day of her discharge, she went through a period of severe depression. I guess it was understandable, almost predictable: For the first time in her life, she wasn't unique; she was suddenly surrounded by people who had problems as complicated and distressing as hers, people who had, apparently, come to terms with those problems and begun to cope with them in a positive way. Just being Denise was no longer enough to gain her special attention; she had to try to be something more than an eighteen-year-old patient with brittle bone disease. Also, she was the "new kid on the block," and, at least during the first few months, must have felt like an outsider, an invader in a tight, closed world. The discovery of these facts, coupled with the loneliness she must have felt after leaving the only home she'd ever known, must have been too much for even this tough young woman to bear.

She received some psychiatric help, and it did some good, but from what I heard, she never fully recovered. In addition, her asthma became much worse. No longer an occasional problem, Denise began wheezing every day. Whether the deterioration was due to her depression, to exposure to new kinds of pollen in the rural air, or to a combination of these factors was never determined. But for the first time in her life, Denise became dependent on her asthma medication. She was forced to take it constantly, and even with good compliance, she still suffered fairly frequent flare-ups, some of which required treatment in the emergency room at the local hospital. God only knows what the doctor on duty in that emergency room thought the first time he was faced with treating this particular asthmatic.

It was ultimately an asthma attack that killed her. It must have been exactly like the one she'd suffered during the month I was senior resident on 8 East, an attack we'd managed to treat successfully only because we'd been within a minute away from her bed. This time, when she awoke wheezing one night in January, there weren't any interns or residents around. And by the time one of the group home's caretakers was awakened, got the car warmed up, and made it to the emergency room, it was too late. There was nothing, the doctor said, that could be done.

I didn't hear about her death until after the funeral. I'm sorry I missed it, but it doesn't really matter; I'll never forget Denise. And there are a lot of other people who feel as I do: I've figured out that, during the eighteen years she spent at Jonas Bronck Hospital, Denise Sanderson interacted with over six hundred pediatric and orthopedic surgery residents, and more than fifteen hundred medical students. In addition, there were countless nursing students, nurses' aides, and patients who came into contact with her. She taught all of us not only about the rare disease that deformed every one of her bones, but, more importantly, about what life was like when you are young and afflicted with a horrible, debilitating, chronic disease. And for me, whenever I hear mention of osteogenesis imperfecta, I see a clear picture of the disheveled back room on 8 East at Jonas Bronck Hospital, where a deformed little person sitting in a motorized wheelchair is asking me, in that strange voice, what the hell I'm doing in _her_ room.

Kevin's Question

• • •

I WAS EXHAUSTED. It was the Friday of what had been a very busy week, and I was hoping that the afternoon would turn out to be relatively quiet. I arrived at the outpatient department of the Garwood Children's Hospital at a little after noon, praying that no patients had been scheduled for me, that I'd be able to just take care of the paperwork I knew would be waiting, and then would be able to go home and get some rest.

By that point, I had been working at Garwood, a rehabilitation hospital for children that was located in northern Westchester County, on Friday afternoons for about a year and a half. The hospital's outpatient department had become the site of our spina bifida program when the clinic had become too crowded to remain at its old home, University Hospital, in the Bronx. Having been appointed coordinator of the spina bifida clinic a few months before the move, I'd been offered a part-time staff appointment at Garwood. Although the clinic, which was attended by a neurosurgeon, orthopedic surgeon, urologist, rehabilitation physician, social workers, and, most importantly, over one hundred patients who'd been born with spina bifida, met formally only once a month, I came to Garwood every Friday, to take care of the problems that had come up concerning our patients, to see infants who were being registered at the clinic for the first time, and to sign the charts, fill out the school and camp forms, write the prescriptions, and do the rest of the endless reams of paperwork that were part and parcel of running the program. I usually hated spending the hours and hours needed to take care of the mindless, mechanical, time-consuming paperwork, but on days like that Friday, when I was so tired, activities that didn't involve thinking or talking with patients or their families were about the only kind of work I was capable of doing.

When I reached the outpatient registration desk, I found that I wasn't going to get off so easily. "We don't have any new patients scheduled for today," Julia, the nurse practitioner who was the assistant coordinator of the clinic, said when I asked what was going on, "but Kevin O'Connor's been looking for you all week. He says he's got to talk to you about something, and that it's very important."

"What's it about?" I asked, a little disappointed that I wasn't going to be able to get out as soon as I'd hoped.

"I don't know," she replied. "He won't tell me. He won't tell anyone. He says it has to be you, and it has to be in private."

I smiled and nodded, thinking immediately that I understood what Kevin wanted. I'd known Kevin, a fifteen-year-old with spina bifida, for about five years. He had been an inpatient at Garwood for a little over a month at that time; I thought I knew what he wanted because I'd had quite a bit more than one other private little talk with fifteen-year-old boys who, like Kevin, had spina bifida. He almost certainly wanted to see me in order to get an answer to what I had come to refer to as the Big Question.

Spina bifida is a condition that's caused by a defect in the way the spinal cord forms during early embryonic life. Because, in this condition, the spinal cord never closes, the nerves that come from the lower part of the spine, the ones that control the muscles of the legs, as well as those that regulate the workings of the bowels and the bladder, never develop properly. As a result of these neurological defects, infants and children with spina bifida frequently are unable to walk, and are often incontinent of urine and stool. In males, sexual dysfunction is a frequently associated problem. And that was the key to the Big Question: I was sure that Kevin wanted to see me that day because he wanted to know if he was impotent, and, specifically, if he'd ever be able to father a child.

"Is it okay if I bring him down now?" Julia asked.

"Yeah, I guess we might as well get it over with," I replied. "I'll be waiting in the office."

I went to the room in which I usually spent Friday afternoons, the office in which the paperwork that had built up over the preceding week had already been assembled for me. I tried to get down to work right away, but I was having a hard time concentrating. My mind kept wandering back to an early morning, five years before. . . .

•   •   •

It was about three o'clock in the morning. The pediatric emergency room of Jonas Bronck Hospital, which was usually about as restful as the floor of the New York Stock Exchange, had been uncharacteristically dead for the past hour or so, and I was taking advantage of this luxury by sitting in the nurses' station, reading a copy of that week's mind-numbing edition of *People* magazine. I'd considered getting up out of my chair, sneaking into the ER's isolation room, curling up on the examining table, and taking a nice nap, but like most senior residents, I was very superstitious; I knew that even thinking seriously about getting into a horizontal position would immediately draw a busload of critically ill children into the ER's registration area, patients who quite easily could keep me up on my feet and running around like a chicken with its head cut off until the day crew arrived at nine o'clock. And so, not wanting to take a chance on jinxing my luck, I continued to sit there in the nurses' station, drinking cup after cup of industrial-strength emergency room coffee in an attempt to stay awake, and studying that stupid magazine, the only reading material available in the place other than the even more mind-numbing pediatric textbooks, from cover to cover.

I was working as the night float, and since starting this two-week rotation, the situation I was in had been scaring me to death; from the moment I came on duty at midnight to the moment the relief arrived at nine o'clock in the morning, it was my job to single-handedly see and treat any and all patients who arrived at the threshold of the Jonas Bronck ER, no matter how sick those patients might be, or how many of them showed up. The realization that I could make a really stupid and horrible mistake that might very well wind up causing the death of one of these patients was weighing pretty heavily on my mind. On that night, I had made it through the halfway point in the rotation, and although thus far I'd done pretty well and no one had died or come to any real harm, this fact didn't make me feel a whole lot better. Always lingering in the back of my mind was the realization that, no matter how well I had done, and no matter how quiet and settled things might appear, disaster could strike at any moment.

And then, suddenly, what could have been a disaster actually did strike. I heard some stirring around the registration desk, usually a sign that someone was checking in to be seen. And then I heard the nurse call my name, and I knew there was going to be trouble. Putting down the magazine and rushing out to the desk, I found a boy sitting in a wheelchair with a woman whom I assumed to be his mother leaning over him. "This kid's a spina bifida patient who's got a shunt in his head," the nurse said upon seeing me, referring to the fact that he had a ventriculoperitoneal shunt, a piece of plastic tubing that drained spinal fluid from his brain into his abdominal cavity; patients with spina bifida frequently have hydrocephalus, a buildup of cerebrospinal fluid in the brain, and these shunts are implanted to drain out this excess fluid. "His temperature is 102.8, and he looks terrible," she continued. "I think his shunt's infected."

I nodded my head; I agreed the boy looked terrible. He had the appearance of someone who had a serious, life-threatening infection, perhaps an infection of the shunt that originated in his brain, which would mean that he also had an infection of the spinal fluid and of the brain itself, and that he needed to be treated immediately, ac-curately, and aggressively, or else he might very possibly die. I also noticed that the boy had some odd facial features: his eyes were very small, and the bridge of his nose and his cheeks were unusually flattened. I got the feeling that I'd seen his face somewhere before; I just couldn't, at that moment, figure out where.

I asked the nurse to help me get him back into one of the treatment rooms so I could perform a complete examination. I was searching through my memory banks, trying to review what needed to be done, but rather than finding the protocol for diagnosis and treatment of a ventriculoperitoneal shunt infection, all my tired brain cells were able to call up were items from the story on Barbra Streisand I had just been reading in _People_ magazine. Realizing almost immediately that this wasn't going to be of much help, I decided instead to try to get some history of the present illness from the boy's mother; I turned to her and asked, "How long has your son been sick?"

"That's a stupid question," she slurred in response, with anger in her voice. "He's been sick all his life. Kevin was born like this. Everybody knows spina bifida is something you're born with. What kind of a doctor are you, anyway?"

I may have been tired, and I may have been a lowly resident who was having trouble figuring out what was wrong with his patient, but I sure as hell knew immediately what was wrong with my patient's mother: she was about as drunk as a human could possibly get while still retaining some semblance of consciousness. So, rather than pursue my questioning of her, I decided to turn to the boy himself: "How long have you been sick, Kevin?"

We had reached the treatment room by that point, and I sat on the room's desk chair, looking into the boy's eyes. "I only got the fever a couple of hours ago," he said, "but I've been feeling bad for a couple of days now."

"What hurts?"

"Everything," he answered.

"Well, what hurts you the most?"

"My back, mostly," he replied, "and my stomach." By this time, Kevin's mother, who had staggered onto the treatment room's examining table, had fallen into a deep, sound sleep, and was snoring loudly.

"Does your head hurt?" I asked.

"No, not too much," he replied. "I don't think it's my shunt, Doc; I've had shunt infections before, and they feel a lot worse than this."

I breathed a sign of relief. "What do you think it is?"

"I think it's my kidneys," Kevin replied. "I think I got another kidney infection."

Over the next few minutes, I was amazed and relieved to find out that Kevin, who was then only ten years of age and carried a diagnosis of mild mental retardation, not only knew his complete medical history—including what medications he took, when and how much of them had been prescribed, who his physicians were, what operations he'd had in the past, and when he'd had them—but also knew more about his mother's history than any ten-year-old should know. He knew that she drank at least a fifth of gin a day, that she had tried to dry out many times in the past, but that she'd never been alcohol-free for more than a single week, and that she'd been drinking since way before Kevin was born.

That's when I realized where I'd seen this boy's face before; it hadn't been his face exactly, but rather that of someone who looked just like him. It had been in a book by David W. Smith, a clinical geneticist at the University of Washington; Dr. Smith and his colleagues had been the first to describe fetal alcohol syndrome, a spectrum of abnormalities that has been seen again and again in infants and children born to women who had drunk large amounts of alcohol during their pregnancies. Children born to alcoholic woman were often growth retarded; had a characteristic facial appearance that, among other features, included small eyes, a flat bridge of the nose, and poorly developed cheekbones; had a much smaller-than-average head circumference; and were, like Kevin, often developmentally delayed. I knew right then, seeing this boy together with his mother in the emergency room, that all of the problems he had faced in his life had been caused by his mother's drinking. He had been cheated out of the normal existence to which all children were entitled, and every aspect of his life had been permanently and irreparably damaged, because he had spent the entire nine months of his gestation, the period during which he had developed from fertilized egg to fully-developed infant, floating in a sea of gin-laced amniotic fluid.

Because Mrs. O'Connor was sleeping so soundly on the examining table, I decided to check Kevin right in his wheelchair. The protocol for ruling out a shunt infection finally came back to me, and I did everything I was supposed to do; I found the shunt tubing just under the skin on the right side of the boy's scalp and, with my fingers, traced its path through his neck and his chest, and finally into his abdomen. I pushed hard on the shunt's subcutaneous valve, and felt another wave of relief when the thing dented under the pressure of my finger, then immediately refilled when the pressure was removed; I understood this meant that the shunt was working properly. After performing a complete neurological exam, I felt comfortable in agreeing with Kevin's assessment: his shunt seemed to be working fine; an infection of the shunt or of his spinal fluid was definitely not responsible for the boy's high fever.

But then I had to figure out what _was_ causing it. Luckily, it didn't take me long to find the answer: I got a sample of Kevin's urine by catheterizing him, which involved passing a plastic tube into his bladder, and upon examining the urine under the ER's microscope, I was overjoyed to find what appeared to be an entire civilization of bacteria living in it. Kevin's fever, I happily concluded, was coming from a simple, run-of-the-mill urinary tract infection, a common cause of fever in people with spina bifida, and probably the most easily treatable infection I could have found in the boy. I realized that not only did this mean that Kevin wasn't going to die right there in the emergency room in the next few minutes, but that, after a dose or two of an appropriate antibiotic, coupled with a few hours of observation to assure that his fever was under control, I would most probably be able to send the boy home directly from the emergency room, without having to admit him to the pediatric ward for an inpatient stay.

I turned off the microscope and began to make my way back to the treatment room, to tell Kevin and his mother, if I could somehow rouse her back to consciousness, the good news. That's when I heard the thud; it sounded as if an elephant had been dropped out of an airplane, landing somewhere within the usually safe confines of the emergency room. A loud, harsh shriek immediately filled the air; following this shriek back to its source, I found Kevin screaming in horror as his mother lay on the treatment room's floor, bleeding heavily from a gash over her left eye, and rhythmically shaking her arms and legs, apparently in the midst of a grand mal seizure.

Along with the nurse, who also had come running when she'd heard the thud, I began to tend to Mrs. O'Connor while she was still lying on the floor; the nurse pressed a sterile gauze pad to the deep laceration just above the woman's left eyebrow, while I assembled the material needed to start an IV and yelled out for the clerk to call down to the adult ER to get some assistance. It was not clear to me exactly what had happened: either Mrs. O'Connor had had a seizure, one of the many side effects of her alcoholism and, as a result, had fallen from the table onto the hard floor; or the fall had been the inciting event, and the seizure had occurred due to the trauma. In any case, I knew what had to be done, and devoted all my attention to doing it. Within a minute, the night float and one of the nurses from the adult emergency room joined us; by that time, I'd already managed to get the IV in (it was a cinch: compared with the veins of little children to which I'd grown accustomed, Mrs. O'Connor had pipelines running up and down her arms) and was pushing a small dose of Valium into the woman's vein; the seizure stopped almost instantaneously. With all of us pulling and pushing, we succeeded in getting Mrs. O'Connor onto a gurney, and within another minute, the staff of the adult ER was pushing that gurney down the hall, toward their own trauma area.

I spent a few minutes trying to calm Kevin. Somewhere between the time we had rushed to his mother's aid and the time she'd been wheeled away, the boy had begun to cry. I felt bad for him: it was rough enough having a urinary tract infection and needing to come to the emergency room in the middle of the night, but it was so much worse to then have to worry about a mother's well-being, to have to be more of a parent to her than she had apparently ever been to him. And on top of all this, it was now evident, of course, that we had no chance of sending Kevin home in the morning; after all, there was now no one for him to go home with. And so, after all the excitement had finally died down, when the pediatric emergency room had returned once again to that eerily quiet state that had held the place in its grasp in the hours before the O'Connors had arrived, I began working on the admission forms necessary to get Kevin a bed on the hospital's pediatric ward.

• • •

When I heard the sound of a wheelchair coming down the hall, I looked up from the stack of charts and papers that I'd spread over the entire surface of the desk in front of me. Within a few seconds, the wheelchair, powered by the arm muscles of a now fifteen-year-old Kevin O'Connor, was making its way into my office. I rose from the chair when I saw him and went to shake his hand. "Hi, Kevin, what's going on?"

"Not much, Doc," he said. He still had all the features of fetal alcohol syndrome: those tiny eyes, that flat nasal bridge, the flattened cheeks. He had grown a lot since that night we'd first met in the Jonas Bronck emergency room, and had matured some, both physically and emotionally. I truly liked Kevin; I'd always found him to be a nice, pleasant, friendly kid; but apparently I wasn't in the majority, because, when I asked, "How are you enjoying your stay at Garwood?" he said, "It stinks. Everybody's always picking on me."

"Why's that?" I asked.

"I don't know. I got into another fight with this kid upstairs. A fistfight."

"A fistfight?" I repeated. "Are you okay?"

"Yeah, mostly. He gave me this cut." He pointed to a little scratch on his right cheek. "It bled a lot at first, but then it stopped on its own. The other guy got into a lot of trouble."

"I don't understand, Kevin," I said. "What'd you fight about this time?"

"He's the one who started it," the boy answered. "I was just sitting in the hall outside my room, minding my own business, and this big guy came up to me and called me stupid. Just like that. He said I was stupid, and funny-looking, and he didn't like the way I smelled. So I told him he was going to have to take it back or I was going to tell the nurses on him. And that's when he hit me."

"Why'd he say those things?" I asked.

"I don't know," Kevin responded, looking up toward the ceiling. "He isn't so smart or handsome himself. He looks like a pig, actually. Everybody says so."

"Kevin, did you ever tell this guy he looked like a pig?" I asked.

"Well, no, not really, I never really said it to him, but I did say it to some other guys. But everyone's been saying it. He's got a pig nose and everything."

I signed. I'd been through this kind of thing with Kevin before, and I thought I understood what had happened. "Kevin, was everyone really saying it, or were you the first one who said it?"

He was silent for a few seconds. "Well, maybe I was the first one to say he looked like a pig," he finally replied. "But everyone's been saying it ever since then. It's true, it really is."

"Kevin, you've got to be careful what you say about people. Even if you think this guy does look like a pig, even if he goes around saying 'oink, oink,' you shouldn't tell other people that. You've got to keep stuff like that to yourself. You're going to get into a lot of trouble, like you did last time you were here. You don't want to get thrown out of Garwood again, do you?"

This was Kevin's fifth admission to this hospital. The last admission had occurred when the boy was fourteen. That stay had been cut short because of Kevin's behavior problems; he'd become so argumentative, had gotten into so many fights with other patients and with staff members, and his presence had been so disruptive, that the hospital's medical director had decided to send him home. And that had led to a whole group of other problems.

Although Kevin's first three admissions to Garwood had been for purposes of rehabilitation following surgery on his legs and feet, both of these last two stays had been arranged mainly for a nonmedical reason: Kevin had been admitted because he simply had no other place to go. Before the first of these two admissions, the Bureau of Child Welfare, the state agency charged with protecting the interests of children, having received a tip from a neighbor, had brought charges against Mrs. O'Connor; it had investigated the situation and had concluded that because of her heavy, unending alcoholism, the woman had been chronically neglecting her son's needs. She had been offered two alternatives: either voluntarily enter an alcohol rehabilitation program and dry out, or permanently relinquish custody of Kevin, thus making him a ward of the state. No matter what else she was guilty of, Mrs. O'Connor truly loved Kevin, and would not even consider giving him up. So she decided to enroll in yet another program; and trying to offer his support for an old patient, the medical director of Garwood had offered Kevin a bed at the hospital for the period during which his mother would be away. But when it had become apparent that the boy had outstayed his welcome, he had been sent home, and his mother, having no choice but to leave her program prematurely, had suffered a relapse very shortly thereafter. The present hospitalization, also arranged by the Bureau of Child Welfare and the medical director at Garwood, was to be the O'Connors' last chance. If Mrs. O'Connor failed to dry out this time, the boy would be placed in foster care; Kevin, through his behavior, seemed to already be booby-trapping the outcome.

In answer to my question, Kevin said, "No, I want to stay here. But sometimes I can't control myself. I'm trying to be good. I just can't help it."

"All I can tell you, Kevin, is you've got to try hard," I responded. "Julia told me you've been looking for me. What's been going on?"

"Well, there's this question I've been wanting to ask. I've been thinking about it for a long time, but it's kind of embarrassing. . . ."

"I think I know what you want to ask about," I interrupted, trying to make this as easy for him as possible. "You know, lots of other kids have asked me about it. . . ."

"They have?" he asked. "Other people are like me?"

"Sure," I replied. "So you don't need to feel embarrassed." I was on the verge of launching into my speech about how some men with spina bifida were fertile and others weren't, and how there were a bunch of tests we could do to find out into which group Kevin fit, but I figured I'd allow him the chance to get the question out. "Just ask," I concluded after a brief pause.

"Okay. I've just been wondering, Doc. Am I the way I am," he waved his hands back and forth over his wheelchair, emphasizing the lower half of his body, "because of my mother's drinking?"

It took a few seconds for his words to sink in, but when they did, my mouth dropped opened. Not only was Kevin's question completely unexpected, it had been the first time in my career that a patient had ever asked anything like this. Sure, I'd thought abstractly about what I'd say to a child with fetal alcohol syndrome, or with any of the other birth defects in which a clear cause-and-effect relationship with maternal drug use had been established. I'd argued in my own mind whether it would be best to tell the truth, to inform someone like Kevin that his mother's uncontrollable, incessant alcoholism had almost definitely caused most of the problems he'd already faced in the past, as well as those he would inevitably have to face in the future, knowing that by doing so, by telling the truth, I would risk damaging whatever relationship the boy and his mother had managed to salvage through the difficult, preceding years. Or was it better to lie, to tell Kevin and other people like him that there was no correlation between his mother's drinking and any problems he might be having? I recognized that in doing the latter, I would be breaking a promise that all doctors had established with their patients; by deceiving someone who had, by tacit agreement, come to trust me, and who, in the future, would need to continue to trust me, I would be breaking a moral code, and doing both of us a great disservice. I had argued these points repeatedly in my mind, and had never come up with a clear conclusion. Now, suddenly, the situation was no longer an abstraction, it was reality, and as of that moment, I had no idea what I should do.

When thirty seconds had passed and I hadn't said anything,

Kevin continued. "I've just been thinking about it; you know, drinking isn't so good for the person who's doing it. I figured it couldn't be too good for a baby who's inside somebody who's doing it either."

"Well, what difference would it make one way or the other?" I asked, trying to bluff my way through. "If I were to tell you that all your problems were due to your mother's drinking, what would you do?"

"Nothing," he replied. "It wouldn't change anything. I just want to know; I have to know."

I took a deep breath and made a decision. "Let me show you something, Kevin," I said, and, reaching up to the bookshelf over the office's desk, I took down the copy of David Smith's textbook. "There's this disorder called fetal alcohol syndrome," I continued, turning the pages of the book until I came to the appropriate section. "It occurs in children whose mothers drink a lot during their pregnancies. You can see the kids who are shown here look a little bit like you." I showed him the photographs and he sadly nodded his head. "And over here, there's a list of a whole bunch of symptoms that occur in children with this problem, things like slow development and poor growth . . ."

"And spina bifida?" Kevin interrupted.

I put my finger on the section headed "Occasional Abnormalities." The last item listed in that section was "spina bifida." "I knew it," this boy, who had a diagnosis of mild mental retardation, who had trouble figuring out how much change he should get from a dollar when buying a candy bar, said sadly. "I knew it was her fault all along. If she wasn't such a drunk, I wouldn't have to be in this wheelchair now!"

"Listen, Kevin; first of all, you were born in 1972, right?"

He nodded his head.

"Well, the first article on fetal alcohol syndrome didn't come out until 1973. When your mother was pregnant with you, we didn't even have a clue that drinking could harm the fetus. And besides, do you think your mother wants to be an alcoholic? Do you think she actually likes having to go into these programs all the time, and forcing you to come up here to live by yourself at Garwood?

"If she doesn't like it, why does she do it?" Tears were beginning to form in his eyes, but he was doing his best to hold them back.

"Because she doesn't have a choice. It's a disease she can't do anything about. She can't control her drinking any more than you can control the fact that you've got spina bifida. It was something she was born with, and whether she likes it or not, that's the way she is."

"Well, I don't have to like it. I hate her, and I'll always hate her!" And then he couldn't stop the tears anymore. He put his hands over his eyes, leaned forward in his chair, and was convulsed with crying. I put my arm around his shoulder and held him, but I didn't interfere, I didn't try to stop him; I knew it was something he had needed to get out of his system for a long time. He didn't say a word, he just cried. At some point, Julia came into the office, saw what was happening, and, without asking why or what, joined me in trying to comfort Kevin.

He cried for nearly fifteen minutes. When he could control himself again, after he'd blown his nose, dried his eyes, taken a deep breath, and calmed himself down, he thanked me for the talk and began to wheel himself out of the office. "Kevin, are you going to be all right?" I asked.

"Yeah," he responded. "I'll be fine. Thanks, Doc."

After he was gone, back up to his room on one of the wards on the hospital's second floor, I told Julia everything that had happened. I told her about my own doubts, that I wasn't so sure that in giving Kevin the facts, I'd done the right thing. She responded by saying something about honesty being the best policy, but in spite of her reassurance, I spent the rest of the afternoon at Garwood finishing my paperwork, and praying to God I hadn't permanently screwed up whatever chance the O'Connor family had to survive intact.

•   •   •

It's now been a year and a half since Kevin came down to my office and asked the question that had been on his mind for so many years. Sometime after our talk, the staff at Garwood noted a marked improvement in the boy's behavior; he didn't exactly become an angel, but at least the number of fights in which he was involved decreased dramatically. In looking back on it, I have to believe there was a definite relationship between the talk we had that Friday afternoon and the noticeable change in Kevin's attitude; the answer I'd given him somehow allowed him to cease acting out so much of the hostility that had secretly been building up inside him.

And because Kevin's behavior was so much improved, it was possible for his mother to finally complete her alcohol rehabilitation program. According to the social worker who's a member of our spina bifida clinic team, Mrs. O'Connor, with close follow-up and frequent counseling, has, for the first time since her childhood, remained dry for a little over a year.

I see them a few times a year, when they come up to Garwood for Kevin's routine checkups. The change in Mrs. O'Connor is remarkable; well-groomed and impeccably dressed, she's a far cry from the scattered, belligerent drunk I first ran into in the pediatric emergency room at Jonas Bronck during my rotation as night float. And for the first time in years, Kevin has shown up on time for all his appointments, and has been well dressed and clean every time I've seen him.

During the first visit to the clinic following his discharge from Garwood, I asked how things were going at home. "Great," he responded. "Better than they've ever been. And Doc?"

"Yeah, Kevin."

"I've been thinking a lot about that talk we had. You know, you didn't have to tell me about fetal alcohol syndrome. You could have told me anything you wanted."

I smiled and said, "I know, Kevin. Do you think I should have lied?"

"No. I'm glad you were straight with me. Now I know I can trust you."

There are rare times when a physician must ask himself whether telling a patient the entire truth is in that patient's best interest. We're taught in medical school the concept of *Primum, non nocere* (First, do no harm), and in the case of Kevin O'Connor, informing him of the effects of his mother's alcoholism had the potential of causing harm to the already tenuous relationship that existed between the boy and his only parent. I could have lied or bent the truth that afternoon when Kevin came to me with his question, but I didn't. I told the truth, guided not by knowledge, but rather by instinct, not knowing whether I was doing the "correct" thing or not; it wasn't until that day in the spina bifida clinic at Garwood that I finally became convinced I had done the right thing.

The Baby Who
Had No Face

• ● •

*T*OMMY RAMA WAS NEARLY TWO MONTHS OLD the afternoon
he was brought to the office of Ed Johnson, our hospital's pediatric
neurosurgeon, for evaluation. A couple of days before, the neurosurgeon had called to tell me he had a complicated patient coming in
who'd been born with serious skull and facial defects, and asked if
I'd be able to come over and check the child out. I agreed immediately, and then promptly put the whole thing out of my mind until
the afternoon of the visit. But even had I spent the entire week
thinking about the craniofacial defects Ed had briefly described to
me over the phone, there would have been no way for me to have
adequately prepared myself for the experience of meeting Tommy.
My first sight of the infant just about knocked the wind out of me.

He was the most grotesque living human I had ever seen. Because
of a severe abnormality in the development of his craniofacial structures, he had been born without a face. Tommy's eyes had never
formed: there were lids, and even lashes, but these structures, which
were placed way over near his relatively normally formed and posi-
tioned ears, covered only nonspecific fat and muscle, connective tissue
that had nothing whatsoever to do with the sense of vision; rather,
they were empty slits that opened and closed as normal eyelids should
but blinked blindly, without consciousness or recognition of the scen-

ery around them. He had no nose: in its place were two deep clefts, one on the left, the other on the right; these clefts, which originated in scar tissue at the forehead and ran downward into the top of the gaping hole that served as the infant's mouth, also extended back into that mouth, splitting its roof into three separate pieces.

And perhaps worst of all, Tommy's skull had not formed. The top of his head was covered with skin, but under that skin, instead of the normal hard bone that's supposed to protect the brain from injury and infection, lay only the meninges, the tough, pliable membranes that serve as a bag for the cranial components. The meninges and their contents, which included cerebrospinal fluid and brain tissue, free from the normal constraining forces of the skull, had formed three odd conelike projections called encephalocoeles, horns that stood out from the surface of the boy's head—structures that, taken together with his facial anomalies, had transformed this infant into a freak, a chilling, nightmarish image that might have been manufactured by a Hollywood makeup artist for the worst, cheapest horror film, a character that couldn't possibly be taken seriously as a living, breathing human being, let alone a cuddly human baby. But there he was, big as life, held in his mother's arms before me, and the realization of this caused me to stumble back clumsily into one of the examining room's empty chairs.

I tried not to stare; I tried to concentrate on the history Ed Johnson had already begun to obtain from the boy's parents and from their minister who had accompanied them on this visit, and although it was difficult to keep my mind focused on the discussion, I did manage to catch most of the important facts. Tommy had been born at a community hospital in northern Westchester county, his parents' first child. His mother was twenty-nine years old; she and the baby's father, thirty-one, had emigrated from Thailand, their native country, when Mrs. Rama had been four months pregnant. They'd come to New York to begin a new life: having both worked in a restaurant in Bangkok, they'd saved every penny they could manage; when enough money had been put away, they'd left their home and their families, and had come to Westchester, where, with a friend who had emigrated a few years before, they'd opened their own restaurant. The Ramas must have been on top of the world around the time of their arrival in New York: in the prime of their lives, looking forward to beginning an enterprise they'd been told was almost guaranteed to be a success, living in the lap of luxury, relatively speaking, and expecting their first child, they must have imagined that they had it all. But within seconds of the delivery of their child, their dreams, their entire universe, had suddenly and completely come crashing down on them, like a poorly constructed house of cards.

In telling us the story of the baby, Mrs. Rama spoke slowly, carefully choosing her words; she was not yet completely comfortably conversing in English, but the emotional distress she was suffering was obvious on her face and in her eyes. All through the discussion, she cradled the hideous baby in her arms, occasionally stroking his arm or, when he let out a whimper, placing the nipple of a bottle of formula in the opening that was his mouth. Tommy took the nipple and sucked contentedly; apparently, he could breathe and suck at the same time without difficulty. He sucked vigorously for a few minutes until, appeased, he faded off to sleep.

The pregnancy, Mrs. Rama assured us, had been completely normal; nothing out of the ordinary had occurred during the entire nine months. At no time during the gestation, either in Bangkok or in Westchester, had a problem with the fetus ever been suspected. It had only been in the delivery room, immediately after birth, that the child's severe defects had been recognized.

"As soon as Tommy came out, they knew there was something wrong," Mr. Rama said. He was more comfortable expressing himself in English. "They took him away immediately. They wouldn't let us see him, and they wouldn't tell us what was wrong with him. They only said that he was very sick, and that someone would come and speak with us later. That was the worst part: the not knowing. We didn't know what to think, or what to do. We felt helpless, completely helpless."

Those few minutes after the baby's delivery must have been terrifying, a situation that couldn't have been completely avoided, but might have been made easier if the parents had received some sort of information from a doctor or a nurse. But can you imagine what must have gone on in that delivery room? Can you imagine the scene that must have occurred when the staff, all of whom fully expected everything to be fine, none of whom had even the slightest clue that an infant like Tommy would emerge from the birth canal, realized what this woman had delivered? I can; I've been there.

• • •

I was a junior resident, doing a month of hard labor in the nursery at University Hospital. As part of the rotation, I was responsible for carrying the delivery room beeper. Anytime the obstetricians suspected there might be trouble at a delivery, they would call that beeper, and upon hearing the squawking of the box that was strapped to my waist, I would drop whatever I was doing and rush down to the DR.

I was doing physical exams on healthy newborns in the well-baby nursery one morning when the beeper went off. I ran down the hall, through the double doors that separated the delivery area from the rest of the hospital's sixth floor, and was told by the clerk to get into Delivery Room 1 stat. Upon reaching the room, I saw an obstetrician, perched on a stool, looking up at a woman's perineum. He turned when he heard my voice and said only, "Thick mec. Get ready to suction."

The passage of meconium, the baby's first bowel movement, is a completely normal phenomenon when it occurs after the infant has been born. When meconium is passed before birth, however, it can have double significance. First, it's a sign of fetal distress, a sign that something has gone wrong with the baby; if the oxygen supply to the fetus is disturbed while it's still in the womb, or if the baby has developed an infection, meconium will pass out of its bowel. So the sighting of dark-stained amniotic fluid when the fetal membranes rupture is evidence that the baby is, or has recently been, in trouble.

But also, the mere presence of meconium in the amniotic fluid can cause serious problems. The stuff is thick and viscous, the color and consistency of tar, and when the baby breathes in, this tarlike material gets stuck in its lungs, causing a stubborn, persistent, difficult-to-treat pneumonia. In order to prevent this from happening, rapid and aggressive treatment is needed as soon as the baby's head emerges from the birth canal. So when that obstetrician told me that he'd seen thick meconium in the amniotic fluid that appeared after this woman's membranes had ruptured, it immediately forced a protocol to the front of my mind, a series of steps that had to be followed in precise sequence in order to ensure the survival of this baby.

I spent my first few minutes in DR-1 getting everything set. I turned on the heater above the room's warming table, the bed on which I planned to lay the infant after delivery; I opened the valve of the oxygen tank, and made sure that gas was escaping through the end of the tubing that had been attached to that valve; I tore into the room's pediatric cardiac arrest cart and removed a suction catheter, an endotracheal tube, a laryngoscope, and an ambu-bag, equipment necessary to provide artificial ventilation; I cracked open vials of medications that I'd use in case the baby needed to be resuscitated and transferred the contents of those vials to syringes; and I asked the circulating nurse to call up to the neonatal intensive care unit to get another resident to come down and give me a hand. I did all of this mechanically, in a stepwise, automatic fashion. I had been trained to perform these tasks in emergencies without having to give them a second thought. When I was done, after I'd checked and rechecked everything and re-reviewed the steps in my head, I placed the mouthpiece of the suction catheter between my clenched teeth and approached the obstetrician; and then we both waited for the baby's head to clear the perineum.

We didn't have to wait long; within a minute, the head was delivered, and before the infant had a chance to take a breath, I used the suction catheter to pull a couple of globs of thick meconium from the baby's nose while most of the body still lay wedged within the confines of the birth canal. The baby inhaled and let out a little cry in response to my suctioning, but it wasn't the normal, healthy, lustful cry that infants normally deliver as their entrance line into this world. And the finding of that meconium had clinched it for me: this baby was in trouble; I was sure he had already gotten some meconium down into his mouth and probably into his lungs, and I was going to have to do everything—intubate, suction, ventilate, and resuscitate—as soon as the obstetrician could manage to clear his body from the birth canal.

But freeing the body from the birth canal turned out to be more difficult than either of us had imagined. The obstetrician was having trouble; something around the baby's abdominal region seemed to be stuck. The obstetrician became red-faced and a little panicked; he manipulated the baby's head and shoulders, moving them to the right, to the left, backward and forward, and each time, a tiny bit more of the baby would become free. Finally, after minutes of this struggle, minutes that seemed more like hours to me, the rest of the baby was delivered, and we both realized instantly what the problem had been: the kid had an enormous bulge in the region just above his umbilical cord. I recognized it immediately as a gastroschisis, a defect in the formation of the wall of the abdomen, a gaping hole through which the baby's stomach, intestine, and liver were bulging. And upon realizing this, in the same way it would happen years later when I saw Tommy Rama for the first time in Ed Johnson's examining room, my knees started to buckle.

I began to carry the infant over to the warming table, but I was having some problems: my hands were shaking, my legs were not answering the calls being sent out by my brain. But somehow, I made it; I managed to get the baby over and placed him down on the table. That's when I discovered that I could no longer remember what needed to be done. I froze, I choked, I was unable to do anything except stand over that infant with my mouth hanging open, staring down at this huge defect in the wall of his abdomen. The baby's breathing was rapidly becoming increasingly labored, I could clearly see that; his skin was turning more and more blue with each passing moment, and his heart rate was dropping. The baby was dying before my eyes, and although I knew I had the ability to intervene, I was failing him; I couldn't do a thing to help him.

I wasn't alone in my paralysis. The normal activities of the delivery room that usually follow the birth of a baby had all been suspended; the scrub nurse and the circulator were both standing beside me, staring down at that abdomen helplessly. The obstetrician, who was trying to concentrate on the mother, attempting to sew closed the episiotomy he had created in order to deliver the child's head and abdomen, kept calling over, demanding to know what was happening. And the woman on the delivery table, the mother of this infant, was crying "My baby, my baby, what's wrong with my baby?" at the top of her lungs.

The scene was finally broken by Susan Falcone, one of the pediatric residents who'd been up in the neonatal ICU when the call had come in from the circulating nurse. Thank God for Susan! She instantly diagnosed my problem, as well as the baby's, and swung into action. She took charge, suctioning the infant's mouth, intubating him, sucking meconium out of his trachea, and forcing oxygen through the endotracheal tube and into his lungs with the ambu-bag. The baby's color began to pink up a little, his heart rate responded, and Susan Falcone announced that, rather than attempt further resuscitation there in the DR, she would take the child up to the intensive care unit right away. She plunked him into a transporting incubator and began running down the hall. I trailed behind them, still useless, but now feeling like shit because I had failed—I had let this baby down, I hadn't done what I was supposed to do, what I'd been trained to do—and I was positive the infant was going to suffer as a result of my incompetence.

That baby spent the first four months of his life in the neonatal intensive care unit. He had a horrible case of meconium aspiration pneumonia, the effect of my not being able to suction him promptly, and he required ventilatory support for nearly a month; the surgery to repair his gastroschisis had to be put off for weeks while we waited for his lungs to heal. But ultimately, no thanks to me, he survived; the child went home, apparently healthy and happy.

In all the time I was in training, that was the only instance when I'd been present at the delivery of an infant who was born with congenital malformations. I've spoken with other people who have told similar stories, good residents who knew what needed to be done, but, under the stress of the situation, had frozen up and had failed their patients miserably. From listening to the Ramas' description of the scene in the delivery room the day Tommy was born, I can't imagine that that picture had been much different.

•   •   •

Although there were similarities between the birth of the baby with the gastroschisis and the birth of Tommy Rama, there were also a great many differences: first, although my patient had a serious congenital defect, he looked in all other ways like a normal baby; none of us would have had any reservations about showing that infant to his mother if he had been healthy enough. Second, and perhaps more important, unlike the case of the baby with the gastroschisis, the bedlam that surrounded the birth of Tommy hadn't resulted in any harm to the infant. Tommy required nothing, no special treatment, no resuscitation or suctioning, no intubation or oxygen therapy. He weighed a little over seven pounds, and as soon as he hit the outside environment, he began to breathe spontaneously, to cry, and to act in the way newborns are supposed to act. He appeared normal in all ways, except for one. But that one difference was bound to create quite a stir.

On whispered orders from Mrs. Rama's obstetrician, immediately after the infant's appearance, Tommy's entire body, including his head, was wrapped in a blanket and removed from the DR by the circulating nurse. The obstetrician unilaterally decided that it wouldn't be in anyone's best interest to allow these parents to see their baby at that moment. So Tommy was whisked off by the nurse to a private room off the well-baby nursery; he was placed in an isolette, and the hospital's neonatologist was paged, stat.

Minutes later, the neonatologist showed up to examine the newborn. She carefully recorded the pattern of malformations present in his craniofacial region and, in addition, was the first to notice his other problem, the unusual defects of his hands and his feet; it looked like a portion of most of his digits had been amputated, as if someone had taken a pair of scissors and snipped off pieces of a finger here and a toe there. She put these apparently disparate abnormalities together and made a presumptive diagnosis: the baby, the neonatologist believed, had a condition called amniotic band syndrome.

Amniotic band syndrome is a mysterious and rare disorder whose etiology is not clearly understood. At the present time, the most widely accepted theory proposes that, early in pregnancy, the amnion, the innermost membrane that forms the sac in which the embryo and later the fetus grows and develops, spontaneously ruptures. This leads to the formation of bands of tissue—sharp, knifelike strips that literally attack the embryo, engulfing limbs and skull and face. Tommy's defects perfectly fit the pattern of anomalies described in this disorder.

"The neonatologist came to us," Mrs. Rama told us, thinking through every word before she said it. "I was in the room where they put you after you give birth and I hurt a lot. This woman came in and told us the baby had this terrible problem. I said I wanted to see him, but she told me it would be best if I didn't, at least not right away. She told us that the baby was going to die. I didn't know what to do. So we started to pray for a miracle."

"And God granted them that miracle," the Ramas' minister interrupted. It turned out that the Ramas were born-again Christians who believed strongly in the healing powers of God. Through the struggle of the last two months, nearly alone in this new and strange country, without family or friends to support them, they had come to rely on their minister for comfort, and on God for strength. The minister had volunteered to accompany them on their visit to Ed Johnson's office that day. "How else can it be explained that this baby has survived for two months, against all odds, so that he was able to come here for this appointment today?"

The minister had a point there; Mr. Rama explained that during the days following Tommy's birth, the neonatologist had convinced the couple that no heroic steps should be taken to keep the child alive. The day after delivery, she had brought them to the room off the nursery to see their son for the first time, and apparently, that visit had gone a long way toward convincing the couple that what the neonatologist was saying made sense. It was agreed that, if the child were to suffer a cardiopulmonary arrest, no resuscitation would be provided, no ventilator assistance would be used, and no drugs or antibiotics would be given. Tommy would be fed, he'd be kept as comfortable as possible, and hopefully the end would come quickly.

But the boy not only didn't die, he thrived. Alone in his bassinet, in the private room off the nursery, he was fed from a bottle and began to gain weight. He proved to be healthy as a horse, and by the time he was six weeks of age and hadn't shown any signs of dying, the neonatologist began to discuss options for the future with the Ramas. "She told us he was getting too old to stay in the nursery," Mrs. Rama said. "She told us we would have to think about taking him home or placing him in another kind of hospital, a hospital that takes care of children with problems like this. Well, we talked it over. . . ." Becoming teary-eyed, unable to continue, she pointed to her husband.

"It's not that we don't want Tommy at home," he continued, less emotional than his wife. "We do want him, at some point. It's our duty to take him. It's just that we're not ready for him, not yet. We need to get ready. It means a lot; it'll mean spending our whole lives, and we . . . we just need more time, just a few more months, and then we'll take him."

"So when they checked with the nursing homes," the minister continued when Mr. Rama also fell silent, "they were told that the boy would only be acceptable for placement if he had those things removed from his head." He pointed to the horrible horns that projected from what should have been a skull. "They were given your name as a physician who might be willing to do the surgery."

"So it's a matter of removing these encephalocoeles for the purpose of placement," Ed Johnson summarized. He'd been taking notes and doodling on a yellow legal pad, and was now rhythmically tapping the tip of his pencil against it. "Technically, it's possible." He put his left thumb and middle finger on the baby's head and began to palpate gently; in response, the baby blinked his eyelids, attempting in vain to see what was happening. "The bone ends here," the surgeon pointed to an obvious demarcating line that ran just above the ears. "We would have to use some rib bone as struts, and lay some blocks of artificial material between the ribs to build a kind of bird cage for the brain. It's not something I've ever done before and it won't be easy. But it could be done. Bob, what do you think? Anything medical we need to worry about?"

I thought for a few seconds. While listening to the story and watching the baby, I had developed some strong emotional feelings about all this. On the one hand, watching Tommy interact with his mother, ignoring his craniofacial defects, hard as that might be, I'd been struck by the fact that the boy acted as any two-month-old would: he sensed his mother's presence, smiling when she held him and crying when she laid him down; he sucked contentedly from his bottle when it was offered; he cried and moved his arms and legs around when the phone rang, things any normal baby would do. And besides, by performing this surgery, we weren't trying to cure him; we were just trying to get him into shape so that he would be acceptable for placement in some chronic care facility.

But on the other hand, I questioned why anything, especially a complicated, ground-breaking neurosurgical procedure, should even be attempted on a baby who had, I believed, virtually no prognosis; why not just leave the kid alone, do nothing invasive, and let nature ultimately take its course? Eventually, the skin of those horns was bound to break down and lead to an overwhelming infection of the boy's central nervous system, and before long, the end would mercifully come. Why should we in any way attempt to interfere with that process?

And by doing this surgery, what message would we be sending to these parents? If Ed were to operate, wouldn't the Ramas think we didn't believe the boy's prognosis was as bad as they'd initially been led to believe? Wouldn't performing this operation send them the message that there was some hope that Tommy might someday be normal, some belief that someday he might be able to go out in public without his head and face being covered to protect him from the stares and the comments of passersby? Is this something we wanted to accomplish? I didn't think so, but I also didn't think it was my place just then to mention any of this. Ed hadn't invited me to come that afternoon to express the emotional reservations I might have had about treating this boy; he'd asked me to consult as a specialist in clinical genetics. So I tried to fight off my emotions and to answer the neurosurgeon's question in my role as an academic pediatrician. "I think we need to do some studies," I replied. "Before you do anything, we need to make sure there are no serious internal malformations."

"I'll have to get some tests done, too," Ed replied. "How long do you think your workup will take?"

"About a week," I estimated.

"Great. Why don't we bring Tommy into the hospital today and get started?"

And that's what we did. I called the chief resident and arranged for a bed on the infants' unit. I went down to the ward, called together the nurses, the resident, and the interns, and gently tried to explain the situation: "I'm admitting a patient for an elective workup. He's a two-month-old who was born without a face."

"Right," Eileen O'Neil, the senior resident on the unit, said. "And I'm the queen of England. What's really wrong with the kid?"

"I'm not joking, Eileen," I replied. "It's a kid with the worst case of amniotic band syndrome I've ever seen. He's got severe craniofacial defects, and Ed Johnson's thinking about taking him to the OR to build him a skull. He's coming in now so we can find out if there's anything else wrong with him that might prevent the surgery from getting done."

They all seemed serious for a minute or so, but then the entire group broke into laughter. "Come on, Bob," Eileen said finally. "You're putting us on."

Just at that moment, Mrs. Rama came out of the elevator with the baby in her arms and all conversation stopped. That was the last time anyone laughed about Tommy Rama.

*   *   *

Like a drum major blowing his whistle, Tommy Rama's admission to the infants' unit started a parade of health care providers that seemed to stretch on for miles. Over the course of the next few days, dozens of people came to see Tommy. At first, the visitors were mainly consultants whose opinions had been officially requested by Ed Johnson or me: attendings and fellows from neurology, endocrinology, nephrology, and cardiology came to examine the boy; the ward's social worker and our program's genetic counselor stopped by to meet with the parents and to discuss their plans for the future. But eventually, just about everybody associated with the pediatric and neurosurgery departments passed through the private room into which Tommy had been placed; although our hospital is huge, rumors travel fast, and when word got around that there was a baby on the infants' unit who had been born without a face, there was no keeping the curious away. The room became like the sideshow of a circus, and almost everyone who came to see the "freak" inside had an opinion about what should be done with him: leave him alone, let him die, they all agreed, don't waste the time and money necessary to operate on something that looks like that.

I recognized pretty soon that doing nothing would not be easy. Throughout the workup, Mrs. Rama steadfastly remained with her baby. While enduring the hundreds of questions, the whispered remarks, the gawking stares, she held her child in her arms, fed him when he cried, changed his diapers when he was wet. During my first few visits to their hospital room, I began to appreciate how much this baby meant to her; in spite of the comments made by the neonatologist on the boy's first days after birth, and the attempts by her and others to reinforce those comments at every opportunity since that time, this woman had clearly not been able to come to terms with the fact that her son had absolutely no prognosis for survival.

It was Maggie Walker, the genetic counselor, who finally put all this into perspective for me. A graduate of the master's program in human genetics at Sarah Lawrence College, Maggie is my partner in our hospital-based practice. Over the years we've worked together,

I've come to depend heavily on her levelheadedness and her instincts; she has a terrific knack for being able to key in on the heart of a problem almost instantaneously. And the Rama case was no exception: after her very first meeting with Tommy's parents on the Friday morning following the infant's admission to the hospital, Maggie had already sorted out the whole situation. "Tommy's not the patient we have to concentrate on here," she said to me when she returned to our office following that first meeting. "There's nothing we're going to be able to do for him. It's the mother we have to work on. She's the most important patient now."

I thought about it for a second, and then agreed. "So what can we do?" I asked.

"It's simple. It's our duty to help her come to terms with the fact that this child is going to die. Once she's accepted that, and stops denying the problems he has, she'll be able to separate a little and begin to get on with her life. As long as she believes he's going to be fine, we're going to be doing this family a disservice. In just talking to her for a minute, I get the sense that she's filled with guilt about this whole thing."

That afternoon, Maggie began to work with the parents in earnest. Through her years of training and experience, she'd developed a style, an effective means of breaking through the wall that almost always surrounds the parents of children who have been born with serious defects. While Tommy slept in his hospital crib, Maggie simply sat and, in a nonjudgmental way, led the Ramas through a discussion of their feelings. It was amazing to see: once the Ramas began to trust Maggie, once they realized that here, for the first time since Tommy had been born, was a person who seemed to honestly care about them, they began to open up.

About an hour into her discussion with them, Mrs. Rama felt comfortable enough to make a confession she had not shared with anyone else, except her husband, since the baby's birth. "It was early in my pregnancy, before I even knew I was pregnant," she said in her halting style. "I was at work one day and an old friend from school came into the restaurant. We hadn't seen each other for nearly ten years, and I was very happy to see her. The restaurant was quiet at that time, so we sat at a table and talked for two hours." Her eyes began to cloud over with tears at this point, but she continued talking: "I brought over a bottle of wine at the beginning, and we drank that whole bottle, all of it, just the two of us. Then, a few days later, I found out I was pregnant. . . ." Her tears now spilled over her eyelids and began running down her cheeks. She could not continue.

"And you think that drinking that bottle of wine caused Tommy's problems?" Maggie asked.

"The doctors at the other hospital told us that Tommy's defects occurred very early in the pregnancy," Mr. Rama replied, nodding his head, "maybe even before my wife knew she was pregnant."

Maggie was silent for a few seconds; she signaled to me, and I knew it was now time for me to speak up and sound scholarly and professorial. "We don't know a lot about what actually causes amniotic band syndrome," I began softly, "but we do know about some things that don't cause it, and one of those things is alcohol. The effects of drinking during pregnancy have been carefully studied, and although a lot of problems have been associated with maternal alcohol use, amniotic band syndrome is not one of them. I can positively assure you that drinking that wine did not cause Tommy's problems."

Mrs. Rama cried for a few minutes longer, but then when she stopped, we were able to move on. Once this hurdle had been surmounted, Maggie began to make larger strides. It turned out that the Ramas had been feeling a mixture of guilt and anger and frustration since Tommy's birth, that they'd been manipulated by the people they'd turned to for support, people who meant well but who always had their own agendas. Most important, the couple expressed real ambivalence about the surgery that had been planned for their son. They wanted it done so he'd be able to be placed in the chronic care facility, but they felt badly about putting the boy through the pain and discomfort the operation would undoubtedly cause. This ambivalence, which would emerge as the most important issue during Tommy's hospitalization, was not easy to resolve.

The workup continued on schedule. Tommy had a battery of sophisticated radiological studies: a CAT scan and an MRI scan of his brain; an angiogram, to look at the composition of blood vessels that fed his brain; and ultrasound studies of his head, his heart, and his kidneys. He had dozens of blood tests, all of which turned out to be normal. We discovered that, below his neck, the boy's internal functioning was completely normal; above his neck, however, everything was severely screwed up.

The appearance of the boy's brain on the radiological studies was so bizarre, so abnormal, that it was almost beyond description. Although most of the essential parts seemed to be present, literally nothing was where it was supposed to be. Each radiologist who was asked to comment on the various studies remarked about how a brain like this couldn't possibly function normally.

This opinion was echoed by Samuel Scheinfeld, the neurologist who had consulted on the case. He said that, although the baby did appear to have some developmental functioning, the things Tommy was able to do were all attributable to brain stem reflexes. Tommy was doing nothing more than an infant with anencephaly, or congenital absence of the brain, would be expected to do. The consultation note that Scheinfeld placed on the chart ended with this phrase: ". . . The possibility that this unfortunate child will exhibit any signs of higher cortical functioning in the future is nearly nil."

On the day Tommy's evaluation was completed and all the opinions had been collected, I happened to run into Ed Johnson in the hallway. "What's the next step?" I asked after reviewing the latest findings with him.

"Tommy's on the schedule for Monday," he replied. "We're going to fix him up."

"You're still going ahead with the surgery?" I asked.

"Sure," he replied. "Why shouldn't I?"

"Well, the parents aren't sure they want it done. . . ."

"That's not what they told me," Ed replied. "They signed the consent form this morning."

"Well, how about his prognosis? Didn't you read Scheinfeld's note?" I asked.

"Sure, I read it," Ed responded. "Hey, I'm not doing this surgery to cure the kid. I'm doing it so he doesn't wind up living out the rest of his life in a private room on the infants' ward. Taking off those encephalocoeles is the only way we're going to get him into that nursing home, remember?"

•　　•　　•

It's now been nearly a year since Tommy Rama was operated on by Ed Johnson. That operation was viewed as a success of sorts: the boy came back from the operating room still resembling a crea-

ture out of a science fiction movie, but at least he no longer had
horns. He spent a little over a month in our hospital following his
surgery, his recovery punctuated by three serious complications: first,
an episode of meningoencephalitis, a serious infection that surely
destroyed whatever higher cortical function the boy might have once
had; second, a leak of spinal fluid from the site of the incision; and
third, a wound dehiscence, a splitting open of the surgical site, a
phenomenon that was probably related to the infection. Normally,
any one of these problems should have been enough to kill this infant;
but somehow, Tommy survived. Finally, when he was a little over
three months of age, the baby was transferred to a pediatric nursing
home in Putnam County, a facility located about a half hour away
from his parents' house in Westchester.

Tommy's been back on the infants' unit twice since that initial
hospitalization. At five months of age and at one year of age, his
wound dehisced again, and on each of these occasions, blocks of the
artificial bone Ed Johnson implanted in an attempt to build the boy
a skull had worked their way to the surface; each time, the complication required another trip to the operating room, and each time,
we argued about the ethical implications of performing that surgery.
During both of these inpatient stays, I've had the opportunity to
examine the boy, and have found that Samuel Scheinfeld's prognosis
was completely correct: the boy has shown absolutely no developmental progress; every function he is capable of performing requires
no higher cerebral cortical input. He is, according to all parameters
tested, a functional anencephalic.

Tommy's parents, however, are doing much better. During the
boy's initial hospitalization, Maggie Walker spent some time every
day talking with them. With Maggie's help, Mrs. Rama began to
separate herself from the boy: she no longer spent every moment of
every day with him, and she began to work again in the now-
successful restaurant she and her husband had opened. She and her
husband have been able to move on with their lives.

On the day Tommy was transferred to the hospital in Putnam
County, Mrs. Rama thanked all of us who had been involved in her
son's care during his rocky stay on the infants' unit; she shook our
hands and offered each of us a broad smile. But for Maggie Walker,
she had a different way of saying good-bye: she embraced the coun-

selor for a long time and kissed her on the cheek, vowing that she'd stay in touch and would send periodic reports on Tommy's progress. It was obvious how much she cared for our genetic counselor.

And after all, that was the way it should have been. Because, of all the many health care providers who had seen Tommy Rama during his stay in our hospital, of all the superspecialists and hotshot consultants who had been involved in the case, Maggie Walker had been the only person to even figure out who the patient was.

Drawing Blood
From Randy

• • •

I HAD BEEN DREADING this moment. During the initial three weeks of my rotation in pediatrics, the first of the clinical clerkships through which I would pass as a third-year medical student, I'd been careful to avoid any situation in which I might be called on to perform a technical task. I'd participated in just about every other part of the day-to-day activities of our ward team on 8 East, the general pediatric ward at Jonas Bronck Hospital to which I'd been assigned, and had been nearly deliriously overjoyed to do anything I was asked. After all, having somehow survived the torture and drudgery of the first two years of medical school, during which the rest of my class and I had been forced to sit in lecture halls day after day, listening carefully as some of the best (not to mention most boring) minds on the faculty droned on and on about their research on subjects I could barely understand, material that obviously had little or no relevance to anything in the real world, I was finally getting the opportunity to take care of living, breathing patients. At last I was learning how to treat human diseases, which was, after all, the reason I'd come to medical school in the first place. So during those first three weeks, I had done everything with a smile on my face, from presenting the histories and physicals of my patients at attending rounds in the morning, to running out to the cafeteria to pick up dinner for my intern and the rest of the staff when we'd been on call at night. But when I knew there was blood to be drawn, or an IV to start, or a spinal tap to be performed, I disappeared as fast as I could. The reason was simple: I was terrified. Although I'd repeatedly watched interns and residents do these things, I'd never done any of them myself. My inability to perform these tasks, the fact that I could harm one of my little patients while simultaneously making a complete jackass of myself, was just too much for me to bear. And so, whenever I knew or anticipated that some test needed to be done on a patient, I made myself scarce.

I did so, that is, until that night three weeks into the rotation when, as I sat at the desk in the nurses' station, innocently writing an enormously long and overdetailed admission note on a three-year-old with asthma who'd come in a short time earlier, my intern, Mike Weinstein, snuck up behind me and said, "Randy needs a set of 'lytes. Would you mind drawing them?"

Mike startled me, and I had to think fast. I understood what he wanted: a small sample of blood for evaluation of the level of electrolytes in Randy's blood. Without a great deal of delay, I reached into the breast pocket of my short white coat and pulled out a three-by-five file card. I handed the card, on which I'd previously drawn pictures of two very crude light bulbs, to the intern, and said, "Look, Mike, I already drew the lights."

The intern didn't even smile. In a desperate attempt to avoid just this situation, I'd been pulling this "joke" on him for the last week or so. It hadn't exactly been hysterically funny to begin with, and it certainly hadn't improved much with age. "I'd do it myself," he went on, ignoring my feeble attempt at humor, "but I've got to start an IV on the new asthmatic, and according to the protocol, Randy's electrolytes are supposed to be checked right now. Unless you'd rather have a go at the IV . . ."

I shook my head and began to rise out of my chair. I was trapped, there was no doubt about it, and I could figure no reasonable way out. "Oh, well," I thought to myself after Mike had walked out of the nurses' station, "it was bound to happen sooner or later. But why does it have to happen to Randy?"

•　　　•　　　•

Randy Moore, who was five years old at that point, was one of my favorite patients. He had been in perfect health during early infancy, but then, at about three months of age, he inexplicably became dehydrated and lapsed into profound shock. His mother had rushed him to the emergency room at Jonas Bronck, where he was found to be suffering from two major disturbances: a very low level of sugar and a very high level of lactic acid in his blood. These metabolic abnormalities, coupled with the finding of an enlarged liver, had been unusual enough to earn Randy a million-dollar workup; blood, urine, and spinal fluid had been taken from him and sent to experts around the country; pieces of his skin and liver had been surgically removed and studied in all sorts of laboratories. As a result of all this, Randy was found to be suffering from von Gierke's disease, a rare, inherited metabolic disorder in which, because of a defect in the way a single enzyme, glucose-6-phosphatase, functions in the liver, the patient is unable to break down glycogen, the complex storage form of glucose, which is the sugar that provides fuel for the activities of the human body.

Normally, what happens in the human body is that during meals, extra glucose is stored away in the liver as glycogen, and then, between meals, as the blood sugar level gradually drops, the stored glycogen is slowly broken down, providing a kind of time-released energy source. This mechanism is especially important during the night, when ten to twelve hours can pass between meals. What happened in Randy's body, though, was that although he had no trouble making and storing glycogen, once the stuff was deposited in his liver cells, he could never again break it down into its component parts. As a result, over the years Randy's liver had gradually grown larger and larger, its cells packed to the brim with unusable glycogen, and between meals he had suffered repeated drastic drops in the level of sugar in his blood. This latter problem, in turn, had caused the buildup of lactic acid, a substance that's as harmful as poison, and which ultimately had led to severe retardation of Randy's growth. The overall effect of this was that the boy now more closely resembled a pregnant two-year-old than a healthy five-year-old, his growth stunted and his abdomen protuberant.

But in spite of the weird metabolic disturbances that were occurring within his body, Randy was as smart as a whip. He could read some simple books and write his own name. His mother had bought him a portable transistor radio, and he spent hours with his ear glued to that thing, listening to the Top 40 radio stations. As a result, he knew the words to almost all the popular songs. It was pretty strange to see this tiny kid with his belly sticking way out, wearing pajamas decorated with cowboys and horses, as he strutted up and down the corridor of the ward holding a miniature radio up to his ear, bopping his head to the beat, and trying unsuccessfully to snap the fingers of his right hand while singing the words to the theme song from the movie *Car Wash*, which that week had climbed to the number one position on the charts.

He had been in the hospital for about a month at that point; he was being tried on a newly developed treatment for von Gierke's disease. Every night before he went to sleep, a feeding tube had to be passed through his nose and into his stomach; the tube was then hooked up to a special pump that constantly dripped a small volume of a glucose-containing solution at the rate of about an ounce or so per hour. The reasoning behind this treatment was simple: if a small amount of sugar could be constantly introduced into Randy's system, even when he was asleep, his metabolic disturbances should spontaneously correct themselves, and he'd begin to grow.

The protocol seemed barbaric, both to Randy and to Mike Weinstein and the other interns who were caring for him. In addition to the daily ritual of passing the tube through his nose, it was necessary to draw blood from him three times a day: right before the pump was switched on in the early evening; in the middle of the nocturnal infusion, at about 3:00 A.M.; and in the morning, when the tube was finally removed for the day. Thinking back on it now, it seems as if this protocol could be considered a perfect method of torture.

But also thinking back on it now, I have to admit that Randy was actually pretty lucky. The prognosis for patients with von Gierke's disease prior to the time this new treatment had been developed was extremely poor. Most affected individuals never reached adulthood, dying in their early teens, their lives destroyed by the overwhelming toll these complex metabolic disturbances took on their bodies and their brains. Until shortly before Randy was admitted to the hospital, no therapy at all was available for von Gierke's disease; the fact that he'd survived long enough for a treatment of any kind to become available, no matter how barbaric that treatment might seem, was extremely fortunate for him. Of course, Randy shouldn't have understood any of this; by all rights, he should have responded to being turned into a nasal-tubed human pincushion the way any normal five-year-old would: with a lot of yelling and screaming and fighting. But amazingly, he'd remained fairly outgoing, reasonably happy, and disgustingly good-natured all through this month of torture. He even had taught himself to pass the nasal tube without help. For some reason, he almost seemed to be enjoying the treatment.

•   •   •

I went into the treatment room and, with a mixture of dread and hopelessness, began to gather all the supplies I knew I'd need: alcohol swabs, gauze pads, a rubber tourniquet, a couple of needles, a small syringe, an empty, red-stoppered test tube, and a couple of Band-Aids. I could feel butterflies start to flutter in my stomach and my hands begin to shake as I put these supplies into an empty cardboard box and proceeded to make my way out of the treatment room and down the hall to Randy's bedside.

He had the middle bed in one of the boys' rooms near the end of the hall. He was lying in his bed when I reached him, wearing his famous cowboy pajamas; I noticed he had already passed the feeding tube through his nostril for the night. He was watching television, but seemed glad to see me. "Oh, it's Doctor Bob," he said as soon as I passed through the door. "What are you doing here tonight? You on call or something?"

I told him that I was, and that I'd come to take some blood from his arm. "Not another needle!" Randy replied, but without hesitation, he rolled up the left sleeve of his pajama top, covering up two or three cowboys and at least a couple of horses.

I thought it would be best if I were straight with him from the very beginning. "Randy," I said firmly, "this is the first time I've ever tried to take blood from a patient. Is that okay with you?"

He shrugged his shoulders and looked back up toward the TV screen. "Maybe he's not as smart as I think he is," I mumbled to myself as, with my hands shaking even more than they had in the treatment room, I tied the tourniquet tightly around the upper part of the boy's left arm. "What are you watching?" I asked. I figured if I made some small talk, he'd think I was more at ease than my hands might indicate.

"Muppets," he answered, watching the TV intently now. "They're my favorites."

I searched the elbow and, amazingly, found what appeared to

be a large vein. "Which one's your favorite Muppet?" I asked as I
tried desperately to tear open the alcohol swab's package, finally
managing to control my hands enough to break the seal and to tear
the thing in two.

"Kermit," Randy answered. "He's a frog. He's green."

"I know," I replied as I tore open packages holding a needle and
the syringe. "He's my favorite, too."

"You know, there's a Doctor Bob on this show," Randy said as
I connected the needle to the syringe. "He's the doctor for all the
Muppets."

"And your doctor is Doctor Bob, too," I said. I had finished with
all the preparations by that point. "Does that mean you're a Muppet?"

"No," Randy replied, looking away from the television screen
and back up at me. "I'm not green, and I'm not a frog. Are you
going to give me the needle now?"

I didn't reply. Concentrating all my effort on trying to steady
my hands, I scrubbed the area around the inside of Randy's left
elbow with the alcohol swab, and, holding my breath, slowly passed
the sharp tip of the needle through the skin just below the big vein.
Randy let out a little yelp, but barely budged his arm, and when I
looked into the tubing coming from the needle, miracle of miracles,
I saw blood! Brownish red, liquid blood, coming directly through the
tubing from Randy's venous system. With a big sigh, I pulled back
on the syringe's plunger, and blood began to fill the inner cavity.
When the "3 cc" mark had been reached, I covered the skin with a
gauze pad, and pulled the needle out of the boy's arm.

I had done it! I had successfully drawn blood from a living,
breathing, human patient. There'd no longer be any need for me to
hide when Mike or anybody else had some blood tests that needed
to be done; no more need for excuses, or silly jokes, or pictures of
light bulbs on file cards. I had done it once, and I was sure I'd be
able to do it again.

Now proudly, smiling, my hands no longer shaking, my abdominal muscles no longer tense, I expertly squirted Randy's blood from
the syringe into the empty red-topped tube. Putting the stopper back
in, I asked Randy how he was doing.

"I'm doing okay, Doctor Bob, but is my blood supposed to be
dripping out like this?"

I looked up at Randy's elbow, and immediately felt the color begin to drain from my face. "Idiot!" I thought, slapping myself on the forehead. I had forgotten to untie the tourniquet from around the boy's arm before removing the needle. Randy's blood, still flowing merrily through the needle hole because of the increased pressure in the vein caused by the tight tourniquet, had long ago soaked through the puny gauze pad I had placed there, had dribbled down his arm, and was now beginning to spread lazily over the bed sheets, forming an abstract design. I quickly yanked the tourniquet off and, pressing the alcohol pad I had used to clean the arm over the still-bleeding vein, tried to make a joke about how things like this never seem to happen when the television version of Doctor Bob gives Kermit a needle. Randy, who had turned his attention back to the TV show, looked up at me quickly and said, "Kermit doesn't ever get any needles. He's a frog."

Pretty soon the bleeding stopped, and I released my hold on the now blood-soaked alcohol pad. I covered the whole area with one of the Band-Aids I had brought from the treatment room and, after I was sure the leakage of blood had completely ceased, ran out of the room and down the hall to the linen closet, where I got a couple of clean sheets. Back in the room, I got Randy out of bed, changed the sheets, and tossed the old, bloody ones onto the laundry cart, thereby burying the evidence. "There you go, Randy," I concluded, still embarrassed. "Good as new." And clutching the precious red-stoppered tube in my hot little hands, I turned to go.

"Doctor Bob?" I heard Randy call as I reached the door. I looked back in time to hear him say, "You did a good job. You didn't hurt me or anything."

I remained silent, but my face turned bright red. I headed back to the nurses' station, where my intern, having already finished starting the new patient's IV and pushing the first dose of medication into his vein, was sitting at the desk, working on the nursing orders for the patient's further care. "You get those 'lytes?" he asked.

"Right here," I replied, producing not a three-by-five file card, but a tube of genuine blood. I pulled up a chair next to his and began filling out the necessary chemistry lab slip.

"Any problems?" Mike asked nonchalantly, not even looking up from his writing. Embarrassed, I shook my head.

"That was the first time you drew blood from a patient, wasn't it?" he asked, and again I didn't say a word. "I remember the first time I ever had to do it," he continued, still scribbling away. "I was a brand-new third-year student, doing the surgery rotation here at Jonas Bronck." He stopped working on the orders and finally looked up at me. "The patient was this fat old woman who had a bad gall bladder that was scheduled to be taken out the following day, and the intern had sent me in cold to get her pre-op blood work. I didn't know what the hell I was doing. I somehow found a huge vein in her arm, but when I stuck a needle into it, nothing happened except she let out this horrible scream, like she was dying or something. So I pulled the needle out and tried again on the other arm, and this time she yelled even louder; she sounded like an elephant in labor, but still not a drop of blood came out. I went back to the first arm and tried it a third time, and missed again, but this time the woman yelled so loud that the chief resident and one of the big attendings came running to see what was wrong. The woman told them I was trying to kill her. 'I'm only here to get her pre-op bloods,' I explained to them. 'I'm sure I'm in the vein; I don't understand why the blood's not coming out.' The chief resident took one look at the needle that was still stuck into the woman's arm and said, 'Schmuck, you're supposed to take this little cap off the end before you try to use the damned thing.' He took the safety cap off the end of the tubing, and the blood started flowing like a babbling brook. I was so embarrassed, I wanted to crawl under that woman's bed and die. I'll never forget that as long as I live."

By the end of Mike's story, I had finished filling out the paperwork, and I rose from my chair to take the specimen down to the lab on the sixth floor. Mike had immediately gone back to concentrating on his work. It was then that I thanked him. I didn't tell him why; but somehow I was sure he knew exactly what had happened when I tried to draw blood from Randy.

•   •   •

It's now been twelve years since I first met Randy, and I'm happy to report that he's done well. Even though it seemed like torture at the beginning, the treatment protocol on which he was started when I was a medical student has been a success. While he was still in the hospital during that initial stay, we had already seen a change in him: his blood sugar level stabilized, his lactic acid level fell back into the normal range, and more important, he had an increased amount of energy and seemed to be growing before our eyes. I'm not sure if we were just imagining it because we were all pulling for him, but he actually seemed to become a tiny bit taller every day. Near the end of my rotation in pediatrics, about ten weeks after he had first been admitted to the hospital, Randy was discharged, returning home armed with a lifetime supply of nasogastric tubes, gallons of glucose solution, and his own, personal Harvard pump.

Since his discharge, Randy's spent most of the rest of his life healthy and happy, living at home, steadily growing and developing. On occasion, it's been necessary for him to come back into the hospital, when minor modifications have been made in his treatment protocol, or during those periods when his pump malfunctioned and had to go into the shop to be fixed. I've seen him off and on over the years, during these short stays in the hospital, or at other times when he'd come into the emergency room for some unrelated reason. I've watched him grow and have seen his protuberant abdomen shrink back to a more normal size. I've even had to draw blood from him on some of these occasions. Thankfully for both of us, my technique has improved dramatically over the years.

Galactosemia

• • •

I MET CASSANDRA GIOVANNI early on the morning of her ninth day of life. She'd been brought into the pediatric emergency room at Jonas Bronck Hospital by her mother, who told the nurse at the triage desk that something was terribly wrong with her daughter. "She's not acting right," the mother said. "I put her to sleep last night, and she didn't get up to feed or anything. And then when I went to wake her up this morning, she was lying there like this. I can't get her to move, or to even open up her eyes." The triage nurse took one look at the little girl and immediately realized that Cassandra was critically ill. Without hesitation, she grabbed the infant out of the mother's arms and, holding the baby as if she were a football, yelled for the residents on duty to come stat, then ran to the back of the emergency room, to the critical-care area, the site where cardiopulmonary resuscitations were performed, and laid the baby down on the stretcher.

It became clear almost immediately that Cassandra was in profound shock and near death. Her heart was beating only about forty times a minute, around a third of the number one would expect in a child of that age, and no blood pressure was initially detectable. The infant's body felt cold and stiff, almost as if she'd spent the night in a refrigerator; this impression was borne out by the reading of the thermometer that one of the nurses placed in the child's rectum: it registered less than 95 degrees Fahrenheit. Apparently, the mother had gotten Cassandra to the hospital just in the nick of time: the child was hanging on by a thread, and that thread was beginning to unravel.

An all-out cardiopulmonary resuscitation was begun: the senior resident in charge that morning worked on getting an IV into Cassandra's left arm, while another resident drew blood for baseline testing from the infant's right arm; the ER's head nurse glued cardiac monitor leads to Cassandra's chest; and the nurse who had first seen the infant at the triage desk hooked the girl up to an electrocardiogram machine. Once the IV was affixed in place with adhesive tape, the senior resident injected a dose of atropine, a drug that increases the heart rate. Next, in an attempt to expand the girl's volume of circulating blood, a bolus of normal saline solution was forced through the IV tubing and into Cassandra's vein. The effects of these two maneuvers were obvious almost immediately: the beeps emanating from the cardiac monitor became more frequent, rising to sixty, and then eighty, until they finally surpassed one hundred beats per minute, signaling that the girl's heart rate had returned to an acceptable range; checking the blood pressure again, the head nurse found that this time it was not only recordable, but was just slightly below normal. And then, within another minute or two, Cassandra opened her eyes for a few seconds and let out a weak cry. That was all the ER staff had to see. At that moment, they knew that the resuscitation had been a success; the infant was now stable enough to be transferred up to the pediatric floor.

Cassandra had apparently come into the emergency room severely dehydrated, and had been in hypovolemic shock (that is, shock caused by a deficiency of circulating blood volume). Although the shock had been relatively easy to diagnose and treat, the cause of the dehydration wasn't so obvious. But the ER staff didn't have to worry too much about that; figuring out the girl's underlying problem would be the job of the people upstairs, the staff assigned to Jonas Bronck's pediatric ward that month. So once it was clear that the infant had been adequately stabilized, the senior resident in charge of the ER called the senior resident on the pediatric ward and asked him to send down the intern who was next in line for an admission.

That intern was Mike Weinstein, the doctor to whom I'd been assigned less than a week before. I was a third-year medical student, doing my first clinical rotation and was anxious for patient contact. So when Mike told me there was an admission waiting for us down in the ER, I was raring to go.

When I first saw her, Cassandra still looked to me as if she were about to die; she was definitely the sickest patient I had ever laid eyes on up to that moment. A large baby with a puffy reddish face, we found her lying limp on the stretcher on which she had been placed at the start of the resuscitation, hooked up to an oxygen mask, an IV bag, and the cardiac monitor, which continued to beep about 120 times per minute. Her mother, a thin, sickly-appearing woman with long, stringy brown hair, stood hunched over the stretcher, sobbing quietly as she looked down at her daughter. After briefly taking in this scene, Mike and I sought out the senior resident; we found him in one of the ER's treatment rooms, beginning to examine another patient. When he saw us at the door, the resident excused himself and slipped out of the room. He told us as much of the girl's history as he knew: what had brought her to the ER, and what they had done to stabilize her. Then, looking straight into Mike's eyes, he asked, "What do you think's wrong with her?"

"I guess the first thing I'd be worried about is an infection," Mike replied, without any hesitation. "Regardless of what else we find, we have to treat her as if she's septic."

"I don't understand," I butted in. "She doesn't have a fever, does she?" I'll admit I didn't know much at that point, but I did know that people who had serious infections, such as sepsis, an overwhelming bacterial infection of the bloodstream, were supposed to have very high temperatures. "How could she have a serious infection if she doesn't have a fever?"

The senior resident looked at me for the first time. "Who's this?" he asked the intern.

"Bob," he replied, "my medical student. This is his first rotation."

"Oh," the resident responded, as if this explained everything. "Well, Bob, it is true that adults and older children get fever with infections, but babies frequently don't." Then turning back toward Mike, he said, "I agree. I'm worried about infection, too. What bug do you think she's got?"

"Well, she's at just the right age for Group B Strep, and her symptoms are right." I was later to learn that Group B Streptococcus is a bacteria that frequently inhabits the birth canal. If a fetus happens to come into contact with the bacteria, either during the birth process or prior to delivery, an overwhelming, life-threatening infection can result.

"I agree," the resident responded. "Group B Strep sepsis is definitely the first thing on my list, too. So we've done all the work for you: we've cultured the kid up," meaning that the ER staff had obtained blood, urine, and spinal fluid samples to test for the presence of bacteria, "and we gave her a whopping dose of ampi and gent." ("Ampi and gent," I already knew, was residentese for "ampicillin and gentamicin," two commonly used antibiotics.) "So all you guys have to do is make sure her IV stays in and check her cultures once a day. Any other diagnoses you want to consider?"

"Well, I guess she could have some sort of weird metabolic disease," the intern continued. "It seems a little late for a lot of them, though. I'd have expected her to show some symptoms in the first couple of days of life if she had maple syrup urine disease or something like that."

"Maple syrup urine disease?" I thought to myself. "There's actually something called maple syrup urine disease?" Of course, I didn't say anything out loud; I'd been far too intimidated by my last exchange with the ER resident to risk another question. So I bit my tongue and just listened as the resident said, "That's true. And anyway, most of those things would've been picked up on the neonatal screen. So I think any of those metabolic diseases is unlikely."

"So the kid's probably septic," Mike concluded. "No other explanation makes any real sense."

After finishing our chat with the senior resident, Mike and I walked back to the stretcher in the critical-care area. The intern asked me to get some history from Cassandra's mother, while he made arrangements to take the baby up to the ICU. I immediately panicked; I had talked to the parents of some of my other patients, but those children had been relatively healthy, not at death's door, as this baby appeared to be. I had no idea what I could say to this distraught woman, who was still hovering over the stretcher, still sobbing to herself, that could possibly make her feel the least bit better, that could possibly reassure her that everything was going to be all right with her daughter. The fact of the matter was that, so far during my medical school years, I'd been taught about physiology and pathology, I'd sat through endless lectures on anatomy and histology and biochemistry and genetics, but I had not been exposed to a single minute of instruction on what a doctor is supposed to say to the parents or other family members of a patient who is critically ill or dying. But I had been assigned this task by my intern, and I didn't want to disappoint him. So trying to remain calm and put these thoughts out of my mind, I approached the woman and introduced myself.

"She's going to be all right, isn't she, Doctor?" Ms. Giovanni asked.

Hemming and hawing, rambling on barely coherently, I told her that we really couldn't answer that question right then, because we weren't exactly 100 percent positive what was wrong with the baby, and that we were doing all sorts of tests that would give us more information, but that it might be a few more days before we knew anything for sure.

"It's all my fault," the woman said immediately. "It must have been something I did that caused this. She's my first baby, I've never been around children before, and I don't know what you're supposed to do with them. It must have been the bath I gave her last night. She vomited yesterday afternoon, and she didn't seem to be acting exactly right, but I gave her a bath anyway. I'm sure she got sick because of that. Or maybe it's the way I've been feeding her; no one showed me how you're supposed to feed a baby; they tried showing me while we were in the hospital, but I was too excited to listen. It must be the way I'm feeding her, or that bath. I'm sure I've done something terribly wrong."

"I don't think any of that could have caused what's wrong with the baby," I told her. In fact, I really didn't know; I had no idea whether a bath could cause a baby to become septic, or whether improper feeding techniques could have possibly been responsible for bringing on dehydration and shock, but I figured that it wouldn't be in either this woman's interest or my own to agree with her conclusion; and besides, logically, I couldn't see how feeding or bathing a baby could have caused any damage. "She must have been sick from the time she left the nursery," I continued. "Why don't you tell me the whole story from the beginning."

My reassurance seemed to calm her down a little, and she was able to give me the child's complete history. She explained that

Cassandra had been a perfect baby until the night before. She had been discharged from the hospital at four days of age, kept an extra day because of a little bit of jaundice, and had done everything a baby was supposed to do. But on the evening before Cassandra's arrival in the emergency room, the woman noticed that the baby seemed a little sleepier than usual. "And then she didn't wake up at three o'clock like she usually does," she continued. "And then this morning . . ." She started crying again, not able to utter another word.

At that point, Mike reappeared. He had finished making all the necessary arrangements, and after introducing himself to Ms. Giovanni, he, the nurse who had been guarding the baby ever since she had first seen her at the triage desk over two hours before, and I began to move the stretcher bearing Cassandra—as well as the pole from which her IV solution was hanging, the cardiac monitor to which she was attached, a portable oxygen tank, and a small tackle box filled with equipment to be used in case of cardiac arrest—out the back door of the ER, down the corridor toward the bank of patient elevators, and up to the eighth floor, where the pediatric intensive care unit was located. Ms. Giovanni, still sobbing occasionally into a crumpled handkerchief, followed close behind.

• • •

Over the next two days, Cassandra rallied. In the ICU, she was monitored closely and treated with large doses of intravenous antibiotics, and slowly, her level of consciousness and activity returned to normal. Because of the vomiting on the night before her admission, she was given no feedings by mouth, receiving all her fluid requirements through the IV in her arm. And when the results of the lab tests that had been sent off at the time of the infant's initial emergency room treatment began to come back, they confirmed Mike Weinstein's impression: Cassandra Giovanni had been suffering from a serious, life-threatening infection in her blood. But oddly, the organism that had grown in the culture medium hadn't been the expected Group B Strep; rather, who was infected with the more unusual but equally virulent _Escherichia coli_.

E. coli, a bacteria that normally resides in the intestinal tract, actually serves a beneficial function in humans by aiding in the digestion of food. _E. coli_ is the most common cause of bacterial infections of the urinary tract, but is only rarely found in the blood of babies or older individuals. If caught in time, it is amenable to treatment, the majority of times responding to the widely used antibiotic Ampicillin.

That this organism was found in the bloodstream of Cassandra Giovanni caused a small amount of concern to those of us who were caring for the child, but the fact was, she was responding terrifically to the treatment. By the morning of the third day after admission, Cassandra was stable enough to be transferred out of the ICU. She was sent to 8 East, where the child's formula feedings were reinstituted, and the antibiotics would be continued for a full ten-day course.

With the apparent recovery of her daughter, Ms. Giovanni's outlook also improved. She still looked tired, drawn, and sickly, but at least she had ceased her constant crying. She was relieved when I was able to tell her that the child's infection had in no way resulted from anything she had done to Cassandra following her discharge from the nursery. Now that the baby was on the ward, where visiting hours for mothers were unlimited, Ms. Giovanni spent most of her time sitting on a chair beside the baby's crib, holding her daughter in her arms, making sure not to disturb the IV through which the antibiotics were running, and feeding her bottle after bottle of Similac. Cassandra responded to Ms. Giovanni's attention by gazing at her face and hungrily sucking down any and all formula her mother offered.

Being so inexperienced in the ways of medicine, I found myself with a lot of free time. There wasn't much I was able to do to help Mike get his work done beyond running samples down to the lab for him and searching the record room for results, errands that weren't all that time-consuming or important. When it came to doing the things that really made internship tedious, because of my inexperience I was absolutely no help to Mike. Most days, out of frustration, he sent me off to the library to read, but that's not what I wanted to do; I had just spent the last two years reading. What I yearned for was some actual contact with patients and their families. And so, roaming the hall of the pediatric ward, looking for action, I came across Ms. Giovanni sitting by her baby's bedside. She seemed as anxious to have someone to talk to as I was to listen. And so, during the next few days, I spent a great deal of time learning about Cassandra's mother.

Asking me to call her Antoinette, she told me things that had not been part of the initial history, stories about her life that had nothing to do with the child's illness, but that I realized were going to have plenty to do with what Cassandra's life was going to be like after she ultimately left our care. Antoinette told me that she and Cassandra were basically alone, sharing a one-room, basement apartment in a private house about a mile from the hospital. She was eighteen years old, and the baby's father was seventeen. They had met in high school and had started dating. Antoinette's parents had disapproved of him from the beginning. "They're kind of racist," she explained, "and he's kind of black. So when they found out about us, they told me either I stop seeing him, or else they'd kill me. But that didn't bother me." She laughed. "Nothing bothered me."

Things went from bad to worse when Antoinette became pregnant. "My folks went completely nuts," she told me. "They called me all sorts of names. We're Catholic, and they couldn't tell me to go and have an abortion, so they did the next best thing: they threw me right out of the house. I had no place to go; I was out on the street, I had no money, nothing. So I went to my boyfriend's parents' house, but it turned out they hated me as much as my parents hated him. They had no idea their son was even going out with a white girl, and then one day, boom, I turn up at their door, pregnant and with no other place to go. So they told him, 'Either she goes or you both go.' And what do you think he did?"

I shrugged my shoulders, and she continued: "He told me to get out. Can you imagine that? Here I am, completely alone and pregnant with his baby, and he tells me that he never really liked me that much in the first place. He told me I should go get an abortion. God! He didn't even offer to help pay for it. He just said I should go and have it done, and then go home to my parents. And to think I once thought I loved him. What a jerk!"

"Did you think about getting an abortion?" I asked.

She frowned. "It's really hard when you've been raised in a family like mine. Anyway, I'm glad I didn't get one. If I had gotten an abortion, I wouldn't have little Cassandra here."

"How did you come up with her name?"

She smiled. "Right before I left high school, we were doing a chapter in Greek mythology in English. I don't know, the name really stuck with me. Right after I got pregnant, I decided the baby's name would be Cassandra if it turned out to be a girl, and Jason if it was a boy."

She told me that after leaving her boyfriend's house, she got a job as a checkout clerk in a supermarket near her parents' house. "It was pretty weird. Here I was, working in this store, and all my mother's friends would come in to do their shopping, and they'd all see me there, but none of them ever said a word to me. They treated me like I didn't exist." She took a one-room apartment in the basement of a private house, and got ready for the baby to come. When she started having labor pains, she showed up in the emergency room at Jonas Bronck. "I know they're not allowed to turn anyone away. It doesn't matter whether you have any money or anything. If you show up at Jonas Bronck, they have to treat you."

"I didn't know that," I said, and smiled, realizing that this eighteen-year-old knew more about the medical care delivery system in the Bronx than I did after two years of medical school. "How are you going to support yourself now that Cassandra's here?"

"I don't know," she replied. "I can't work anymore. I'd have to leave the baby with someone and I can't afford a baby-sitter. I guess I'll have to go on welfare or something. I haven't gone down there or anything yet. The most important thing now is to make sure Cassandra gets all better."

Later, I talked with Mike about Antoinette's financial problems and he told me to get the social worker involved. He said that since the girl would have to remain in the hospital for two whole weeks to complete her course of intravenous antibiotics, there'd be plenty of time to at least apply for help. The ward's social worker met with Antoinette and told her she'd help her fill out the paperwork for financial support. Everything went extremely well with the baby and her mother, until the morning of the seventh day after Cassandra's admission. At about eight o'clock, just as our ward team was starting work rounds, the nurse assigned to her noticed that the child had a fever. Within ten minutes, her cardiac monitor alarm went off: the infant had suffered a complete cardiopulmonary arrest.

Having no idea why this had happened, our team sprang into

action. The ward clerk announced a Code Blue over the loudspeaker system, and within seconds, people started running into the infant's room from all over the floor. The nurses pushed the ward's code cart from the treatment room to the side of Cassandra's bed, and opened all the drawers; Mike began to perform chest compressions, pushing down on Cassandra's breastbone with his thumbs to force her heart to beat about a hundred times a minute; Peter Uris, our senior resident, intubated the baby, passing an endotracheal tube through her larynx and down into her windpipe, to facilitate artificial ventilation; and after affixing an ambu-bag to the end of the endotracheal tube, Peter ordered me to pump the bag. Andy Stewart, the chief resident, appeared, and began ordering medications that the nurses drew up and shot through the infant's IV tubing. All of this occurred while Antoinette, horrified, stood by watching.

We got her back. It took a while, and two full rounds of atropine, epinephrine, calcium, and bicarbonate, medications that reverse cardiac arrest, but eventually, Cassandra's heart and lungs began working on their own again, and her blood pressure gradually returned. When the code was finished and she was stable enough to be moved, her crib was pushed back into the ICU, and she was reconnected to all the monitors; blood, spinal fluid, and urine specimens were again taken, and sent back to the lab. And then the greatest minds of the pediatric department got together and tried to figure out what had happened.

"She's still septic," was the opinion of the chief resident, Andy Stewart. "She's got a bug that's not completely sensitive to the antibiotics she's on. We have to start again and treat her more aggressively."

"Yeah, she's definitely septic," Peter Uris agreed. "But don't you think it might be another bug this time?"

"It'd be hard to imagine how something like that could happen," the chief resident replied. "Unless she had some weird congenital immunologic deficiency. And those things are pretty damned rare. No, it's most likely to be a resistant strain of _E. coli._"

"So what should we treat her with?" Mike asked. As the intern responsible for doing the work, he had to try to bring the discussion back from these lofty heights to a more practical level.

"Add chloramphenicol," Andy responded, mentioning an antibiotic that has a great many potential side effects, such as aplastic anemia (lack of formation of all blood elements because of failure of the bone marrow); Peter and Mike nodded their heads.

After this conversation, I went out to find Antoinette. She was still in Cassandra's room on 8 East, sitting in the chair on which she had sat for so many hours over the previous few days, crying hysterically, saying "My baby, my baby" over and over again. I felt terrible: it was bad enough that Cassandra had suddenly gotten so sick; it was worse that the woman had witnessed the entire resuscitation. "She's okay," I told her, and she looked up at me for the first time since I entered the room. "She's all set in the ICU. They'll let you in to see her in a couple of minutes."

"What's wrong with her, Bob?" she asked. "She was doing so well and then, my God, she nearly died again. Why did something like that happen? I'm so frightened."

"The chief resident thinks it's because we weren't treating her infection aggressively enough," I explained. "We're adding another antibiotic. Everybody's convinced this'll clear things up for good."

This seemed to raise her spirits a little. I led her down the hall, toward the ICU, where, after another minute, a nurse led her in to see the baby. Antoinette began crying again the moment she laid eyes on her daughter. I left her there like that, and went to have a talk with Mike Weinstein.

He was sitting in the ICU's nurses' station, writing a note in Cassandra's chart. After apologizing for interrupting, I quietly asked if maybe there were things other than infections that might be causing Cassandra's problems. "Things like what?" he snapped at me. He wasn't in a terrific mood; the events of the morning had obviously made him more than a little irritable.

"Well, I've been doing some reading," I replied meekly, "and I came across the fact that sometimes metabolic problems predispose infants to *E. coli* infections."

"Oh, so you've been doing some reading, huh?" he asked. "Okay, so let's hear it: what kind of metabolic diseases cause *E. coli* infections?"

"Galactosemia," I replied.

"Right," he said, slowly nodding his head. "At least you've been reading the right books. Now, do you really think it's possible that this baby has galactosemia?"

"Sure," I replied. I had done a lot of reading about this disease. It was a rare, inborn error of metabolism, an autosomal recessively inherited disorder caused by the absence of a single enzyme, galactose-1-phosphate uridyltransferase. The enzyme is essential for the breakdown of galactose, one of the two components of lactose, the sugar found in both human and cow milk. Without the enzyme, the infant cannot use the sugar, a main source of energy, and even worse, toxic levels of galactose build up in the blood, causing damage to many organs. "She's got this infection that's not getting better, she had low blood sugar when she first came in, she even had jaundice in the first few days of life. Those are all things that happen to babies with galactosemia. And it's easy to test for: all we have to do is get a sample of urine and . . ."

"Absolutely," the intern cut me off. "You're absolutely right about everything, Bob. But it's still impossible for this child to have galactosemia."

"Why?" I asked.

"Because this is New York State. And in New York State, there's a neonatal screen for metabolic diseases that's done on every baby before discharge from the nursery. Since galactosemia's one of the diseases that's tested for, there's not a snowball's chance in hell that this kid could have it. But if you'd like to waste a couple of minutes of your precious time doing a Clinitest on this kid's urine to check for reducing sugars, be my guest!" And with that, Mike went back to writing his note.

Feeling like an idiot, I left the ICU and headed for the nursery. Finding one of the neonatal fellows, I asked very nicely if he would tell me about the screen. He explained that, on the third day of life, just before a baby is discharged to go home, a nurse, using a tiny lancet, pierces the skin of the heel. The few drops of blood that result are collected on a special piece of filter paper, which also contains the baby's name, the hospital of birth, and the home address and telephone number. These filter paper samples are collected at the end of each day and mailed to a lab in Albany, where the actual testing is performed. The fellow explained that, if an infant born at Jonas Bronck Hospital is found to have an abnormal screen, the director of neonatology is immediately informed, and tracking down that infant becomes his responsibility. The majority of babies found to be abnormal on the initial neonatal screen turn out, on subsequent testing, to be "false positives," having no real problem. But a small fraction of the babies found to have abnormalities on their initial sample will ultimately be found to have one of the dozen or so disorders for which testing is performed. "We take this stuff very seriously," the fellow explained to me, "because all of the diseases they test for are treatable with either medication or special diets. If they're not treated, the kids wind up neurologic disasters. So it's our chance to be real heroes. That's why we make sure to find and treat every single damned one of them!"

The neonatal fellow's explanation convinced me. There was no way Cassandra could have galactosemia. No way.

•   •   •

It took a little longer this time for Cassandra to return to normal. After her arrest, she was a very sick little girl. As expected, another pure culture of *E. coli* grew from the sample of blood that had been taken at the time of her readmission to the ICU. The chloramphenicol slowly began to take effect, and four days after her cardiac arrest, Cassandra was again well enough to be transferred back to 8 East.

I helped move her back to the ward that day. She screamed all the way down the hall during the short trip. Her mother assured us that the little girl was starving: "How do you think you'd feel if you hadn't been allowed to eat anything for four whole days?" Sure enough, as soon as she was told it was okay, Antoinette stuck a nipple into her daughter's mouth, and the girl sucked down eight ounces of formula in less than five minutes.

Things were really looking up for the Giovannis that day and the next; the baby appeared fine, and seemed to have finally beaten this infection that had plagued her for nearly two weeks now. With the help of the social worker, the mother had filled out and filed an application for welfare assistance, and had been assured that benefits would begin by the time the infant was discharged from Jonas Bronck Hospital. Everything was going along fine.

And then it happened again.

A little after midnight on the night after Cassandra had been sent back to 8 East, the cardiac monitor that was still attached to her chest began to alarm. Mike and I happened to be on call that night, along with Peter Uris, and we all came running. We found the girl with a heart rate of twenty-five. Antoinette wasn't around; according to the ward clerk, she had been seen leaving the pediatric floor a few hours before, and hadn't told anyone where she was going.

We worked on Cassandra for hours, most of that time in the cramped, overcrowded room on 8 East, but near the end, we managed to get her down to the ICU. We gave her round after round of medication; she was intubated and hooked up to a ventilator; we gave her a bolus of electrolyte solution, attempting to reverse dehydration, although no real signs of dehydration were present. We managed to get her heart rate up to about seventy, and we got her a low blood pressure, but she never again breathed on her own and never regained consciousness.

At four o'clock in the morning, after everything had been tried and nothing had been very successful, Cassandra's heart gave out. She simply died, and there was nothing any of us could do to get her back. Andy Stewart, who had been stat paged out of his sleep and had made it into the hospital a little before one o'clock, after finally becoming convinced that all resources at his command had been completely and utterly exhausted, sadly declared her dead at ten minutes after four.

There was an almost palpable feeling of gloom in the ICU. Andy Stewart, Peter Uris, and Mike Weinstein slumped down into chairs in the nurses' station, trying to figure out why this had happened. I stood leaning against a storage shelf, listening to the conversation. "It doesn't make sense," Peter said slowly. "She got sick, came into the ICU, got better, went out to the floor, got sick again, came into the ICU, got better again, went out to the floor, and got sick and died. In the ICU she's healthy; on the floor, she crumps. It just doesn't make sense."

"How is being on the ward different from being in the ICU?" Mike asked. "Answer that question, and we'll probably know why this happened."

That's when the light bulb went on in my head. Without another word, I left the nurses' station and walked over to the crib that held Cassandra's body. With a syringe, I sucked a 3 cc sample of urine from the bag that was connected to the catheter that had been placed in Cassandra's bladder at the start of the resuscitation. With the syringe in hand, I walked to the ICU's small laboratory. I took a glass tube, placed a Clinitest tablet into it, and, following the instructions posted on the lab's wall, added three drops of urine and three drops of tap water to the tube. An immediate chemical reaction began. The fluid began to fizz and change color: in five seconds, the liquid was green; in fifteen seconds, the liquid turned dark brown.

Still with the tube in my hand, I walked back into the nurses' station. All three doctors looked up. They saw the dark brown color in the test tube. And all, as one, said a single word: "Galactosemia."

•   •   •

Now, thirteen years later, I still have trouble believing all this really happened. It's not just that she was the first patient I ever cared for who died; it's much more than that. The death of Cassandra Giovanni should have never occurred, certainly not in the way it did; she died as the result of a series of mix-ups and blunders; she and her mother, inexplicably, had fallen through a series of nooks and crannies that run through the huge and unwieldy medical care delivery system. And she died because I had been intimidated by my intern, because I had allowed myself to be put off by an assumption that should never have been made.

In checking it out over the next few days, I discovered the reason why Cassandra had not been found, on the neonatal screen, to have galactosemia. It wasn't because the test was faulty or unreliable; rather, it was because a sample of her blood had never been received in the state lab in Albany. It might have been because the blood was never taken; it might have been because the filter paper sample had never been sent, or had been lost in handling, or had been thrown away before it was logged in, but when I called to ask for the results, I was informed by a very concerned lab technician that not only was there absolutely no record of a sample taken from any infant named Giovanni who had been born at Jonas Bronck Hospital on Cassandra's birthday, but there had been no infants in the state of New York who had been found to have galactosemia in the past few months.

After that first blunder, the others fell smoothly into line; because we had come to rely on the neonatal screening program, it had been assumed that no child with galactosemia could possibly escape detection. So in Cassandra's case, the diagnosis was never really seriously considered. And even when I suggested the diagnosis to my intern, even though I knew that only a simple urine test was needed to confirm the diagnosis, I hadn't done it. I hadn't had the courage or the confidence in myself to follow through until after it was too late; and quite probably, my failure had caused this infant her life.

But the mix-ups didn't stop there. Despite the missed diagnosis, there was the chance that some good might have come of all this. Because galactosemia is an autosomal recessively inherited disorder, it meant that both Antoinette and the infant's father were obligate carriers of an abnormal gene, and that the potential existed for the same thing to happen to their children in the future. The two of them needed genetic counseling. But providing it proved to be impossible.

I never saw Antoinette Giovanni again. She returned to the hospital around eight o'clock, four hours after Cassandra had died. Upon seeing the empty space where Cassandra's crib had stood, she began to scream. A nurse came running and, without saying a word, led the mother into the ward's family room. Andy Stewart was paged and, after arriving in the room, broke the news to the woman. She was inconsolable for over an hour, an hour during which I was off in the on-call room, sound asleep. And then, after hastily signing a permission-for-autopsy form, the woman left the hospital, and apparently walked off the face of the earth.

We couldn't find her anywhere. She had falsified her address on the hospital admission forms and had used the same phony address on the welfare application; from the very beginning, she obviously hadn't wanted anyone in the hospital's billing office to be able to track her down. I checked through the phone book and called every Giovanni in the Bronx; none admitted knowing an eighteen-year-old named Antoinette.

I can still vividly remember the moment during the predawn morning when the connections finally came together in my head. In an instant I understood that, in spite of what my intern and other superiors on the staff had told me, Cassandra Giovanni had become sick every time she'd been transferred back to pediatric ward, not because she had received shoddy care, but simply because that was when her diet of infant formula, her source of toxic galactose, had always been resumed. It was from that moment of realization that I learned to trust my own instincts, and to not be intimidated by what others who are older and possibly wiser than me might believe. And whenever I'm attending on one of the pediatric wards, I make sure to tell the interns, residents, and medical students about Cassandra, and to teach them the lesson I learned from her. By telling and retelling her story, I like to think I'm helping to ensure that what happened to Cassandra never happen to another child.

Teaching Rounds

• ● •

I WAS BEGINNING TO DOUBT MY ABILITY. As the attending physician assigned to the pediatric ward at University Hospital in January, it was my responsibility to spend at least an hour every day with the interns, residents, and medical students who were working on the unit, in order to teach them something about my specialty. But during the first two weeks of the month, I had been faced with a real problem: although University Hospital, a nationally known tertiary care facility, had been filled to capacity with an assortment of interesting cases, there had been a real shortage of good clinical genetics teaching material. I had found myself showing up for rounds every morning, only to discover that there was nothing new or extraordinary about which I could lecture the house officers. That's why I became so excited when I walked into the pediatric conference room that Thursday morning, and was told by Eileen Barrett, the senior resident on the unit that month, that a great teaching case had come into the hospital the evening before: a five-year-old girl with Gaucher's disease had been admitted for medical management of her apparently intractible seizures.

I immediately found an empty chair at the room's conference table, around which the three interns, one resident, and two medical students who made up the ward team that month had already assembled, and took a seat. To me, a fresh case of juvenile Gaucher's disease, a rare autosomal recessively inherited disorder that afflicts children sometime after infancy and before adolescence, was like manna from heaven. Because of the rarity of the disorder, it was a subject about which I was sure the house staff knew very little; in addition, it was a topic on which I could lecture off the top of my head for at least an hour. So, relaxing and settling into my chair, I listened carefully as Don Schwartz, the intern who had been on call the night before, began presenting the girl's history.

The patient, whose first name was Sarah, had been in excellent health during her first year of life. Her development had apparently been textbook normal: she had rolled over at four months of age, had sat without support at six months, and had taken her first unassisted steps a few days before her first birthday. And during that first year, she had suffered not a single illness, not even an upper respiratory or ear infection. But then, when Sarah was about sixteen months of age, her mother noticed that the child seemed to be having trouble with her balance; she was clumsier than she had been just a few months before, always falling to the ground after taking a step or two. Sarah's mother brought this to the attention of their pediatrician during the girl's routine eighteen-month visit to his office. He had done a complete physical exam and, having uncovered no hard signs or symptoms of disease, had been reassuring, saying that this type of behavior was not unusual in toddlers, that it was a normal developmental stage that would undoubtedly pass.

But the clumsiness didn't pass; in fact, it seemed to become worse. Within a month, Sarah was back in her pediatrician's office; the doctor repeated his examination, and this time noticed that the little girl's liver and spleen were both slightly enlarged, that her muscle tone was mildly increased, and that her deep tendon reflexes were abnormally brisk. Appropriately concerned, he immediately referred Sarah to Dr. Alice Robbins, a pediatric neurologist at our medical school, for evaluation. Dr. Robbins saw the girl the following week and, alarmed by Sarah's symptomatology, immediately began a comprehensive workup for disorders that cause degeneration of the central nervous system. According to the intern, the diagnosis was made when a blood test revealed that Sarah had a deficiency of beta-glucosidase, the enzyme that's absent in patients with Gaucher's disease.

By twenty-one months of age, Sarah had become so clumsy that she couldn't take even a single step without falling to the ground; her abdomen, because of the enlargement of her liver and spleen, had become so protuberant that clothes that had previously fit perfectly now barely stretched across her widening tummy. And it was around that time that her mother noticed that Sarah's breathing had become very noisy and labored, as if she had developed a bad case of croup. Dr. Robbins confirmed that the girl had inspiratory stridor, but knew that this symptom wasn't due to simple spasm of the trachea, the cause of common childhood croup; rather, it was due, like many of the other manifestations of Gaucher's disease, to the buildup of a complex chemical called glucocerebroside in the cells of the little girl's windpipe.

The seizures had begun when Sarah was nearly two. In the beginning they had been short, lasting only a minute or two, and they had occurred relatively infrequently. But as time passed, their severity and periodicity increased dramatically; Sarah's arms and legs would flail uncontrollably for ten, fifteen, or even twenty minutes without ceasing. And the convulsions, which in the beginning had occurred only once or twice a month, became more common, first once a week, then every other day, until finally, at the age of thirty months, the little girl was having three or four seizures every day. Dr. Robbins experimented with varying dosages and combinations of all kinds of anticonvulsants; at one time, Sarah had been on five separate medications. Although some of the combinations tended to decrease the frequency of the seizures, and some had shortened the length of time each one lasted, none had been completely successful in eradicating them. Most of the time, the mix of drugs enabled the convulsions to be controlled well enough for life to continue in Sarah's house with only occasional disruption. But when the child developed a cold or a fever, the seizures would flare up out of control, completely overtaking the lives of Sarah, her mother, and her father.

That's apparently what had happened this time. "She was in her usual state of health," Don, the intern, said, coming to the end of the history, "until the day before admission, when she began tugging on her left ear. Her mother brought her to the pediatrician's office yesterday, and he diagnosed an ear infection and started her on an antibiotic. But then in the afternoon, she developed a fever of 101, and started seizing. She's been seizing ever since; it's been," he looked at his watch at this point, "about sixteen hours now. Dr.

Robbins is trying her on a new anticonvulsant called Depakene that's just been approved for use in children. So far it hasn't even touched her."

"Anything unusual on the physical exam?" I asked.

"Well, she's a wasted little girl who's actively seizing," he replied. "She has an enormous liver; it's at least twice the size it should be for a kid her age. She does have an ear infection, and we're giving her Amoxicillin for it, but her fever's staying up. That's about all, really."

"It's an unusual story," I said, beginning the lecture I had been planning the entire time the intern had been telling the little girl's story. As I had suspected, it had turned out to be a great teaching case, filled with all sorts of clinical findings that correlated well with the disease's basic genetic defect; I spent the next twenty minutes lecturing about the clinical, biochemical, and pathological features of Gaucher's disease. I explained that, although all patients exhibited deficiency of the enzyme beta-glucosidase, there were three distinct clinical forms of the disorder, and that these forms could usually be distinguished by the age of onset and the types of symptoms. Type I, the chronic form of the disease, occurred mainly in adults and caused enlargement of the liver and spleen, but always spared the brain; Type II was always seen in infants, caused severe damage to the brain, the liver, and the spleen, and inevitably led to death by the end of the first year of life; and Type III, the juvenile form, struck later in life than Type II but earlier than Type I, and often involved the brain. I concluded my talk by saying that this patient's story seemed most compatible with Type III Gaucher's disease, but that there were some real inconsistencies with this diagnosis. I then suggested that, before continuing the discussion any further, we all go and examine the patient.

Don, the intern, led the way out of the conference room and down the hall toward the patient's bed. She had been placed in the room adjacent to the floor's nurses' station, the room in which the patients most in need of constant, close monitoring, were inevitably placed. The intern stopped in front of a bed and, when the rest of the team pulled up behind him, said, "This is Sarah."

The girl had been propped up in the bed on a pillow, and was obviously in the midst of a partial seizure: her right arm and leg were shaking rhythmically, but her left side was at rest on the mattress. She was small, looking more like a three-year-old than a five-year-old, and her skin was a pale bluish-white, the color of fine bone china. She had been covered with the paraphernalia of intensive care: there were two IVs plugged into her emaciated arms, cardiac monitor leads attached to her chest, and prongs stuck into her nostrils through which oxygen was flowing. When she breathed, it sounded as if a seal was barking in the room, a sound caused by the narrowing of her trachea, which, for the past three years, had apparently served as a constant reminder of her disease. In her left hand, she clutched an old, obviously frequently used, stuffed animal; faded gray and threadbare, the thing looked as if it had, at some point in the far distant past, been a floppy-eared puppy. I noticed something familiar about the little girl's face; I couldn't put my finger on what it was at first, so I assumed it was just something in her expression, the look of sadness or despair I had seen over and over again in other patients like this, children who were dying from the effects of a chronic, debilitating disease.

I was beginning to examine the girl when the door to the room's bathroom flew open, and a panicked voice screamed out the words, "What's wrong?" Sarah's mother, who, thinking this crowd had formed around her daughter's bed because the child had gone into cardiac arrest, was running toward us at top speed. It was then that I realized who Sarah was.

•   •   •

It had been four years since we had last seen them. My wife, Beth, had met Sarah's mother, Laura Hamilton, in a "new mothers" group at the Mother and Child Center in New Rochelle. Every week from September through June, the group met for two-and-a-half hours, the mothers sitting upstairs, discussing the changes that had occurred in their lives following the recent birth of their first child, and trying, collectively, to solve some of the problems these changes had caused; meanwhile, in a well-stocked, closely supervised playroom in the basement, the children ran or crawled around, literally tearing the place apart, and generally having a terrific time. Our daughter, Isadora, and Sarah Hamilton had become fast friends during these sessions, and Beth and Laura had arranged for the girls to get together for play dates at least once a week.

After the program ended that June, we moved to a new house

in a neighboring town, and because of the distance, Beth didn't return to the center the following September. As time passed, she completely lost touch with Laura, and since then, we hadn't heard a thing about either Sarah or her mother.

I had met Laura and Sarah a few times when the kids had played at our house. There hadn't been anything unusual or different about this little girl: she had been a cute, playful toddler. I remember one specific Saturday when Beth and Laura had gone shopping, leaving me at home to baby-sit; this was during the late spring, and because the weather was so surprisingly warm, I took the girls out into the backyard of the building in which we were then living. I sat on a lawn chair and watched as they crawled around the grass, playing together, having a great time. Sarah had no trouble keeping up with Isadora; looking back on it, there had been nothing obvious wrong with her. Was it possible that that cute, playful, nearly-one-year-old girl, who had been my daughter's best friend, had turned into this patient, a wasted, terminally ill five-year-old who sat unresponsive, gripped by an unending, uncontrollable convulsion, in the bed in front of me? I suddenly felt dizzy; trying to talk, to explain to Laura what we were doing there, I found that I couldn't manage to get even a single word out of my mouth.

By this time, Laura was standing at her daughter's right side. Having heard the steady "beep-beeps" coming from the girl's cardiac monitor, which signaled that the child's heart was still beating, she waited impatiently for some explanation for why this group of doctors had invaded the sanctity of her daughter's hospital room. "Nothing's wrong," Don Schwartz said matter-of-factly. "We're just here on rounds."

"Well, Sarah's not feeling very well right now," Laura responded. She was much thinner than she'd been the last time I had seen her. She obviously didn't recognize me, just another anonymous doctor among the many who had briefly passed through the life of her child. "I wonder if you'd mind not bothering her too much," she continued.

Feeling uncomfortably light-headed, and having trouble catching my breath, I was happy to comply with Laura's request. I rapidly turned away from the bed and walked, nearly ran, out of the room. The rest of the team followed, and, with the "beep beep beep" of

Sarah's cardiac monitor gradually fading in the background, we headed for the conference room.

"So you do still think the diagnosis is Type III Gaucher's?" Eileen Barrett asked as soon as we were all settled around the conference table.

I tried to speak, but I was still having trouble forming words into sentences. After a brief delay, the only thing I could manage to get out of my mouth was "I know her."

"That isn't very surprising," Don Schwartz responded. "She's been here a lot. This is her eighth or ninth admission to University Hospital. Everyone runs into her sooner or later."

"No, you don't understand," I said, shaking my head. I had recovered a little; my breathing had become better and I was able to speak again. "I knew her when she was a normal kid. Before she was like this." And I told the whole team the story of Sarah and Isadora.

Somewhere along the line, I realized then, I had lost something. I had learned, from the lessons of some of the attendings who had been my teachers, academic subspecialists who had devoted their lives to the education of young physicians, that the training of interns and residents needed to rely heavily on the tried-and-true method of presentation and discussion of interesting, informative "cases." In pediatrics, a good teaching case is often one in which the patient, more often than not an infant or young child, is afflicted with a rare, often horrible, debilitating disease that has already caused a tremendous amount of suffering to the child and to his family, suffering that, in many cases, can be relieved only by the inevitable death of the patient. I had learned that, to the teacher, the subspecialist acting as ward attending, the patient's pain and suffering often had to take a backseat to the lesson his disease could teach the house officers; the patient as person becomes less important than the patient as specimen, an object to be carefully dissected under a microscope into tiny bits of informative facts, for the education of the interns, residents, and medical students who have, out of necessity, come to rely upon these bits of facts to form them into good clinicians. In my desire to do a good job, to be a good teacher, and to be what house officers considered "a good attending," I had somehow lost my perspective. In lecturing on Gaucher's disease, I had covered the biochemical defect, the clinical course, and the pathological findings, but I had forgotten that there was a child attached to the diagnosis, a unique person, who was seizing uncontrollably as a result of what the disease had done to her; that there was a man and a woman who were desperately trying to hold their lives together as they watched their only child slowly deteriorating before their eyes, unable to do anything to help her, or to prevent it from happening, or to even slow the steady downward progression the disease caused; and that there was a whole family in turmoil, a family that surely didn't need or want a team of six or seven doctors or doctors-in-training walking through their lives every day, staring at and judging their misery, simply because the child they loved happened to have a rare disease, happened to be what was considered "a good teaching case." Somewhere along the line, I had forgotten all this, and it had taken the jolt of realizing that the debilitated child convulsing uncontrollably in the room off of the nurses' station was a child I had known during better times, to hammer this message home to me.

I didn't spend the rest of that hour lecturing about Type III Gaucher disease, as I had planned. Instead, we talked about some of the other children who were patients at University Hospital that day, many of whom, like Sarah, had rare diseases, many of whom were constantly treated more like specimens by those of us in the academic medicine game than like the children they really were.

When rounds ended, I went back to talk with Laura. She recognized me only after I introduced myself. We spoke for only a short time that morning, and the conversation was forced and uncomfortable. I felt somehow guilty for being the father of the friend who had survived unscathed, while Sarah had gone on to become devastated by this disease, and I sensed the same discomfort in Laura. Neither of us knew exactly what to say. We exchanged addresses and phone numbers, and promised that we'd stay in touch. And then I shook her hand and headed sadly for the stairs, and back toward my office across the street from University Hospital.

•　　•　　•

A little over three years after I finished that month of attending rounds, I was called to University Hospital's newborn nursery to see an infant who had been born with a cleft palate. It was an easy case, apparently just an isolated defect in the roof of the mouth of an otherwise healthy baby, a problem that could easily be repaired by a plastic surgeon. After spending some time explaining the problem to the baby's parents and reassuring them about the future, I was making my way toward the staircase when I heard someone call out my name. Turning, I saw a woman pushing a bassinet toward the nursery. It took me only a second to realize that the woman was Laura Hamilton.

Walking back toward her, I noticed an expression on her face that hadn't been there the last time we'd met: no longer pale or pasty, she seemed radiant. In the bassinet lay a beautiful baby boy. "I'm sorry I never got around to calling," were her first words to me. "We've been kind of busy."

"I can see that," I said, now taking a close look at the infant. "Well, this guy looks great. You don't think he needs a genetics consult, do you?"

"No, thank you," she replied, smiling broadly. "You can come and visit him anytime you want, but only as a friend."

I walked with her as she dropped the baby off at the nursery, and then came back with her toward her room. As she told me what had been happening to her and her family over the past three years, I recalled what our past meeting had been like.

Sarah had stayed on the pediatric ward at University Hospital for a little over a week following the morning during which I saw her as part of teaching rounds. I spent a fair amount of time that week sitting by the girl's bedside with her mother and father, getting to understand a little about what life had been like for them since Sarah's diagnosis had been made. And during those days, almost miraculously, as her blood level of Depakene, the new anticonvulsant that Dr. Robbins had prescribed, increased, Sarah's seizures gradually came under control. They had stayed under control for a fairly long time: following discharge from the hospital, Sarah had a nine-month interval during which she remained healthy, active, and almost completely seizure-free. It was during this period that Sarah, as part of a therapeutic program in which Laura had enrolled her, learned to ride a horse. "Those nine months were probably the best in Sarah's life," Laura said, her smile disappearing as she thought back on the past. But unfortunately, those good times hadn't lasted forever.

The girl began convulsing again about a week before her sixth birthday, and this time, nothing at all could be done to stop or even to control the constant and violent jerking. Dr. Robbins, realizing that there was nothing left to offer Sarah, sat and had a long talk with Laura and her husband, Bill. Yes, they understood that Sarah was dying, and yes, they agreed that she should be allowed to go peacefully. Together, they agreed to a "Do Not Resuscitate" order, and a note was written in the chart that said that Sarah should be made comfortable and as pain-free as possible, but that if her heart were to stop beating, or if she were to stop breathing, no heroic efforts should be made to bring her back. After three days of seizing, during which her level of consciousness waxed and waned, the girl died quietly in her mother's arms.

Laura told me that she viewed Sarah's death with ambivalence. "On the one hand, it was horrible to watch her get worse and worse like that during those last few days. It was so slow and drawn out, and so inevitable. On the other hand, it was really a relief to all of us. There just wasn't anything for us to look forward to in the future except for her to get worse and worse and finally die. I think we were all ready for it when it finally happened. At least we had some good months with her near the end."

They had a small private funeral, and then Laura and her husband began to get on with their lives. Because Gaucher's disease could be diagnosed in the second trimester of pregnancy through amniocentesis, they decided to try to have another child. Their first son, Eric, a healthy boy who, as predicted by the amniocentesis, did not show any of the signs of Gaucher's disease, had been born nearly a year after Sarah's death. And now the Hamiltons had another boy, also apparently free of the disease.

"Sarah will always be an important part of our lives," Laura said as I got up to leave. "But it's kind of funny: neither of our boys will ever have known her; all they'll know is that they once had a sister whose name was Sarah, who died of a terrible disease before they were born. But I'll guarantee they'll never forget her; we have a lot of pictures in our family album."

Jaundice

• ● •

*I*SADORA COULDN'T HAVE PICKED a better time to be born. It was the second month of my third year of residency, and I had just started a relatively easy rotation in the outpatient department at Jonas Bronck Hospital. I had been on call in the emergency room on Saturday, and had managed to get some important rest on Sunday. So when Beth went into labor early Monday morning I was ready: after calling the chief residents and telling them I wouldn't be coming in, I left with Beth for the labor and delivery ward at University Hospital. I stayed with her all through the day, and a little after six that evening, our first baby was born without complication.

Although the delivery was relatively easy for Beth, it proved to be pretty taxing for me. During the time just before the baby's birth, my whole demeanor changed dramatically. Within minutes, I was transformed from a calm, complaisant husband and expectant father into a semicrazed, overeducated future clinical geneticist, who understood just about everything that could go wrong during fetal life, and fully expected all of these things to have happened during the gestation of his first child. I nearly hyperventilated in the delivery room, and could not be consoled by anyone until I'd had a chance to fully examine the baby. I breathed comfortably again only after I had convinced myself that all of Isadora's important parts were present and seemed to be hooked up in more or less the correct order.

A few hours after the delivery, Beth convinced me that she and the baby would both be better off if I got some rest, so reluctantly, I left the hospital. I went home and got into bed, but falling asleep proved to be more difficult than I had imagined; I still had a massive dose of adrenaline pumping through my veins. I spent most of that night tossing and turning, and when the alarm clock went off at six-thirty on Tuesday morning, I had gotten a total of only about one hour of sleep. I got out of bed slowly, showered and dressed, and left for another day of work at the hospital, and another night on call.

Luckily for me, things were fairly quiet that day in the pediatric emergency room. It was the beginning of August, and it seemed as if we were between epidemics. I was still running on that adrenaline high from the night before, and actually made it through the day and evening in pretty good shape. I spent my lunch hour with Beth, and when our on-call crew was finally relieved by the night float at a little after one in the morning, I stopped back at University Hospital to say good-night to Beth and the baby before heading home to New Rochelle. I got to bed that night at a little before three and managed about two-and-a-half hours of uninterrupted sleep; not what you'd call a tremendous amount, but, as we residents liked to say, every minute of it was strictly quality time.

My adrenaline rush finally gave out with a vengeance on Wednesday. Beth was being discharged by her obstetrician, and the baby had been cleared to go home by our pediatrician, Alan Cozza. I showed up early on Wednesday morning to take my little family home. But when I reached the maternity unit, I noticed that something was wrong with the baby. She was as yellow as a Checker cab!

As a pediatrician, I knew that jaundice was a common problem in infants, one that, in the vast majority of cases, causes no harm. I had been taught during my rotations in the neonatal intensive care unit that the liver of most newborns doesn't usually begin to work at full strength until the third day of life. Since this organ is the one responsible for removing bilirubin, the yellow breakdown product of red blood cells, from the circulating blood, the canary-hued chemical tends to build up to fairly high levels in the blood during the first three days of life. The bilirubin, however, almost never reaches a concentration at which it can cause problems, and once the liver begins to function normally, the bilirubin level drops dramatically, and the jaundice rapidly disappears, never to be a concern again.

But I also knew that if an infant has a problem that might lead to the unusually rapid destruction of red blood cells, the bilirubin might reach very high levels, dangerous because it then can cause a condition called kernicterus, in which severe brain damage occurs. And I knew that Isadora could have a condition that might lead to the unusually rapid destruction of red blood cells; she had a 50 percent chance of having inherited my gene for a disease called hereditary spherocytosis.

•   •   •

It had happened in January of my internship. Jonathan, a one-year-old, had been admitted to the general pediatric ward in the middle of a Tuesday afternoon for evaluation of his severe anemia. He had, according to his mother, always been in excellent health, but about a month before admission, she had noticed that he was looking a little pale. She hadn't thought much of it at first; it was, after all, early winter, and people in New England were supposed to be pale in winter; but when she brought him to the pediatrician for his one year checkup, the doctor also noticed the boy's pallor. He examined Jonathan carefully, and found that the toddler seemed tired and listless and that his heart was beating 140 times a minute, a rate much too rapid for any human older than a newborn. The pediatrician immediately ordered a blood count; it showed a hematocrit, or percentage of red blood cells in whole blood, of only 18 percent, about half of what it should have been. Without delay, he referred Jonathan and his mother to the pediatric hematologist at the Massachusetts Medical Center for a complete evaluation.

I was on call that Tuesday, so Jonathan became my patient. I had finished taking the history and examining the boy, and was sitting in the nurses' station busily writing my admission note, when Ernie Lewin, the hematology fellow, appeared in front of me. He handed me a sheet of progress notepaper and said, "These are the tests Dr. Donahue wants done on the new anemic."

I looked at the piece of paper. On it were printed the names of at least twenty-five different blood tests. Scanning the list rapidly, I identified some tests that were very common—everyday things that get done at one time or another on just about all hospitalized patients, no matter what their underlying diagnosis is; but some of the tests were so obscure I'd never even heard of them before, let alone knew what purpose they served or what they were supposed tell us about Jonathan's condition. "Do you have any questions?" Ernie Lewin asked impatiently as I continued to scan the list.

I knew better than to ask for an explanation about the importance of the tests. By January, I had been an intern at the medical center long enough to know that teaching the interns about the conditions that afflict the patients entrusted to their care was not anywhere in the fellow's or attending's job description. And frankly, I was so tired and busy and annoyed with my life by that point that I just didn't care much about learning anymore; all I really wanted to do was get my work done and get the hell out. So I limited my questions to just one very practical one: "What labs do I send these things to?" I asked.

Irritated, Ernie sat down next to me and hurriedly wrote the names of a dozen different laboratories, each, it seemed, in a separate building of the medical center. After he had finished, the hematology fellow stood up and, without another word, ambled off the floor.

I remained behind in the nurses' station, calculating the amount of blood I was going to have to drain from my patient in order to get enough to do all those tests. And then, speculating that even if he hadn't been anemic before this workup had begun, he sure as hell was going to be after I got through with him, I went to draw the 50 milliliters of precious fluid that were required. Getting lucky, I made a direct hit of the artery that ran under the boy's right wrist. The blood, which seemed more like water, flowed freely in spite of Jonathan's screaming and squirming, and I managed to get every drop I needed. After shooting appropriate amounts into the rack of test tubes I had lined up before beginning the bloodletting, I spent about an hour back at the nurses' station, filling out an endless parade of lab slips, and then began my odyssey around the medical center, distributing little tubes of Jonathan's blood as if they were Christmas presents.

One of my stops along the way was at a place called the Osmotic Fragility Lab. It was in the gloomy basement of a building I had never been in before, and it was kind of spooky down there. I dropped off a tube and the appropriate lab slip and was heading for the door when the technician looked up at me and said, "Did you bring a control for that sample?"

I turned and looked at the man in bewilderment.

"We can't run a test for osmotic fragility without a control," he continued. "The results won't mean anything."

I had no response. But the technician had what he thought was a terrific solution: I would serve as the control. He volunteered to draw my blood and, sitting me down at the laboratory's blood-drawing station, produced a mammoth 16-gauge needle and proceeded to stick the thing into my arm. It hurt like hell, and when he was done, he smiled warmly and told me the results would be available the following Monday afternoon.

For the rest of my journey around the medical center complex, I could think of nothing other than the incident in the Osmotic Fragility Lab. "This damned internship has turned me into an exhausted wretch," I mumbled to myself like a madman as I walked along. "They've drained me of all my energy, and now they're trying to drain me of all my blood. Why did I have to be the control? Why couldn't someone else do it? And what is osmotic fragility anyway?" Angrily, I finished my three-mile walking tour, ultimately returning to the general pediatric ward.

I had delivered one of the tubes to the blood bank for a type and cross match. Soon after, the bank released a unit of packed red blood cells for use in Jonathan. I started an IV, we infused the blood slowly over six hours, and by the end of that time, the boy was looking and acting a whole lot better: his skin got some color in it, his heart rate came down into a more acceptable range, and he started bouncing around the crib as any normal one-year-old would. And even before any of the blood test results came back from the lab, we established a diagnosis: the boy had had a bowel movement, and as is standard care, a guaiac test for occult blood (that is, a test for blood that is not visible, but is concealed within the stool) was performed by one of the nurses. The test, one that hadn't even made Dr. Donahue's top twenty-five, revealed a large amount of blood in the boy's stool. The gastroenterologist was immediately consulted, and he made the diagnosis over the phone: Jonathan had milk intolerance. He had been drinking cow's milk since the age of six months, and apparently it had caused damage to his intestinal tract; the boy's intestines were actively bleeding. We took the toddler off all milk and milk products, and over the next few days, his stool samples became free of blood. Jonathan, it seemed, was cured.

As expected, all the tests came back negative. But the following Tuesday morning, the day after Jonathan had been discharged to home, I got paged to an unfamiliar number. After dialing it, I found myself talking to the technician in the Osmotic Fragility Lab. "Is this the Dr. Marion who brought a sample of blood to our lab last week?" he asked.

"Yeah," I responded. "Don't tell me the kid has an abnormal osmotic fragility! We've already figured out what was wrong with him and he's fine now. We sent him home already. If there's something wrong with his osmotic fragility . . ."

"Not so fast," the technician interrupted. "The patient's osmotic fragility was fine, but your sample was definitely abnormal. Your red blood cells showed marked fragility when exposed to any greater than normal osmotic load."

I was silent for a few seconds, trying to understand what the man was saying. "Are you sure?" I finally asked.

"Absolutely," he replied. "I didn't believe it myself, so I repeated the run three times. The patient's blood was fine; your blood was abnormal each and every time."

"Are you sure you didn't mix up the samples?" I asked, now getting desperate.

"I'm positive," the guy answered. "I drew your blood in a large tube. The patient's sample came in one of the small pediatric tubes. There's no doubt about it. Have you been in good health?"

I had been in good health, but suddenly, now that he mentioned it, I wasn't feeling all that well. My heart was beating too rapidly, my palms had begun to sweat, and I was feeling light-headed. There was something wrong with me, perhaps something terribly wrong, a problem that, at the very least, could cause severe, life-threatening anemia in a one-year-old. My red blood cells were very fragile—this technician had told me there was no doubt about it, and the tests had unequivocally shown that. For all I knew, they could be violently breaking apart even as I stood there gabbing on the telephone to this sadistic lab technician.

I got off the phone and immediately walked down the hall to

the library. I needed to find out right away what dread diseases were associated with elevated osmotic fragility. I got to the library and located the textbook of pediatric hematology, but I found that I just couldn't read: my eyes kept going out of focus, I was getting dizzier by the minute, and I thought maybe I had developed a fever. I decided I couldn't go on, that I needed to rest, and so I went to lie down on one of the bunk beds in the interns' on-call room. Before hitting the sack, I paged Ernie Lewin stat to the number of the on-call room's phone.

By the time the hematology fellow called back, I was beginning to plan my own funeral. I must have sounded terrible because, after he heard my voice, the fellow didn't even yell at me for using the sacred "stat" code that was usually reserved for true medical emergencies. "What the hell's wrong with you?" he asked with what sounded like real concern in his voice. I described in florid detail what the technician had told me about my very abnormal osmotic fragility test.

He laughed. "Have you ever been anemic?" he asked, and I told him that I hadn't, that as far as I knew, my blood count had always been normal in the past, and that whatever it was that was causing my fragility to be increased now must have hit me while I had been here at the Massachusetts Medical Center, working as an intern.

He laughed again. "Does anybody in your family have any problems with their blood?"

I thought about this for a while. "My uncle has spherocytosis," I finally replied, coming up with the name of his condition, in which, because of abnormalities in the way they're shaped, red blood cells are rendered more susceptible than normal to breakdown by the spleen. "Other than that, nothing."

"Well, Bob, people who have spherocytosis always have elevated osmotic fragility," he answered. "We did the test in that kid because spherocytosis is a fairly common cause of hemolytic anemia. As you may know, spherocytosis runs in families, so if your uncle has it, you probably have it, too."

"But spherocytosis is congenital," I interrupted. "If I have it, how come I've never been anemic?"

"Many people with spherocytosis are asymptomatic," he replied. "You're just another one of the statistics, another nameless, faceless person with a completely asymptomatic blood disease."

I thanked Ernie for his help and got off the phone. Miraculously,

I found that I was suddenly feeling much better. I got up from the bunk bed, went back to the ward, and spent the rest of that night working like a dog, as usual.

•   •   •

I was one of the lucky ones: an asymptomatic carrier of sphero-cytosis. But would my daughter be that lucky? Was the jaundice that we were seeing in Isadora the first manifestation of her spherocytosis? Was she at increased risk for developing brain damage from kernic-terus? I needed answers to these questions, and I needed them right then. And so, for the next hour or so, I made the lives of everyone around me completely crazy.

I called Alan Cozza immediately, and asked him if he realized that the baby was jaundiced. "Yeah, I noticed she was a little yellow this morning," Alan replied, matter-of-factly. "I don't think it's any-thing to worry about."

"You remember I have spherocytosis, don't you?" I asked.

"Yeah, I remember, Bob, and I still don't think there's really any problem. But listen, if you're going to lose sleep over this, why don't you just ask the resident who's on call in the nursery to get some blood for a bilirubin level."

I did just that. The junior resident, Arthur Winninger, was a close friend of mine, a doctor I'd definitely trust with my life. But when I asked him to draw a bilirubin on my newborn daughter, he went white as a sheet. "Are you planning on being in there watching me?" he asked.

"Not if you don't want me," I answered.

"Good," he replied, "because I don't think I'd be able to find a vein with you staring at the kid over my shoulder." So he went to draw the blood, while Beth, who thought all of this was nuts but, through years of experience, knew better than to interfere with me when I got like that, waited in her room with me.

Even with me out of the way, it took the usually competent Winninger three sticks to get enough blood for the test; he was that shook up about having to draw blood from the arm of a friend's baby. When Isadora was brought back to us by the nurse, she was covered with Band-Aids.

Then the waiting began: Beth, who calmly worked on a sweater she was knitting, and I, who was an utter nervous wreck, sat next to each other on the hospital bed; the baby lay sleeping quietly in her bassinet; and Winninger kept flitting into the room, just to make certain that, through his attempts to draw blood, he hadn't inadvertently murdered our child. We sat like that, frozen, for one, and then two, and then three hours. As the time passed, Beth's sweater got closer to completion, I became more and more hysterical, and the baby continued to sleep calmly. And Winninger, finally convinced that he had done no permanent harm, went off to take care of some real problems over in the nursery.

It took the lab four hours to run the damned test, but when the results came back, it was good news: the bilirubin level was only 12.4, much higher than the level that would be acceptable in an adult, but well below the kernicterus danger zone of 20. And so, relieved, I packed Beth and the baby into our Oldsmobile and headed home.

The baby was up most of Wednesday night, and Beth and I were up with her. She fed every two hours; she dirtied her diaper between each of those feedings. We changed her hourly. And even when she did sleep, Beth and I didn't; we stayed up staring at her, not completely believing the fact that this creature was actually our child.

On Thursday, I went back to work, now more tired than I had ever been before. I hadn't slept more than two straight hours during any night since the previous Sunday. I somehow managed to get through my usual clinic patients in the morning and, even more astonishing, through my scheduled afternoon shift in the emergency room. Nearly falling asleep at the wheel, I somehow made it home to our town house in New Rochelle, completely ready to flop into bed and enter a long, satisfying comatose state. But I didn't make it to bed that fast.

Beth was waiting for me in the backyard. I kissed her and went to pick up Isadora, who was yelling her head off in the carriage. "She's been kind of cranky," Beth said as I lifted the kid out. And my heart sank as I looked at her.

She was now as orange as a pumpkin. "Oh, shit," was all I could manage to say, as I immediately ran into the house and toward the phone. Beth jumped out of her lawn chair and, yelling "What's wrong?" over and over again, followed me inside.

"Don't you see how jaundiced she is?" I yelled at her. "And she's been irritable? She's got kernicterus, Beth, there's no doubt about it. She's got it, and we've been sitting on it all day!"

"She's not any more yellow than she was yesterday," Beth said, much calmer than me.

"You don't see it because you've been with her all day!" I continued to yell as I dialed Alan Cozza's office number. "Take my word for it; oh Jesus, is she jaundiced!"

Alan happened to still be in his office and, hearing the concern in my voice, told me to bring the baby in right away. Without another word to Beth, with Isadora still in my arms, I marched back out to the car and began to strap her into her car seat. Beth, sure that this was yet another sign that my screws had worked themselves a little bit looser, followed behind, closed the back door of the house, and took her place in the passenger seat. We drove the ten miles into the Bronx in complete silence; images of the brain-damaged children I had seen and cared for during my training flashed through my exhausted mind, and I began to imagine what our lives were going to be like. Meanwhile, Beth worked on her sweater.

Alan was waiting for us in his office on the eighth floor of Jonas Bronck Hospital. He had his feet up on his desk and was reading a recent issue of a medical journal when I came barreling through the door. He immediately came to attention and asked, "Bob, what happened to you? You look like you've been shot out of a cannon!"

"I'm fine," I mumbled, "but take a look at the baby."

"Well, she is yellow," he said with his usual calm, soothing tone, "but she's not that much different than she was yesterday morning. Do you think she's more yellow, Beth?"

"No, I think she's about the same," Beth replied.

That's when I really lost it. "She looks like a damned pumpkin!" I yelled. "She's so jaundiced, she's past yellow, for God's sake! And she's been irritable. Don't you see it? What's wrong with you two? I've got spherocytosis and she has it, too, and it's causing all her little red blood cells to break down and her poor liver just can't keep up with all of it, and she must have a bilirubin level of at least thirty by now! She's got to have kernicterus, and she's going to be brain-damaged, don't either of you see that?"

Alan just let me go on like that, letting me get it all out of my system. When I was finally done, when I had finally fallen silent, he calmly asked, "Bob, when was the last time you got to sleep?"

I didn't see how the last time I had gotten to sleep had anything to do with our baby having kernicterus, but I answered anyway: "Sunday, I guess."

"Just what I thought. Bob, you haven't slept in four days. You think you might be overreacting just a little bit here?"

"Overreacting?" I asked, knowing that I wasn't, but either Alan's calmness had relieved me, or my last bit of adrenaline had finally given out, because suddenly, everything seemed to be fine.

"I'll take some blood, and we'll send it off to the lab for a bilirubin, but I'm just doing it to make you feel better, Bob. I don't think the level's going to be any higher than it was yesterday."

Alan stayed with us while we waited, and when the lab called with the bilirubin of only 10.6 on Isadora Marion, he said, "When our first baby was born, I tried to work like nothing had happened. She screamed the whole first night after we had brought her home, and I was sure she had meningitis. Our pediatrician just about had to sit up with me the whole night in order to get me to calm down. So I understand what you're going through, Bob. So listen, would you mind doing me a favor?"

"Yeah?" I asked, now greatly relieved and unbelievably tired.

"Go home and get some sleep. Stay home tomorrow, too. I'll tell the chief residents you won't be coming in. Just get yourself back in shape."

I nodded my head and Alan went on: "And Beth, I'd like you to do me a favor, too."

"Anything," she said.

"If Bob ever tries to play doctor for this kid again, hit him over the head with a crowbar."

•   •   •

Isadora's now eight-and-a-half years old. She has a sister, Davida, who's six, and a brother, Jonah, who's one and a half. Ever since the day Alan Cozza suggested that Beth do everything possible to prevent me from playing doctor to my children, I've never so much as looked into an ear when one of the children has had symptoms of an infection. And I think this policy has served us well: it's certainly kept all of us reasonably sane.

I have also never found out whether Isadora, or for that matter, either of her siblings, inherited my gene for spherocytosis. None of them has demonstrated symptoms of the disorder. But when they're older, if any of them seem to be leaning toward a career in medicine, I'm going to insist on one thing: that he or she never, ever volunteer, either willingly or unwillingly, to be a control in an osmotic fragility test. Internship and residency cause enough problems in a physician's life; there's no need to go looking for trouble.

Peter and Paul

● ● ●

I HEARD THE PHONE BEGIN TO RING as soon as I got the key into the lock. "Not today," I groaned, as I pulled the door open and entered the outer office. It had been a hard weekend, a sad weekend; one of my patients had died in the intensive care nursery at Jonas Bronck Hospital, and I needed a little time to decompress before starting this new week. But I knew that a call coming in at just after eight o'clock on a Monday morning usually meant trouble. And so, reluctantly, after throwing my briefcase down on the secretary's desk and pulling off my coat, I picked up the receiver on what had to be the sixth or seventh ring, and said hello. "Dr. Marion?" the female voice at the other end asked, and after I had responded in the affirmative, the voice continued: "This is Rita in the nursery at University Hospital. There's a baby here whom Dr. Cooper would like you to see."

Feeling the tiny, visceral squeeze in my gut that usually accompanies the news that an abnormal infant has been born in one of our affiliated hospitals, I asked Rita, the nursery's clerk, what the problem with the baby was thought to be. "Dr. Cooper's worried about Down syndrome," she answered.

As anticipated, this information wasn't exactly a great way to start off a Monday morning; bringing news that would undoubtedly send the lives of the parents of a newborn into complete chaos just wasn't a very enjoyable experience. But it was my job, and so, without hesitation, I assured Rita I'd be over as soon as I could make it. Then, after moving my briefcase to my own desk and pulling my coat over my shoulders, I headed out, back toward the parking lot.

On the drive over to University Hospital, I reviewed silently exactly what needed to be done. The job was fairly straightforward: I had to examine the infant, confirm in my own mind that the child did, in fact, have Down syndrome, and then inform the parents of my opinion.

Through the nine months of pregnancy, all parents, whether they will admit it or not, form a firm impression of what their baby is going to look like, what he or she is going to act like. They may imagine a girl, they may think it will be a boy, but all expect the child to be completely normal in every way. And when that baby is born, if he or she is not normal, the parents must go through a mourning process, lamenting the loss of the perfect baby they had imagined. Informing the parents of the baby's problem is the step that launches them down this long and very difficult path.

Occurring in about one in eight hundred infants, Down syndrome is probably the most common disorder clinical geneticists see. In a sense, it has to be considered the "bread and butter" of the medical geneticist's practice, playing much the same role that ear infections or asthma play in general pediatrics. So, as I parked my car in the attending physician's lot at University Hospital and started up the walkway to the main entrance, I felt, if not exactly happy, then at least confident; I knew what needed to be done, and I'd had a great deal of experience doing it. But still, I hoped that Dr. Cooper had been wrong. I prayed that, after examining this baby, I'd disagree with the pediatrician's impression: that I'd find that the infant didn't have Down syndrome, and that he and his parents would be spared the inevitable turmoil that necessarily follows the confirmation of this diagnosis.

The nursery was quiet when I arrived; no physicians were present, and I could find only one nurse, who was supervising things. In addition, most of the fourteen babies who were housed in the large room that morning were silent, each of them presumably deep in sleep. After putting on one of the sterile yellow paper gowns that all individuals who come into contact with the newborns are required to wear, I introduced myself to the nurse, explaining that I'd been called to see one of Phil Cooper's patients. "Baby Warren," she responded, nodding her head and she walked toward the back of the room. I followed close behind.

Baby Warren was sleeping when I first saw him, lying face down in a bassinet, but even without turning him over to look at his face, I knew he had Down syndrome. Caused by an extra chromosome, a structure that carries the genetic material from parent to child, the disorder has associated with it a whole host of minor alterations in physical appearance, abnormalities that are called dysmorphic features. Looking at the baby's head, I noticed the flattening of his occipital (or back of the skull) region and the redundancy of skin around his neck, features I'd come to recognize again and again in infants affected with the disorder. Phil Cooper had undoubtedly been correct; I immediately felt my heart sink.

Turning the baby over then, I went down the checklist of facial features that occurred in Down syndrome, noting that this child had virtually every one of them. His head circumference was slightly smaller than it should have been, indicating that the brain hadn't grown as well as expected during later fetal life; his eyes slanted slightly upward, and there were flaps of skin, called epicanthal folds, covering the inner corner of each eye; the bridge of his nose was flat, and its tip was turned slightly upward; his jaw was small and his tongue was thrust out, as if it were too big to fit into his mouth; his ears were also small, and the upper part of the cartilage that formed them was flattened down. Although it's never been fully explained why children affected with this disorder—infants whose body cells contain three copies of a twenty-first chromosome instead of the normal two—should have all of these abnormalities, they've been observed repeatedly, since the initial description of the disorder by John Langdon Down in 1866, by physicians who've provided care for newborns. These features form the tried-and-true basis of making the clinical diagnosis. This infant had Down syndrome; there was little doubt about it.

The rest of the exam was really unnecessary, but just to be complete, I went through it anyway. Unswaddling him, I noted that the child was extremely floppy, his muscle tone markedly decreased, a nearly constant feature in newborns with Down syndrome; his skin texture was doughy, and the skin itself was cracked and dried out, as if the baby had spent too much time in the womb; his hands were short, the fingers stubby, and each palm had a so-called simian line, a single crease running through the center of it, a crease that I knew occurred much more commonly on the hands of individuals with Down syndrome. The exam did nothing other than confirm my impression.

After reswaddling the baby in his receiving blanket, I went to the nurses' station and called Phil Cooper. I told him I agreed with his diagnosis, and asked what the parents knew about our concern. "Not much," he replied. "I didn't tell them anything about it. I figured I'd wait to see what you had to say."

"Okay," I sighed, cursing this guy in my head for not laying a shred of groundwork for the difficult visit I'd be having with the family. "I'll go and tell them what we think." After hanging up, I left the nursery and headed for Mrs. Warren's room.

Over the years, I've developed my own style for informing parents that their baby has Down syndrome. In the very beginning of my career, I used to spend a great deal of time hemming and hawing, laying all sorts of informative, but exceedingly unnecessary, groundwork for the "punchline" I'd ultimately be delivering: for instance, I would start off by telling the parents all about chromosomes, their structure, their number, their significance, where they come from, what they do, and on and on, giving a complex overview of the entire field of human cytogenetics (the branch of genetics that deals with chromosome abnormalities), until both the parents and myself were thoroughly and hopelessly bored. And then, after I'd finally informed them of the diagnosis, the parents very often would not even be able to remember anything I'd said. I've learned from these early mistakes; more recently, I've figured out that the news should be given immediately, as rapidly as possible, without making eye contact, without allowing the parents or myself time to think. It may seem brutal, but I'd learned, from talking with parents in the months and years following their informing interview, that it was the most humane technique. And so, as I approached Mrs. Warren's room, I took a series of deep breaths, preparing my mind for the task ahead.

She had been placed in a private room on the corridor opposite the entrance to the nursery. She was lying in bed talking on the telephone when I knocked and entered the room. Her husband was sitting on the bedside chair next to her, gazing blankly up at the TV that was mounted on the wall, on which a rerun of "Bewitched" was playing. The mother, seeing me standing just inside the door, still dressed in my sterile yellow gown, and probably thinking I was yet another of the bothersome house officers who had, since the delivery of her child, been sent to torture her for no good reason, said, "I've got to hang up now, a doctor just walked in," and replaced the phone onto its cradle.

"I'm Dr. Marion," I said, trying to sound as upbeat as possible. "I'm from genetics. Can I talk with you for a few minutes?" I had walked into the room by this point and, hoisting myself up, took a seat on the room's large windowsill.

"Is something wrong?" the father asked, turning off the TV.

"Well, Dr. Cooper noticed some things when he examined the baby, and he wanted me to come over and take a look." In the direction of Mrs. Warren, I asked, "How are you feeling?"

But it was Mr. Warren who answered. "He didn't mention anything wrong when he talked to me. Is there a problem?"

Here it comes, I thought. Keeping my eyes on the wall between the two of them, I said, "Well, there are some things that suggest the possibility that the baby might have Down syndrome. Do you know what that is?"

"What things?" the father asked, using a hostile tone.

"Little things," I answered, now looking toward the father's face. "The way the baby's eyes slant upward, the way his ears are formed, things like that, that don't mean anything in and of themselves, but, taken together, give us the impression that the baby might have Down syndrome."

"Yeah, eyes, and ears; what else?" he asked, challenging me.

"Well, a lot of things," I responded, going on the defensive but trying to sound conciliatory. "His muscle tone is decreased, the back of his head is flattened . . ."

"Well, if you haven't noticed, my wife's eyes slant upward," the man interrupted. I looked at the woman, who hadn't said a word since she had hung up the phone. I didn't agree with him: there was not even a hit of an upward or downward slant to her eyes. "And I have an uncle who has exactly the same-shaped ears as Paul. And when our daughter was born, they told us her muscle tone was decreased, also. But she's fine now. What else?"

I realized, from past experience, that arguing with this man would prove fruitless. "Mr. Warren, it's not any one thing that makes us think the baby might have Down syndrome. It's just an overall impression based on all his findings. The way to be sure, one way or the other, is to do a blood test to look at the baby's chromosomes. I think Paul—that's the baby's name, right—?" The man nodded and I continued: "I think Paul has enough of the features to at least warrant doing the test."

"How long will it take?" Mr. Warren asked.

"About a week," I replied.

"Does he have to stay here until it's ready?" the man asked.

"Not necessarily," I answered. "If it's okay with Dr. Cooper, and there should be no reason it isn't okay, I don't see why Paul wouldn't be able to go home at the usual time. My secretary will call you when the test results are ready, and regardless of the results, we'll make arrangements to see you in my office next week. In the meantime, I'll stop by while you're here to check on the baby. Do you have any questions you want to ask?"

They were silent for a few uncomfortable seconds, and I added: "I guess it's difficult to know what questions to ask until we have some definitive answer. I should tell you, though, that if Paul does turn out to have Down syndrome, it was something that was present in him at the moment he was conceived; nothing that either of you did or didn't do, either before or after conception, could have in any way made a difference." I stopped talking then, and waited for questions.

I had begun to search through my shirt pocket for a copy of my business card to leave with them, when Mrs. Warren finally spoke. She had been completely silent, staring up at me from her bed, while her husband had done all of the talking, but now she had a question: "Doctor, how sure are you?" she asked.

"It's hard to put an exact number on it," I replied. This, of course, was probably the most commonly asked question during the initial session. I had learned that, even when the diagnosis was fairly certain, leaving some room for doubt was always best; it seemed to help the bonding process between parents and child. So I answered in the way I always did: "If you pushed me, I'd say I'm about 75 percent sure Paul's got it. Even if he does, I should point out now that he'll be pretty much like any other infant. He'll feed and cry and need to be changed. You most likely won't notice any difference in him until he's about a year old, when his milestones are delayed."

She nodded her head, and after they'd been silent for a few more seconds, after I'd finally managed to find a copy of my card and placed it on the table by the mother's bedside, I shook their hands and headed out of the room. Walking toward the exit sign, I didn't stop to talk to anyone in the nursery about what had just occurred. Angrily slamming the heavy metal door behind me, I began walking down the stairs toward the hospital's main entrance.

•　　•　　•

On my way to work on Tuesday morning, I stopped again in the nursery at University Hospital. Paul Warren had done fairly well through the night. The nursing notes revealed that he'd been able to suck fairly vigorously, keeping his formula feedings down with only a very small amount of vomiting, and that he had, the previous afternoon, passed a large mass of sticky, black meconium, the baby's first bowel movement. All of these facts reassured me that the infant didn't have a serious gastrointestinal malformation, an abnormality that occurs in about 10 percent of newborns with Down syndrome and requires immediate surgery in order to insure survival. Further, when I listened to Paul's chest with my stethoscope that morning, I was happy to hear only normal heart sounds; the fact that he had no murmur was a good sign, evidence that no congenital heart defect, a serious, life-threatening complication that occurs in a third to a half of all affected babies, was present. I was beginning to believe that maybe this infant was going to be one of the lucky ones, a child with Down syndrome who had no complication, a patient who would have a better than even chance of doing well over the next few years.

So I was optimistic as I walked toward Mrs. Warren's hospital room that morning. I was also pretty sure I knew what the couple would be thinking. Having seen their son do so well over the preceding twenty-four hours, having watched him guzzle down bottle after bottle filled with formula without difficulty, they had to figure I couldn't possibly be right, that I had alarmed them about their son having Down syndrome for no good reason, that I was incompetent and shouldn't be allowed to work with infants or with other fragile individuals, such as the parents of newborns. I had borne the brunt of all of these thoughts and emotions in the past; I understood that they were normal reactions, healthy defense mechanisms on the part of parents going through a very difficult crisis, and I had grown, if not exactly comfortable with them, then at least able to accept them for what they were. But when I entered Mrs. Warren's room that morning, I was in for a surprise.

They were both there, fixed in exactly the same positions in which they had been the day before. Mrs. Warren's eyes were red and puffy; Mr. Warren looked exhausted, his clothes wrinkled, his face lined, bags under his eyes. It seemed to me as if they'd been up all night, gazing straight ahead like that, frozen in time. And when I said good morning in a falsely cheerful tone, I was met with sad, blank looks. "How are you doing?" I asked, getting only nods as a response. I continued: "I just came from examining the baby. He's doing very well. There are no signs of any problems. I just stopped by to see if you had any questions."

"Let's say he does have Down syndrome," Mr. Warren finally said after some uncomfortable silence. The anger that had been in his voice the previous day seemed to have gone, having been replaced, it seemed, by intense fatigue. "Let's say you're right. What's he going to be like?"

"Well, it might be a little too premature to have a discussion like this," I began, wanting to put this off until the following week, after the couple had had a chance to care for their infant at home for a few days. "I wouldn't want you to go through this if you don't really need to."

"Look, let's cut out all the small talk," the man interrupted. "Let's just get to the bottom line: what's our life going to be like if the baby has Down syndrome?"

"I would think it'd be pretty much the same as it is now," I replied, a little surprised by the father's frankness. "As I told you yesterday, babies with Down syndrome are pretty much like any other baby; they have the same needs and desires. But on top of those needs and desires, there are some additional problems, both medical and developmental. You both probably know that children with Down syndrome all have some degree of developmental delay." This was usually a devastating statement for parents; it typically brought tears instantly to their eyes. But my words didn't seem to cause any change in Mr. Warren. "The range of delay is very wide; some kids have borderline normal intelligence and some are much more severely retarded. If Paul does turn out to have Down syndrome, there'd be no way of predicting right now where exactly he'll fall within the spectrum. But if we do find that he has it, we'll probably refer you to one of the local infant stimulation programs, a place where he'll be able to go to school at a very early age, so that he can be the best Paul possible."

"What'll all that entail?" Mr. Warren asked. "These infant stimulation programs you're talking about: Do they meet every day? Will we have to go to it with him?"

"It depends on what program he winds up attending," I replied. I was beginning to realize something was very wrong here; Mr. Warren was asking questions I'd never heard anyone ask before, certainly not at this stage in the newborn's life. And I was concerned about Mrs. Warren: still silent, she stared straight ahead; occasionally, her eyes would fill with tears, but then she'd wipe them away and replace them with that stony, glazed stare. I didn't have a clue as to what was going on in her head.

"And what else?" the man asked. "What about the future? What's his life span likely to be?"

This was really weird. Asking about how long the baby would live while the infant was still in the nursery? I didn't know exactly how to respond. Not able to think all of this through, not able to come up with a rational plan to get to the bottom of what Mr. Warren was trying to tell me, I simply continued offering what I viewed as helpful answers: "It's hard to say; some babies with Down syndrome have congenital heart disease, and that's something that might shorten their life expectancy. If Paul does have Down syndrome, we'll have to test him for heart problems. He's been okay so far, but sometimes symptoms don't appear until later. . . ."

"Let's say he doesn't have heart disease," the man interrupted. "How long will he be expected to live?"

"Oh, I don't know," I responded uneasily. "I've seen fifty- and sixty-year old people with Down syndrome. There's no reason to think. . . ."

"How about our other kids?" the man interrupted again. I knew from reading the chart that the Warrens had two older children, a boy, age five, and a girl, age three.

"How about them?" I asked, not trying to be funny, but simply not knowing what he was asking about.

"What will this mean to them?" he rephrased his question. "What will the fact that their brother has Down syndrome do to their lives?"

At last, a reasonable question, a question that I'd been asked many times before, a question to which I had a ready answer: "Usually, older siblings just come to accept newborns with Down syndrome as if they had no problem," I began. "They don't even know there's a problem until . . ."

"Won't he be a burden to them?" he asked then. "Won't they always have to defend him and wait for him? Won't that bother them? Won't they someday wind up having to take care of him?"

"I haven't heard of that being a problem," I answered.

It continued on like that for a good half hour; the man cross-examined me about the impact Paul's having Down syndrome would have on just about every aspect of their lives, and when it was finally over, after I'd finally said good-bye and left the room, I felt horrible, wasted and exhausted. It took a while, but it eventually dawned on me what was happening here: Mr. Warren was looking for a way out. He and his wife had been handed this baby who we all, by that point, knew was affected with Down syndrome. He wanted to find a good enough reason, a rationalization, that would allow him to abandon the infant without looking like an inhuman beast. I had no experience to guide me through this; I hadn't known how to proceed, and as a result, the meeting had drained all the strength out of me.

Reaching my office finally at around ten o'clock, I checked the appointment book. My spirits lifted immediately when I saw Peter Gonzalez's name penciled into the one o'clock slot.

•   •   •

Over the past seven months, I'd grown to love Peter Gonzalez, and to respect the strength his parents and sisters had shown. Peter's life had begun much the same as Paul Warren's had: Within hours after his delivery at University Hospital, his pediatrician had suspected the diagnosis of Down syndrome. I'd received a call from Rita in the nursery, had gone over to see the infant, and, after confirming the diagnosis, had spoken with Mr. and Mrs. Gonzalez. But that was where the similarity between the two ended.

The Gonzalezes' behavior had been much more what I'd come to expect from parents following the initial counseling session. The boy's mother and father had both cried when I told them of our suspicion; they had questioned me carefully about the cause of Down syndrome, and asked how sure I was that Peter had it. In talking with them, I'd learned that Peter was very much wanted by this family: he was the couple's fifth child, and their first son. Mrs. Gonzalez assured me before she left the hospital with Peter three days after his birth, that, regardless of whether the infant had Down syndrome or not, he was sure to get a tremendous amount of attention: "I've got four girls at home who are dying to take care of this little boy."

Peter had thrived during the first seven months of his life. Following the family's initial visit to my office when the infant was six days old, a tear-filled session during which, by showing all the Gonzalezes (including Peter's sisters) the report from the chromosome lab, I had confirmed the diagnosis of Down syndrome, they had returned at least once a month for follow-up checks and encouragement. There was little I needed to do for Peter during that time; he had been the picture of health, acting pretty much like any other baby, eating and stooling, crying and laughing, growing and developing, although he did the latter at a slower pace than had any of his sisters. No, most of my work during those seven months had been directed toward Mr. and Mrs. Gonzalez, who, with the help of the people at the infant stimulation program in which Peter had been registered during his first weeks of life, had finally managed to come to grips with the fact that their son had a chronic, lifelong medical condition. The couple had weathered this as well as any couple could; they had a strong support network, lots of family members and friends who were always available, always willing to help out. By the time of that visit, when Peter was seven months old, they had pretty much made their way out of the woods. So I looked forward to seeing them; I figured an office visit from the Gonzalezes, all seven of them, might be just the thing I needed to take my mind off the problems I'd been having with the Warrens.

But Mrs. Gonzalez came alone that day, just her and the baby. After a big hello, I ushered her and Peter into my office. "How's everything going?" I asked as she got settled into a chair.

"Fine, everything's been fine," she began. "Peter has this rash, that's the only thing I have to tell you. Otherwise, he's perfect."

Rashes, within the purview of the general pediatrician, were usually not my strong suit. "Let's see it," I said, hoping it would turn out to be one of the easy ones I could still recognize from my training.

They were all over him. When Mrs. Gonzalez pulled off his coat, I could see them, small dots of red, on his arms, on his face, on his neck. And as she undressed more of the boy, I saw that they were everywhere, his trunk, his legs, his buttocks. I pressed on one to confirm my impression. Holy shit, they don't blanch, I thought, hoping that my face wouldn't betray my worst fear. I knew he was covered with petechiae.

"How long has he had these?" I asked, as casually as possible.

"They started last night," she replied. I don't know if she sensed my panic right then. "I was going to take him to the emergency room, but I figured, since I had the appointment with you today, I'd wait."

"Has he been sick?" I asked. "Any fever?"

"No, he's been his old self," she replied. "Is it anything serious?"

Yes, I wanted to tell her, very, very serious. But I held that in; panic was not going to help this situation. "These are called petechiae," I said, pressing on one to show that their red color didn't disappear with pressure. "They're caused by small leaks in the capillaries, the blood vessels just under the skin. They can be caused by all sorts of problems. . . ."

"Like what?" she asked, seeming alarmed for the first time.

"Sometimes infections . . ." I began.

"But Peter's been fine," she interrupted.

"I know," I replied. "Other things like not having enough platelets . . ."

"What are those?" she asked.

"Things that help the blood to clot. As I said, it could be all sorts of things. Most of the causes are nothing to worry about. But sometimes, these can be a sign of bad diseases. Even though it's probably nothing, there are some blood tests we have to do, just to be on the safe side, and the tests should be done right away. After we get some of the results back, we'll have a better idea of what's going on. Okay?"

She nodded and said "Okay."

I took her and the infant into the treatment room and went to work. "Please don't have leukemia," I kept repeating in my head as, with Peter lying comfortably on his back, I stuck a butterfly needle into a vein I'd found in his left elbow. I needed to get a large quantity of blood; I intended to do a complete blood count, bleeding times, and, even though he hadn't had any symptoms, a culture, to rule out infection. After making a direct hit, I knew immediately, as the blood began flowing slowly into the syringe, that my worst fear had been realized: the stuff coming out of Peter's vein had the consistency and appearance of dilute cherry Kool-Aid. I was sure the baby had to be anemic, that the petechiae had been caused by thrombocytopenia (an abnormally low platelet count), and that all of this almost certainly had to be caused by some form of leukemia.

For some reason that's as mysterious as the rest of the features of this disorder, individuals with an extra twenty-first chromosome are at twenty times the risk of developing leukemia at some time during their childhoods, when compared with normal children. Leukemia is a diagnosis to be dreaded in infants and children with Down syndrome; it's frequently highly resistant to therapy, a phenomenon that's especially true in patients as young as Peter Gonzalez. I was almost positive that the results of the blood count were going to be very abnormal, and that, in the next few days, during the evaluation that would follow, the pediatric hematologist would hand Peter what basically amounted to a death sentence.

After sending the specimens off to the lab, I returned to my office and sadly began making arrangements to immediately admit Peter to the hospital's infants' ward. I called the pediatric chief resident and the clerk in the admitting office, giving each of them the appropriate information. Then I spoke with the pediatric hematologist, informing him of what was happening; he said he'd be by later in the day to see Peter, after the baby had been settled into a crib.

When all the arrangements had been made, when everyone in the hospital who needed to know about Peter's problems did know, it was time to have a talk with his mother. She had been sitting in our waiting room while I had made all these calls, cradling her baby in her arms, and worrying. When I called her back into my office and offered her a seat, I sensed that she was near tears. "None of the lab tests are back yet, but I'm very concerned," I told her bluntly. "There's a chance Peter might have leukemia."

The word, probably the one she had been thinking all the time she had been sitting out in the waiting area, instantly brought her tears to the surface. I knew that, following Peter's birth, Mrs. Gonzalez had gone to the public library and read everything she could find about Down syndrome. At some point during the course of that reading, I was sure she had come across information about leukemia, and by the tears and the look in her eyes, I knew she understood exactly what this diagnosis might mean. "I've made arrangements for Peter to be admitted to the hospital," I continued. "The hematologist will see him up on the infants' ward later today. By the time he comes around, we'll have the results of at least some of the tests, so we'll have a better idea about the problem."

She was overwhelmed with tears by this point; the baby, who had been quietly asleep in Mrs. Gonzalez's arms, now opened his eyes and looked up at his mother. A wave of depression hit me then, and I wanted to go home, climb into my bed, and forget that the past few hours had ever happened. What a day it had been!

•   •   •

Paul Warren was scheduled for discharge on Wednesday afternoon, so as on the previous morning, I began my day in the nursery at University Hospital. Again, no medical problems had reared their ugly heads, nothing that might require that the boy stay in the hospital for any additional time. So after examining him, I made the walk that I was dreading, down the hall toward his mother's room.

I had thought over the situation during the previous night, and I had come to the conclusion that we were fairly likely to be in for an angry confrontation that morning. Considering everything that had happened in the days before, I figured that either the parents would have backed off by now, or they'd have decided what I was fearing the most, that they definitely weren't going to take their baby home. What would I, an advocate for children with Down syndrome, a person who had very strong feelings about this issue, do in a situation like that? How would I handle it? Would I back off myself, compromising my principles for the sake of preventing a scene, and simply, helpfully inform them of the methods for placing babies in foster care? Or would I become defensive, informing them of what I really thought, condemning them for their principles and their feelings? I wasn't so sure, but, as a result of what had happened the afternoon before, because of the outcome of Peter Gonzalez's hematology consult, I guess I was leaning more toward the latter of the two options.

As expected, Peter's blood count had come back markedly abnormal: he was anemic, with a hematocrit of only 24 percent, about two-thirds of normal, and his platelet count was nineteen thousand, less than a tenth of what it should have been. In addition, the lab found that his white blood cell count, a value that normally ranges between five thousand and ten thousand, was greater than a hundred thousand, and that most of the cells that had streamed madly into his circulation were immature, abnormal myeloblasts. The baby had received a diagnosis of acute myeloblastic leukemia; based on survival figures, there was strong reason to doubt that Peter would survive to see his second birthday.

And so, faced with entering this room and having to talk with a couple who simply did not want to take home, care for, and love their infant who happened to have Down syndrome, while another baby with Down syndrome, a baby who was very much loved and wanted by his parents and by the rest of his family, was lying critically ill and dying in another hospital across the Bronx, I felt anger and rage. I knew that physicians should never allow one patient's problems to interfere with their care and management of another patient; I recognized that fact on a rational and intellectual basis. But I wasn't functioning on either a rational or intellectual basis that morning; I was letting my emotions take over, and those emotions inevitably were getting in the way.

The Warrens were still fixed in the same positions, Mrs. Warren lying on the bed, Mr. Warren sitting on the bedside chair. They were both freshly dressed, and I noticed that a small suitcase, leaned up against Mr. Warren's chair, had been packed, and appeared ready to go. I said good morning and asked how they were feeling. As they had the day before, both nodded their head in response. "I understand you're being discharged this morning," I continued when neither of them spoke. "Are there any questions you want to ask?"

"We've given it a lot of thought," Mr. Warren said, with no emotion at all in his voice. "We've been thinking this over since Monday. My wife and I don't think we can handle this baby at home."

"Can't handle him?" I repeated, not surprised by the message, but amazed at the words that bore them. "I don't understand; there's nothing about Paul that you shouldn't be able to handle."

"We understand that taking care of a child with Down syndrome requires a lot of time and patience," Mr. Warren continued. "You spoke about those infant stimulation programs; it turns out that all of the programs you mentioned require that at least one parent attend every day with the child. That would mean that either my wife or I would have to give up working in order for the child to participate. We simply can't do that. We're at a point in our lives when we both simply have to work."

"I don't understand. . . ." I began to reply, but was interrupted.

"Six months ago, my wife and I started a new business," Mr. Warren continued. "I gave up a very cushy job in a law firm in Manhattan because I wanted to have more time to spend with my kids. The business we started depends on both of us being involved. We figured that after the baby was born, my wife would take two months off for maternity leave and then would come back full-time. That just won't be possible with this child."

"Wait a minute, wait a minute," I said, waving my hands in the air in front of me. "You're not taking your baby home because you both have to be there at work? Isn't it possible to hire someone to fill in?"

"No, I can't hire anyone else," Mr. Warren replied, now getting angry. "I can't trust anyone else. If my wife doesn't come back to our business full-time within the next few months, the business will definitely fail. We might as well have poured our life savings down the toilet."

"But this is your child," I said. "This is your baby. Do you have any idea what kind of message you'll be sending your two older children if you don't take Paul home?"

"Yes, I know exactly the message we'll be sending them," Mr. Warren answered, once again spitting fire at me. "We'll be telling them, showing them how much we love them. Look, since we opened this business, I've been spending a lot more time with my kids. I sit with them every day, reading to them, playing sports with them. Let's say, for argument's sake, that we decide to bring this baby home with us, and that we're going to provide him with everything he needs. What can we expect from him? That someday, if we work very hard, and concentrate all our efforts, he might be able to be toilet trained? And what'll be happening to our other children in the meantime? While we're working with this retarded child, they'll wind up spending less quality time with both of their parents; they wouldn't possibly be able to do as well in school. Look, maybe, if we work with them now, these two kids'll be able to get into Harvard or Yale. You think that'll happen if we wind up spending all our time with a defective infant?"

"Harvard or Yale?" I repeated, my voice raised, completely amazed, terribly angered by this man and his attitude. "My God, it's not a question of whether they get into Harvard or Yale or not. You're going to be telling these kids that if they don't perform up to the level you expect of them, if they're not perfect in every way, that you just might decide to get rid of them, the same way you got rid of their little brother who happened to have Down syndrome. Don't you see that? Don't you understand what you're doing?"

"You listen," Mrs. Warren spoke out at that moment. I was stunned; I hadn't heard her voice since the first day I had entered their lives, and the sound of it, the anger and rage it contained, startled me. "You've stood there, so sure of yourself, for three days now, telling us what we should think and how we should feel. You don't know anything about us. You can't tell me what's right and wrong for me and my family, because you haven't lived my life. My husband and I know what we're doing. We know what's best for ourselves and for our children. And having this baby at home is not what's best for any of us. Now, I'll thank you to leave my room immediately!"

I turned and walked away. I left the room and headed for the elevator. Tearing off the yellow gown I'd been wearing over my clothes since I had examined the baby in the nursery, I forcefully crumpled it into a ball and threw it into the trash can.

• • •

I screwed up that morning, and I knew it. The job of a geneticist is not to force the parents to do what the geneticist wants them to do, but rather to supply the information necessary so that a rational decision can be made, and then, once that decision has been reached and finalized, to support the parents in any way possible. But the Warrens hit me with what I found to be the "wrong" decision at exactly the wrong moment. I let them down at the precise time I should have been there for them.

I never saw Paul Warren again. Although he remained in the

hospital after his mother was discharged, the nursery's social worker had no trouble placing the infant in a foster home in New Jersey. He was gone by the time the chromosome studies had been completed, studies that, not surprising to any of us, confirmed that the child did in fact have Down syndrome. I passed this information on to the social worker, who notified everyone involved.

I haven't had contact with Mr. or Mrs. Warren since that morning, either. I've thought about them frequently, though, mostly about the rage I felt toward them, rage I hardly believed I was capable of mustering under any circumstances, rage that's symptomatic of an underlying, insolvable problem. I had allowed my affection for Peter, and the concern I felt for him following his diagnosis of leukemia, to interfere with my ability to serve Paul's parents, and I knew there was nothing, either then or in the future, that I would ever be able to do to change that. I came to realize that this was one of my flaws, a weakness that would prevent me from becoming Marcus Welby, most people's idealized model of the perfect physician: try as I might, no matter how much experience I gain, there are things about the private "me," things about my values and principles, that simply cannot be separated from the professional "me." My anger frightened me that day; it continues to frighten me now.

And what of Peter Gonzalez? He was begun on a regimen of chemotherapy the day after his admission to the infant's unit. Although he lost his hair and developed a round, moonlike facial appearance as a result of the medication, he responded as well as could be expected. He's been in remission now for four months, living at home and getting as much love from his parents and his sisters as he can handle.

The Most Unselfish Thing

• ● •

*T*HERE WAS NO WAY she could have survived the night. Driving to work that Monday morning, I was sure I'd find Meghan gone, her place in the three-bed room on the infants' ward either empty or already occupied by another, healthier patient. And while I felt some sadness about this child's death, I was also experiencing a sense of relief: Meghan had suffered terribly, struggling with every breath just to stay alive; and for the past two months, we'd known that her passing was inevitable—"only a matter of time" is how I'd put it to her mother over and over again during the previous weeks. But my feeling of relief was due to more than just the fact that this little girl was finally out of her misery: having visited her bedside every week-day morning, having chatted with her mother during my daily rounds, having closely monitored her slipping vital signs that docu-mented her slow deterioration, I realized that her disappearance from the ward would remove what had become an everpresent symbol of my helplessness. So it was with a sense of calm, and what I guess could be called liberation, that I arrived at the hospital that morning.

I'd made a special trip to the Bronx to see Meghan the afternoon before. The resident covering the ward had called to say that the girl's respiratory distress had markedly worsened during the morning, and that the Do Not Resuscitate order I'd written the week before had expired. As Meghan's physician-of-record, writing that order and renewing it every three days was my responsibility. So I'd driven to the Bronx, but I was not overly concerned about this latest deterioration: after all, this was the third call about Meghan I'd received in the last two months, calls from senior residents who were sure the end had finally arrived. Twice before, I'd made trips to the hospital to see her, and on both occasions, she'd looked horrible; but following each visit, after some minor adjustments in her medications had been made, she'd rallied, ultimately returning to her baseline vegetative state.

But this time had been different: I'd arrived to find her lying in her hospital crib gasping for air like a fish that had washed up on the beach. She was breathing ninety times a minute and her heart rate was over two hundred, both about double what would be expected in a healthy nine-month-old. But despite the enormous effort of her damaged heart and lungs, despite the pure, 100 percent oxygen that was being forced into her mouth and nose through the plastic tubing held by Mrs. McGuinness, Meghan's mother, the skin around the child's lips remained blue and dusky. "She's drowning," the mother said softly when she saw me. "She's drowning in her crib."

"It won't be long," I promised. "It can't possibly go on much longer."

The mother, fighting off tears, didn't respond.

I stayed with Meghan and her mother for about two hours during the afternoon. As usual, we tried some simple maneuvers to make the girl more comfortable: Anita, Meghan's primary nurse, carefully suctioned the infant's tracheostomy tube to clear out any mucous plugs that had formed; we injected a dose of Lasix, a diuretic that removes fluid from the lungs, through Meghan's Hickman catheter (the surgically implanted intravenous line through which the girl received all her food and medications); and we gave her an Alupent treatment, an inhaled medication that dilates the breathing tubes. But after all these therapies had been administered, after one and then two hours had passed with no improvement in the child's condition, I had given up. I said good-bye to Mrs. McGuinness, still stationed over her daughter, oxygen tubing in hand, and again promised this poor woman that it was "only a matter of time"; I thanked the resident for his help and reassured him that we'd done all we could; and then I left the hospital for home. I'd spent the rest of that afternoon and evening mindlessly watching television, trying my best not to think about what was happening back in the Bronx on the infants' ward.

But upon reaching the ward on rounds that Monday morning, I found that the inevitable had not yet occurred. Meghan was still there, still struggling to get air into her lungs, still working desperately to move whatever oxygen was available in those lungs to the rest of her body. Her mother, looking exhausted after a night spent without a moment of sleep, continued to hover over her daughter's body. When I arrived in the small room, she looked up, her eyes red but dry, and said, "This is torture. This is worse than anything in the world. Isn't there something you can do to speed this up?"

• • •

It had been a little after six o'clock on a Thursday evening, nine months before. I'd been about to leave the office for home when the phone had rung; it was Steve Benson, a pediatrician with a large private practice in the community around our medical center. "I know it's late," he said after I'd said hello, "but I've got an emergency." He explained that a woman who'd planned to use him as her baby's doctor had just given birth to an infant with multiple anomalies at Pelham Parkway Medical Center, a small hospital nestled in an Irish neighborhood in the north Bronx. "I'm very worried about this kid," he concluded after describing some of the baby's problems. "I don't know exactly what's wrong, but I've got a feeling it's something bad."

I promised Steve I'd be at the hospital within an hour, and he said he'd wait there for me. "No big deal," I thought to myself as I drove over. "How long could a consult on a newborn take?

Meghan McGuinness was already in mild respiratory distress when I reached Pelham Parkway's well-baby nursery. She was lying on the unit's lone warming table, surrounded by bassinets containing a dozen or so healthy, screaming newborns, but it was clear that Meghan herself was far from healthy. A nurse stood guard over the infant, searching for evidence of worsening distress. A quick glance at the baby revealed that, in addition to her breathing problems, Meghan had serious congenital malformations that affected the entire lower half of her body. Her legs, much shorter than they should have been, were withered and wasted; their joints, the hips, knees, and ankles, were contracted, frozen solid in a flexed position; both

feet were clubbed; and the legs themselves were completely para-
lyzed. No matter how hard the child struggled, she was unable to
move those lower extremities even an inch.

I thought I knew what was wrong with her. Running my fingers
across her back, I found that the sacrum, the lower part of her spine,
was absent. This finding confirmed my impression: Meghan had the
caudal regression malformation sequence, an extremely rare and
severely disabling disorder.

At that moment, Steve Benson appeared in the nursery's nurses'
station. He waved and smiled when he saw me, obviously relieved
that help had arrived. "Well, what do you think?" he asked after I
waved back.

"I think we've got trouble," I replied, and Steve nodded his
head. "Is the mother a diabetic?"

The pediatrician seemed surprised by my question. "How did
you know that?" he asked.

"I think the baby's got the caudal regression sequence," I told
him. "For some reason, caudal regression occurs much more commonly in infants of diabetic mothers."

Steve then briefly outlined the mother's story. She was thirty-
two years old and had been an insulin-dependent diabetic for over
twenty years. This baby was her first child. The pregnancy had been
very rough; the woman had required hospitalization for control of
her diabetes on three separate occasions. She'd spent a total of eight
weeks as an inpatient on Pelham Parkway's maternity ward, including the last four weeks of the pregnancy, a period during which she'd
been kept at complete bed rest because of dangerously elevated blood
pressures. Prior to delivery, there had been absolutely no indication
that the fetus had any significant problem. "Did you hear that murmur?" the pediatrician asked at the conclusion of his summary.

I hadn't, but I took the opportunity to pull out my stethoscope
and place it on the baby's chest. The murmur was loud and harsh,
and radiated all over the chest; it was a sure sign that the baby had
significant heart disease. "We've got to get this kid to an NICU," I
said after listening intently to the murmur for a few seconds. "If she
stays here, she's going to die."

Steve agreed, and we walked back into the nurses' station. I
called the neonatal intensive care unit at West Bronx Hospital and
arranged for the transport team to come. After finishing the call and

writing a brief note in the infant's chart, Steve and I went to talk to the mother.

She was lying in bed crying. Her husband was sitting alongside her, trying to comfort her, but it was clear that his efforts were having little effect. I introduced myself and asked how they were feeling. Mrs. McGuinness didn't respond; she simply continued to cry. Mr. McGuinness shook my hand and asked what I thought was wrong with the baby. "I think she has something called caudal regression sequence," I replied. "It's a condition in which the lower part of the body fails to develop properly. It combines absence of the lower part of the spine and abnormalities of the legs with a large group of other problems."

"What other problems?" he asked.

"Babies with caudal regression frequently have malformation of their intestines, kidneys, and genitourinary tracts," I replied, sounding a little too formal. "We don't know whether your daughter has any or all of these other problems. We'll need to do some tests to be sure."

"She has a heart murmur," Steve added. "So there's a good chance she has something wrong with her heart, as well."

"Because of all her problems, both those we know are present and those we suspect," I continued, "Dr. Benson and I think it would be best if the baby were transferred to an intensive care unit."

"We don't have the facilities here to do all the tests she needs, or to take care of her properly," Steve added.

"I've made arrangements to transfer the baby to West Bronx Hospital," I said. "Is that all right with you?"

The parents stared back at me without response. "When will she have to go?" Mr. McGuinness finally asked.

"As soon as they can get the ambulance here to take her," Steve replied. "She's very sick."

"Is she going to die?" Mr. McGuinness asked.

"Probably not," I replied. "Most babies with caudal regression sequence survive. But we'll have to wait and see what kind of other problems she has before we'll be sure."

"Can I see her?" the mother asked.

"Of course," Steve answered, and he immediately went out to find a nurse and a wheelchair.

There was uncomfortable silence in the room after the pediatrician left. "Do you know what causes this?" Mrs. McGuinness finally asked, so quietly that her voice was barely audible.

I hesitated. "I'm not 100 percent sure," I replied. "It has to be due to some severe damage that occurs in the embryo very early in development. Whatever caused this must have happened even before you knew you were pregnant."

"It was the diabetes, wasn't it?" she asked, her crying overtaking her again. I didn't respond, but I was sure she knew the answer.

Steve Benson, pushing a wheelchair in front of him, then appeared at the door with a maternity ward nurse. We helped Mrs. McGuinness into the chair, and then, with the nurse pushing her IV pole and her husband pushing the wheelchair, we slowly made our way down the hall to the well-baby nursery.

The mother's crying ended the moment she laid eyes on her daughter. After the chair was wheeled up to the side of the warming table, Mrs. McGuinness gently began to stroke the baby's face. "Want to hold her?" Steve asked, and the mother nodded. The baby, her respiratory distress visibly worse than it had been minutes before, was placed in her mother's arms. She remained like that, gasping for breath, some extra oxygen from a portable tank blown in her face, cradled lovingly in her mother's arms, until the team from West Bronx's NICU arrived to take her away.

•   •   •

Immediately upon their arrival in the nursery at Pelham Parkway, the transport team took the little girl from her mother's arms and began to prepare her for the trip to West Bronx Hospital. One physician passed a tube into Meghan's mouth, through her vocal cords, and into her trachea; the nurse attached the external end of that tube to a portable ventilator; a second physician inserted a plastic catheter into the girl's umbilical vein and began an infusion of sterile sugar water; finally, the nurse placed the infant in a portable incubator and began to wheel her off toward the elevator. I followed the team, assuring the McGuinesses I'd call as soon as I could to fill them in on everything that was happening.

Soon after the transport team arrived at West Bronx Hospital and Meghan was settled onto a warming table in the NICU, an extensive workup was begun, a workup that continued for nearly two weeks. Dozens of tests were performed, and unfortunately nearly every one revealed evidence of some anomaly buried deep inside the little girl's body. A chest X ray revealed enlargement of the heart and damage to the lungs; an echocardiogram (an ultrasonic examination of the heart) showed that the murmur Steve Benson and I had heard in the first hours of life was due to a ventricular septal defect, a hole that allowed blood to pass between the left and right ventricles, the pumping chambers of the heart; an ultrasound exam of the baby's abdomen demonstrated that the left kidney was absent (the right one appeared to be functioning normally); X rays of her spine confirmed that the sacrum had not formed, but also showed that other defects were present in the thoracic and lumbar regions. About the only test that didn't demonstrate the presence of an abnormality was the CAT scan of Meghan's head. Amazingly, although serious damage had occurred to nearly every other major organ of her body, Meghan's brain had apparently been spared.

Following her discharge from the maternity ward at Pelham Parkway Medical Center on the day after her daughter's birth, Mrs. McGuinness became a regular visitor at her daughter's bedside: she'd arrive in the NICU just after nine every morning and stay through the afternoon. Because of Meghan's respiratory problems, and her dependence on the ventilator, Mrs. McGuinness could not hold her daughter in her arms; but she spent her time sitting beside the infant, stroking her skin gently, and talking to her soothingly over the din produced by the ventilator's air compressor and the cardiac monitor's alarm system. By the end of Meghan's first week of life, Mrs. McGuinness, having learned to pass a feeding tube, had begun to take on the responsibility of feeding her daughter, at least in those early days, when oral feedings of Meghan were still possible.

It was the apparent good news about her daughter's brain that dominated most of my early conversations with Mrs. McGuinness. Every day on rounds, I'd stop by the baby's bedside and report to the mother the results of the latest tests, telling her the significance of each new abnormality found and explaining what, if anything, could possibly be done to correct it. With news of each new defect, through these daily reports of every new complication, Mrs. McGuinness remained steady. "At least her brain's all right," the mother would sigh at the end of each of our conversations. "That means she'll probably have normal intelligence, right?"

My answer to this question was always the same: an unequivocal "maybe."

It was through these conversation during the first days of Meghan's life that I learned just how much this baby meant to Mrs. McGuinness. She and her husband had been married for six years. They'd wanted a large family, and Mrs. McGuinness had become pregnant for the first time less than six months after the wedding. "It was great, those first months," she told me one morning when Meghan was about two weeks old. "It was like heaven. And then I had the first miscarriage."

That miscarriage had occurred when Mrs. McGuinness was slightly less than four months pregnant. "My doctor said it was just one of those things, nothing to worry about or anything. He told me we should wait a few months, let my body recover from the shock of being pregnant, and then try again. So that's what we did: We waited six months, and then we started trying. We tried and we tried, but nothing happened."

Mrs. McGuinness attempted to conceive again for more than two years before seeking further assistance. Finally, after a visit to her obstetrician had confirmed that nothing—other than her diabetes, which had been under good control—was medically wrong with her, she had been referred to a local fertility expert.

The workup that followed had gone on for months; the tests had been painful, expensive, and torturous. "It wasn't all that bad, though," she explained, shrugging her shoulders. "I would've done anything if it meant I'd be able to have a baby. I wanted one so badly. But all the tests turned out fine; the doctor couldn't find anything wrong. I was getting to the point where I was beginning to accept the fact that I wasn't meant to have a baby. And then, just when I was about out of hope, I turned up pregnant again. Just like that, out of the clear blue. My husband and I figured it was a miracle."

The miracle ended less than four months later when, for the second time, Mrs. McGuinness had a miscarriage. "That was about the lowest point in my life," she told me. "Here I'd just about come to accept the fact that it wasn't going to happen; then suddenly I was pregnant; and then, just as suddenly, I lost the baby again. I got very depressed; I went through a long time when I didn't want to leave the house. I just stayed at home and cried."

Her depression had lasted for over a year, lifting only when she became pregnant for the third time. "I figured this might be my last shot. If I had another miscarriage, I wasn't going to try again. I wanted a baby so badly, but I just couldn't go through the pain anymore."

But this pregnancy didn't end in a miscarriage. The fourth month came and went, and Mrs. McGuinness was still pregnant. "It was wonderful," she recalled. "I felt awful, terrible: I was nauseated from morning to night, I had no energy, my sugar was way out of control, but I felt terrific. I know it sounds crazy," she continued. "You can't possibly understand what I'm talking about unless you've gone through it. That feeling of being pregnant, really pregnant, when you've been trying for so long, has got to be the most wonderful feeling in the world."

She told me about the time she'd spent as an inpatient during the latter part of the pregnancy, the eight weeks during which she'd mostly lain on her back, watching the wild undulations that represented the movements of the fetus inside her. "There was nothing else for me to do. I guarded this baby very closely. I wasn't going to let anything happen to her. That's why I spend so much time here now. I've worked so hard to get her, I'm going to make sure she stays here."

During those early months, I rarely saw Mr. McGuinness. When asked about him, his wife offered a series of excuses: he was very busy at his job; he could only come to see Meghan in the evenings; he himself was under the weather. It didn't take long to figure out that the man simply wasn't all that interested in his daughter. This impression was confirmed by the NICU staff. "He's written the kid off," I heard a nurse say one afternoon. "As far as he's concerned, she's not even his child. The only reason he ever shows up at all is because his wife still has the power to shame him into coming." Another nurse added that Mrs. McGuinness was pretty much on her own: "She's just like a single parent," she said. "If you ask me, that marriage is over."

The medical news continued to be bad. After the initial workup was completed, the baby's respiratory difficulties dominated her life. She could not be weaned from the ventilator: the neonatologists tried again and again to remove the infant from the machine, giving her a chance to breathe on her own; but each time, Meghan would sooner or later simply stop breathing, and turn blue, and her heart rate would drop to dangerously low levels. It took weeks of observation to figure out why this happened, but eventually the cause became clear: these episodes always followed a feeding. An X-ray study confirmed the problem: food from Meghan's stomach returned abnormally into her esophagus and spilled over into her lungs. The infant's lungs were being damaged by the feedings her mother lovingly offered her every three hours.

An operation was performed to repair the condition, but it failed; a second operation was done when the baby was three months old, but it also had little effect on Meghan's worsening symptoms. Finally, the decision was made to surgically place a Hickman catheter, and to provide all the nutrition the infant needed through intravenous solution. And so, from the age of four months on, Meghan McGuinness had received no food by mouth.

But by that point, it was probably already too late: Meghan's lungs had been too severely and irreparably scarred. Because of the infant's continuing dependence on the ventilator, a tracheostomy tube was placed in her neck. For a total of five months, Meghan was completely dependent on the ventilator; when at last her lungs had healed enough to wean her from the machine, she still required continuous oxygen supplementation.

Through all this, I tried to be as encouraging with Mrs. McGuinness as possible. She demanded optimism; she let it be known that she needed to be told that Meghan would ultimately do well. She wanted her daughter to come off the ventilator, to begin feeding again so she'd build up her strength; she wanted surgery done to repair Meghan's heart problem; and most of all, she wanted her daughter to come home, to come and live in the nursery she'd started planning years before, a nursery her husband had constructed in the spare bedroom of their apartment during the happy months before Meghan's birth.

I did what I could: I decided that Mrs. McGuinness was as much my patient as was her daughter, and if she needed me to be optimistic, then it was my job to be as optimistic as possible. So whenever there was another setback in Meghan's progress, whenever a lab test came back showing yet another abnormality, I told the woman that, rather than dwelling on the day-to-day disappointments, it was more important to look at the "Big Picture." I talked about how I fully expected Meghan to turn a corner any day now, how, pretty soon, she was definitely going to overcome her medical problems and begin to get well. I offered the mother everything she needed for a full six months. And then the reality of the situation hit me.

Six months is an important age. At six months, babies begin to get the first inklings that they're independent beings, that they're separate from their parents. Developmentally, by six months, a social smile should be well established; the baby should be able to roll over, and to support himself or herself in a sitting position, at least for a short period of time.

On the day she turned six months, Meghan McGuinness could do none of these things: she did not smile; she did not raise her head off the mattress; she could not roll over or sit up. And although, when she'd been younger, I'd chosen to ignore these deficiencies in order to pacify her mother, attributing her delays to serious illness or to lack of stimulation, once the girl turned six months, I found it impossible to continue to be blind to the truth. So when Meghan reached that important age, I accepted for the first time the fact that even though her brain had appeared normal on the CAT scan performed during her first week of life, there was something seriously wrong with the way that brain functioned. And once I became convinced that the child's cerebral cortex, like the rest of her body, had been seriously damaged during early embryonic life, once I realized that she would never develop past the stage of a one- or two-month old, I knew it would only be a matter of time before hope would be lost, heroic medical care would be limited, and Meghan would die.

Armed with that realization, wittingly or unwittingly, I began to withdraw from the baby and her mother. I spent less time each day standing at the girl's bedside. At around this point, Meghan was transferred from the NICU to the infants' ward, a place I visited only infrequently during my morning rounds, so the lack of my presence didn't seem in any way unnatural. I don't know if Mrs. McGuinness sensed the change in my attitude; I only know that it was another month before the day arrived when she, too, realized that Meghan wasn't going to survive.

•   •   •

Meghan was seven months old then. For the past few days, she'd been having symptoms of an upper respiratory infection: nothing major, just a slight fever, cough, and increase in secretions, a common cold one would expect in a child of that age. But then, at a little after one o'clock on a Thursday afternoon, just after her mother had gone down to the cafeteria to get some lunch, the infant's cardiac monitor went off. Anita, Meghan's nurse, rushed in to find the infant blue and not breathing, her heart rate slowed to a dangerously low thirty beats per minute.

They were on her within a minute. The ward's senior resident, three interns, and a chief resident ran to Meghan's bedside; an ambu-bag was attached to her tracheostomy tube and oxygen was pumped manually into her lungs; medications were administered to get her heart pumping again. She was soon out of danger, but because no underlying cause for this near-arrest could be immediately identified, the infant was transferred to the pediatric ICU, placed back on a ventilator, and again worked up.

Mrs. McGuinness, returning from lunch a few minutes later to find her daughter's place empty, began to wail. Anita came running and, after explaining what had happened during the mother's absence, led the woman up to the ICU.

She took one look at her daughter—again placed on a warming table, again attached to a ventilator, with tubes going into her and monitor lead wires coming off her—she gazed briefly at this hectic scene of nurses and physicians sticking needles into her daughter's arms and legs, attempting to get blood, spinal fluid, and God knew what else out of this tiny, suffering, barely responsive body, and she left. She turned on her heel and walked out of the room, toward the elevator, down the hall, and into my office. "Dr. Marion," she said with tears forming in her eyes as she took a seat, "something has to be done. I can't let this go on."

Having missed the events that occurred on the infants' ward, I was at a loss. After Mrs. McGuinness explained what had happened, I called the ICU to get a progress report. "They think she's got pneumonia," I told the mother when I got off the phone. "They're starting her on antibiotics. It doesn't sound very serious. It looks like she's going to make it."

"Make what?" she asked, tears beginning to roll down her cheeks. "Dr. Marion, Meghan never gets any better; she just gets sicker and sicker each day. She's worse now than she was two months ago. Where is this going to lead?"

I didn't know exactly what she wanted of me at that moment; I didn't know if she expected me to come back with an optimistic line, or to be solicitous and comforting. But I simply told her the truth: "I don't know," I said. "Meghan's a very sick little girl."

"She's suffered enough. She's very sick, and she's not getting any better, and I don't want her to have to suffer anymore. No more ICUs, no more ventilators. Is there any way I can make sure she doesn't have to go through this again?"

I took a breath. I had known we would eventually be having this conversation, over the past month and a half I'd imagined the words we'd say; the events that signal the end of a terminally ill patient's life were beginning to play themselves out. "There's something called a DNR order," I replied slowly. "'DNR' stands for 'Do Not Resuscitate.' If the patient, or in the case of a child, the patient's parents, and the doctors agree that the situation is hopeless, an order can be written that says that, in case of cardiac arrest, nothing should be done."

"That means that if what happened a little while ago happens, Meghan will be allowed to die in peace?" Mrs. McGuinness asked, and, after I nodded, she continued: "That's what I want. That's what I want for my daughter."

I didn't argue. "Do you want to talk this over with your husband? This is a big . . ."

"No," she interrupted, not hesitating for an instant. "I don't need to talk to him about it. What do we have to do?"

"Well, there's a form we have to fill out and sign. You're sure you don't want to wait until tomorrow, after you've had time to think . . . ?"

"No, let's do it right now." she said.

We went up to the ICU and filled out the three-page form necessary before a DNR order can be written. During the ten minutes it took to complete the document, Mrs. McGuinness remained businesslike and calm. At the conclusion, after signing my name on the line that said "Attending Physician," I offered Mrs. McGuinness my pen and showed her where to sign. Without hesitation, she took the pen and wrote out her name. And then, without another word, I walked into the ICU nurses' station, picked up Meghan's massive hospital chart, now containing a seven-month accumulation of doctors' and nurses' notes, vital-sign sheets, and lab reports, and, on a clean "Doctor's Orders" sheet, wrote the following words:

Do Not Resuscitate. In case of cardiac arrest, do not place on a ventilator or give resuscitation medications.

I signed the order and returned to my office. Sitting at my desk late that afternoon, I tried to interpret the day's events. The inevitable, I figured, had at last occurred: Mrs. McGuinness had finally realized the hopelessness of Meghan's situation, as I had the month before; she had realized that going on would be pointless, and had done the only logical thing. That's what I concluded had happened that afternoon. It was another two months before I found that my conclusion was dead wrong.

• • •

So, two months later, on that Monday morning when Meghan still hadn't died, and her mother asked if anything could be done to speed the process along, I figured I understood exactly what she was asking: she wanted this all to finally be over, to have this terrible, horrible period of her life mercifully come to an end.

Upon entering the room that morning, I stood next to Mrs. McGuinness, staring down at the infant, who was still working distressingly hard to get air into her lungs. "I'll do anything you want, as long as it doesn't hurt her more than she's already hurting," I said. "Is there something you have in mind?"

"I don't know," she said, shaking her head. "Just something. . . ."

Before I could respond, I saw the infant's face turn black. Her breathing was still labored, but all the color had gone out of her. Glancing at the cardiac monitor, I watched as her heart tracing nose-dived from two hundred beats per minute to less than eighty.

The episode lasted for only a few seconds, and Meghan recovered again, back to her baseline, but I knew the end was very near. "Mrs. McGuinness, did your husband want to be here when Meghan died?" I asked. She shook her head but said that her mother wanted to be with her. "You'd better call her right now," I quickly replied. "It's going to happen any minute."

The cardiac monitor had been set off by the rapid drop in the girl's heart rate, and the alarm brought Anita running. Mrs. McGuinness went to call her mother, while the nurse and I watched the infant's breathing slow to less than fifteen inspirations a minute. "She's going," I said, and the nurse nodded.

We called Mrs. McGuinness back from the phone. After helping her into a chair next to Meghan's bed, I placed the infant in her arms, while Anita repositioned the oxygen hose and removed the cardiac monitor leads from the baby's chest. The nurse and I stood back and watched.

She died like that, in her mother's arms. Her breathing gradually slowed and then stopped. When five minutes had passed and the infant's chest had not moved, I put my stethoscope over her heart and listened: there was nothing; not a single sound was audible. "She's gone," I said.

The mother began to cry. "My baby, you're finally at peace. For the first time in your life you're finally free," she said. "Oh, Meghan, this is the most unselfish thing I've ever done."

I stayed with her for only a few minutes. It was clear that Mrs. McGuinness wanted to be alone with her daughter, and Anita and I, when we were sure she was comfortable, were happy to offer her privacy. I finished my rounds, thinking about Mrs. McGuinness's words; I just didn't understand what she meant by them.

It took me a while to put it together, but it should have been obvious from the very beginning. I'd been wrong about Mrs. McGuinness; I'd been wrong about what had motivated her to sign the DNR order, and about why she had wanted me to do something to speed Meghan's passing. It was not, as I had naively assumed, because she had come to realize that the child's death was inevitable, that her situation was hopeless, or that allowing her to die was the only logical thing to do. She had done all this out of love, love for a baby she had longed for all her life, love for a child she would never be able to take home from the hospital, love for an infant too sick to even know how much she was loved. It was longing for this infant that had allowed Mrs. McGuinness to endure the hardships of her two miscarriages, and the long, painful fertility workup; it was her desire to bear this child that had comforted her during the long weeks spent flat on her back on the maternity ward at Pelham Parkway Medical Center; it was her love for Meghan that had caused her to put the needs of this sick, malformed infant ahead of those of her husband, and had, most probably, cost her her marriage.

And in the end, it was that love that had caused Mrs. McGuinness to realize that, regardless of how much she needed this infant, no matter how much the child meant to her, she had to put Meghan's needs before her own. She had come to understand that forcing Meghan to endure the pain and suffering any longer was mere self-ishness. And so, it was because of her love for Meghan that Mrs. McGuinness allowed her child to die in peace, an act as selfless and as courageous as any performed by one human being for another.

Alex Goes
for a Walk

• • •

*T*HE TRIP WAS AS CAREFULLY PLANNED as a NASA space walk.
Days of preparation had preceded the events that were scheduled to
unfold that morning. A team consisting of Maryanne Holmes, who
was an intensive care nurse, Dr. Len Sutton, the director of the
pediatric critical care unit, and me, the senior resident assigned to
the unit that month, had rehearsed again and again how we would
handle every possible emergency. A large amount of sophisticated
equipment, including a small, portable ventilator, a rubber ambu-
bag fitted with an appropriate-sized face mask, and a cardiac arrest
box filled with the medications necessary for resuscitation, had been
assembled. And now, the day had finally come, and it was time to
proceed: on this morning, Alex Hernandez would go for a walk.

Alex was a little over four years of age on that day. In some
ways, he was a typical preschooler: he watched a lot of television,
never missing "Sesame Street" or "Mister Rogers," his two favorite
shows; he loved to have books read to him, and had a dozen favorites
that he'd ask to hear over and over again until the reader was tempted
to set them on fire; and he liked to play with his enormous assortment
of toys, each of which he'd carefully lay out across the floor in front
of his crib, as if trying to lay booby traps for the adults who would
inevitably walk through the room while Alex was playing. But there
were a lot of things about Alex that set him apart from almost every

other human being: he lived, and had lived his entire life, in an intensive care unit; he had no family, his parents having abandoned him when he was less than three months old; and, most unusual of all, because of a rare congenital disorder, he had never been able to breathe on his own, and had lived his whole life hooked up by about ten feet of plastic tubing to a large, noisy ventilator, a device that blew oxygen directly into his lungs twenty times a minute, sixty minutes an hour, twenty-four hours a day. And up until a month before this morning, in the four years that Alex had lived in Jonas Bronck Hospital, having oxygen forced into his lungs, he had never left the cramped confines of an intensive care unit.

Alex had been born at Jonas Bronck, the first child of a seventeen-year-old woman and an eighteen-year-old man. His mother's pregnancy had been essentially uncomplicated until five days before delivery, when her membranes, the pliable structures that surround the developing fetus, had ruptured spontaneously. This event, which usually signals the beginning of labor, was followed by absolutely no change in Ms. Hernandez's condition; days passed without a single labor pain or uterine contraction. Finally, after she had developed a fever of 102, the obstetricians, fearing that chorioamnionitis, a serious infection of the contents of the uterus, including the baby, was developing, decided to perform an emergency cesarean section.

At birth, Alex had all the symptoms of an overwhelming infection: he was blue, responded poorly to stimulation, and smelled of a foul odor. The pediatric resident who was called stat to the delivery room performed vigorous resuscitation on the infant. He inserted a plastic endotracheal tube through Alex's mouth and vocal cords and into his trachea, and began forcing oxygen into the baby's lungs via an ambu-bag; then he inserted a catheter into one of Alex's umbilical veins and rapidly pushed a solution of glucose water and sodium chloride into the child's circulation. Slowly, the child's color improved, and his heart rate came up into the normal range. Then, Alex was immediately brought to the neonatal intensive care unit; he was placed on a ventilator, and, to discover the cause of the infection from which he was undoubtedly suffering, a sepsis workup was performed. Specimens of blood, urine, and cerebrospinal fluid were obtained and sent to the lab for cultures. Then, large doses of two different types of antibiotics were pushed through the umbilical vein.

The sepsis workup revealed that Alex's blood was infected with

Group B streptococcus, a bacterium commonly found in the vagina, which can cause serious disease and even death in an infected newborn. Alex was lucky, however; his infection apparently had been caught and treated in time, because he made what appeared to be a rapid recovery. Within days, he was eating well and responding normally to stimulation. In fact, he was better in all ways except one: no matter how hard they tried, the staff of the neonatal intensive care unit just couldn't get Alex to breathe on his own for any extended period of time. They gave him numerous chances to come off the ventilator: he'd be disconnected from the machine and would seem to do well for a while; but then, within an hour, the baby would have a long episode of apnea, or absence of breathing, and would turn blue again. He'd immediately be hooked back up to the ventilator after these episodes and, within a few minutes, would be back to his old self.

This went on day after day for the next few weeks. The neonatologists tried everything: they gave him medications that were known to improve apnea, and they put him on special low ventilator settings that sometimes allow patients with "bad lungs" to be weaned off the machine. But nothing helped. After two months, with Alex gaining weight and developing appropriately, but with these episodes of apnea becoming worse and worse, the neonatologist in charge of the intensive care unit decided it was time to call for help. He requested consultations from just about every subspecialty service at his disposal: pulmonology, cardiology, gastroenterology, and neurology, among others. Specialists swarmed all over Alex, examining every part of him, and a massive workup was performed, including chest X rays and fluoroscopic examinations, to look at the functioning of his diaphragm; a barium swallow, to check for gastroesophageal reflux, an occasional cause of apnea; an electrocardiogram, to rule out aberrations of the heart's rhythm pattern; an electroencephalogram, to search for abnormal brain waves that might signal an underlying seizure disorder; and a CAT scan, to check for structural defects of the brain. What seemed like a vat of blood was taken out of Alex's veins to do numerous lab tests; a second spinal tap was performed; and a Prostigmine test, to rule out the possibility of the neurologic disease, myasthenia gravis, was done.

It took two weeks to complete this workup, and when it was over, the specialists concluded that every one of the tests was completely normal. At that point, a meeting was held in the neonatal intensive care unit's conference room. Seated around the table were all of the specialists, as well as the neonatologist in charge of the unit. Huddled together in one corner of the room, looking very young and frightened, sat Alex's mother and father.

Alex's mother had visited her baby every day during the first two weeks after her discharge from the maternity ward. She had made it her business to be present at his feedings, and although his problem seemed intimidating and the equipment to which he was attached complicated, she attempted to take whatever responsibility for Alex's day-to-day care that she could. But when the baby's respiratory condition failed to improve significantly, her visits became less frequent: soon, she was coming every other day, then twice a week, and finally, at the time of the meeting, she was showing up on the ward only about once a week, and would stay with her baby for less than a half hour.

The neonatologist did most of the talking at the meeting. He patiently explained that, after careful evaluation, the doctors had found that every structure needed for respiration was present in Alex and appeared to be completely intact: the baby's heart, lungs, thorax, and muscles all seemed to work perfectly. The specialists could find nothing wrong with Alex; nothing, that is, except for the fact that whenever he was disconnected from the ventilator, he would stop breathing, turn blue, and if left unaided, would most certainly die. The doctors had concluded, the neonatologist explained to Alex's parents, that for want of any better diagnosis, the child was suffering from a difficult-to-confirm condition called central hypoventilation.

Congenital central hypoventilation is an extremely rare condition. It is also known as Ondine's curse, after the sea nymph Ondine, who, according to the play by Jean Giraudoux, willed the death of her unfaithful lover by cursing him with an affliction that destroyed his ability to breathe spontaneously. At the time of Alex's birth, fewer than ten cases had been reported in the world's medical literature. The disorder is caused by the inability of the brain's respiratory centers in the medulla and the pons to respond to the normal stimuli that induce breathing. Breathing is nothing more than a reflex reaction; it is initiated in response to elevated levels of carbon dioxide in the blood or of acid in the cerebrospinal fluid. Levels of these compounds are constantly monitored by the two respiratory centers.

In normal individuals, this control mechanism is exquisitely sensitive. In Alex, the specialists postulated, for reasons they couldn't explain, the mechanism didn't work at all. Alex didn't breathe, they concluded, because his respiratory centers just didn't do their job.

Alex's parents said nothing during the neonatologist's description of their child's problem. Whether they were overwhelmed by the information he was imparting, or whether they simply didn't understand what he was talking about, will never be known. However, when finally asked if they had any questions, Ms. Hernandez said only, "When will Alex be able to come home?"

The specialists hemmed and hawed. They said that, although anything was possible and there are a great many things that doctors don't know, none of the patients described in the literature had gone home or, for that matter, had survived childhood. The woman nodded and the room grew silent. And then the meeting ended.

•   •   •

That was the last time Alex Hernandez's parents were ever seen at Jonas Bronck Hospital. After two weeks without a visit, the social worker assigned to the neonatal intensive care unit tried to contact the mother; calls were made, letters and telegrams were sent, even the police were involved, but the woman just could not be located. It was as if she and the boy's father had vanished off the face of the earth.

Alex continued to thrive, though. Pretty soon, he was the oldest patient in the intensive care nursery, and since he was normal in every way except one, the nurses became very attached to him. They brought him clothes to wear and toys to play with; they picked him up during their breaks and held him. Over time, the nurses became the infant's surrogate family.

But by five months of age, it was clearly time for Alex to move on. He was beginning to outgrow his bassinet, and the neonatologist, against the protests of the nurses, decided it was time for the boy to be transferred out of this unit that had been designed, after all, exclusively for newborns. So at five months of age, Alex was taken to the hospital's operating room, where a tracheostomy was performed, a procedure necessary for any patient who's going to be spending a prolonged period of time hooked up to a ventilator, but one which would render him unable to speak, turning him into a kind of pediatric Harpo Marx. And then, following a short stay in the recovery room, Alex was moved to what would become his new home, a crib in the pediatric intensive care unit, in which he slept and ate and spent almost all of his childhood.

Some things didn't change after Alex's transfer. He again quickly became a favorite of the nurses, especially of Maryanne Holmes, who was the boy's primary nurse. Maryanne and Alex would spend hours together. The nurse established a routine for the boy: she would awaken Alex at seven o'clock every morning when she came on duty, and would get him washed and dressed; then she'd feed him breakfast and, if she wasn't too busy with other patients, would play with him or read to him for an hour or so; then, she'd put him back in his crib for a morning nap. The boy would be fed lunch after awakening from his nap, and would have his visit with the physical therapist. Alex, whose motor function was normal and who had taken his first tentative step on the floor around his crib at a little over fourteen months of age, had had an exercise regimen prescribed for him; the ventilator tubing allowed him to range about six feet from the bulky machine, and within that small radius, he could bend and stretch and even dance. Alex loved his workout; it was clearly his favorite portion of the day.

After the physical therapist departed, the boy would spend most of the afternoon either watching the color TV the staff of the ICU had bought for him, or playing with Maryanne, the other nurses, and the interns and residents who rotated through the unit. Just about everyone who passed through the ICU got to know Alex, and none of us, no matter how busy with other things, could resist stopping and playing with him for at least a couple of minutes.

Maryanne felt that establishing a daily routine for Alex would make his existence seem more normal; but no matter how much normalcy she attempted to impose on him, there was no denying the fact that life in a pediatric intensive care unit was a strange experience. For one thing, critically ill patients don't usually understand that they're supposed to be sick during the day and get better at night. As a result, the unit's lights were never turned off, and for Alex, a child who hadn't been outdoors, the concept of day and night simply didn't exist. Also, although Alex had seen a lot of children come into the ICU, he'd never been able to establish a relationship with any of them. So, from his crib, he watched many of them get better and leave, and a good number of them get sicker and die. He witnessed more cardiac arrests, more failed attempts at resuscitation, and more tearful farewells than anyone, young or old, has a right to see.

I remember one particular incident that occurred in August of my senior residency year; I was on call, it was about four in the morning, and a three-year-old drowning victim, who had come into the hospital dead and had been miraculously resuscitated in the emergency room earlier in the day, went into cardiac arrest. A Code Blue was announced over the loudspeaker, and within minutes, staff from all over the hospital came flying into the unit. We tried everything to save that boy; we worked on him for nearly two hours. But he had been too far gone from the very beginning; and so, at about 6:00 A.M., we declared him dead.

This patient had been placed in the bed directly adjacent to Alex's crib, and sometime near the beginning of the code, I looked up and saw Alex staring back at me. He was sitting up, watching the activity intently. He had a peculiar look on his face, a look I'd never seen on a child before. I realized later that it was due to his eyes: they were wide open and had a horrified, frightened expression in them. I hadn't thought about it much before then, but at that moment, I realized that Alex knew, and that he always had known, exactly what was happening in that intensive care unit; he understood that this boy, who might have been his friend had things been different for both of them, was dying, had been dying since he had been admitted hours before, and that our attempts to save his life would probably be in vain. He knew this from experience; he had witnessed this same scenario repeatedly in the past and would inevitably witness it again in the future, until he, too, ultimately arrested and couldn't be resuscitated by a team of doctors and nurses. With his condition, there seemed to be little hope that he would ever leave this ICU.

But then, when Alex was a little over three-and-a-half years old, Maryanne decided to try an experiment: she began attempting to teach him how to breathe. She reasoned that since the boy was of at least average intelligence, he could probably be taught the mechanics of moving his chest wall, and if he were able to accomplish this goal, air would inevitably fill his lungs. It was more than just worth a try: it was Alex's only chance of escaping from the ICU.

So she started in January. It didn't go well at first; Alex simply had no idea what was expected of him. It was like teaching someone who had never heard a human voice how to talk. But by March, Alex had begun to catch on. He had most of the principles down pretty well, but there were still some huge problems. Moving his chest wall required all of his attention; he literally could not breathe and chew gum at the same time. Also, he still required, and would always require, ventilator support when he slept. But at least he had learned the basics, and now there was a chance that, with close supervision, he could begin to spend short periods of time away from his ventilator.

Alex's first excursion out of the unit took place near the end of March. Tentatively, and with Dr. Sutton in attendance, Maryanne detached the collar that locked the ventilator tubing to Alex's tracheostomy. The boy, equally tentative, held his nurse's hand as tightly at he could as he took a few steps toward the door of the unit. As he reached that door, the nurse said "Breathe, Alex, breathe," and the boy stopped, forced his chest wall to expand, and then exhaled. Within another few seconds, he was out in the hall, beyond the limits of the ICU for the first time in his life.

Like the Wright brothers' first flight, that trip lasted only for about two minutes. Alex demonstrated that he could breathe when reminded, and even instituted a couple of breaths on his own. Over the next month, he left the ICU a half-dozen times, at one point making it all the way down the hall to the elevator before the nurse brought him back. Only once during those trips did Alex turn blue and need to have oxygen forced into his lungs through an ambu-bag: that was when Maryanne had decided to test what would happen if she didn't remind the boy to breathe. But outside of that one episode, things had gone better than expected; so it had been decided that, on the first warm day of spring, an attempt would be made to take Alex out of the hospital for a walk. And today was that day.

•   •   •

The plan of the trip was simple. We would walk down the hall to the hospital's central corridor, take an elevator down to the ground floor, and walk out the back door of Jonas Bronck onto the grass that ringed the building. We'd stay outside in the backyard for a few minutes, and then repeat the journey back upstairs and into the ICU.

We estimated that the total time away from the unit would be no more than thirty minutes.

I was in charge of ventilation; Len Sutton had drilled into me exactly what I was expected to do after we left the ICU. I carried the red ambu-bag, the compressible rubber balloon fitted at one end with a tracheostomy adapter, which I would use to force air into Alex's lungs if the occasion arose. I was also responsible for the cart that held the battery-operated portable ventilator. Len was in charge of resuscitation: he carried a tackle box filled with drugs, needles, and IV solutions that would be used to save Alex's life if the boy happened to suffer a cardiac arrest between the time we left the unit and the time we returned. And Maryanne, of course, was in charge of Alex. When all was ready, when the equipment was in our hands, after we had made sure all the other patients in the unit were stable and we had signed out to the junior resident, after the other nurses had kissed Alex and wished him a safe trip, Maryanne once again disconnected the ventilator tubing from the boy's trach. And we slowly began to make our way down the hall.

This hall that connected the ICU with the central corridor was old news to Alex; as I've said, he'd been down this way a half-dozen times already. But still, he stopped and gazed with interest at the patients who occupied every room we passed. He'd occasionally breathe on his own during these stops, but most of the time, Maryanne would have to squeeze his hand, a signal they had worked out over the past few weeks, to remind the boy that it was time to once again move his chest cage.

The elevator, which had been summoned and held by one of the nurses in the ICU, was waiting for us when we reached the central corridor. We got inside, the doors closed, and a look of panic immediately crossed Alex's face. When the car began moving, his face contorted into a cry; of course no sound came from his mouth, because his open tracheostomy prevented air from passing through his vocal cords. Maryanne picked him up and hugged him until the doors opened. He had no idea what an elevator was, or what function it served; but he already knew that he didn't like it one bit.

When the elevator doors finally opened, Alex's panicked expression was replaced by a look of amazement. The ground-floor corridor was a swarm of activity; people of all ages, in all conditions, were walking, being wheeled, or being pushed on stretchers, back and forth from emergency room to pharmacy to clinic to exit. The boy was so distracted by the sight of all this hubbub that he forgot to breathe, even with prompting from Maryanne. I noticed he was starting to turn blue around the lips, and I pulled out the ambu-bag, figuring that we were going to have to perform a cardiopulmonary resuscitation right there, right in the central corridor of the hospital, with all these people watching. But then, finally, the nurse stood in front of the boy and shouted "Breathe, Alex, breathe!" directly at him. This snapped him back to attention, because the boy took a deep inspiration, and his color instantly returned to its usual pink.

We made it down the central corridor slowly. Alex just didn't want to move; he stopped and looked at everything. We passed the hospital's coffee shop and he spent a minute watching people eat breakfast; we walked in front of the display window of the gift shop and he looked longingly at the toys. Things I had passed every day of my residency and never given a second thought suddenly seemed to hold incredible fascination. But ultimately, with some encouragement from Len and with Maryanne squeezing his hand every few seconds, we finally made it to the double doors that led to the hospital's backyard.

It was a gorgeous early-spring day, the kind that makes everything, even the Bronx, look good: the sun was out, the air was mild, the grass was green, and everything was blooming. Upon setting foot outside, Alex stopped and broke into a grin from ear to ear. It must have been incredible to him: to look out over so vast a landscape, to see firsthand, for the first time, grass and trees and cars and roads, to see other people hurriedly coming and going, to smell the perfume of the flowers, and to breathe, to fill his lungs on his own without benefit of a ventilator, or an ambu-bag, or any other artificial device, with warm, fresh spring air, must have seemed like heaven to this little boy.

We stayed outside for no more than ten minutes. A small group, composed of interns, residents, and nurses from the pediatric department, as well as passersby who couldn't have possibly understood what was going on, gathered around and cheered as Alex got down on all fours. He touched and smelled and rolled in the grass; he pulled some of it out and tried to eat it, but almost immediately spit it out, quickly deciding that it didn't compare with the exquisite hospital cuisine to which he had grown accustomed. He walked over to a car parked illegally nearby and, seemingly awestruck, touched its fender with the fingers of both hands; he had seen cars many times on his television, but had never been so close to one before. Watching him, it seemed to us as if Alex were an astronaut who, having left the only world he had ever known, had traveled to a distant galaxy of which he had no information or experience. All during Alex's explorations through the hospital's backyard, Maryanne kept on top of him, reminding him almost constantly to breathe. The boy complied every time; not once did he turn blue or require any kind of assistance from either Len Sutton or me.

When he was told it was time to go back in, Alex was obviously sad, but he didn't cry. Maryanne, who was a pushover when Alex had his sad face on, picked the boy up in her arms and hugged him, promising that this definitely wouldn't be his last trip outside. So, with Maryanne carrying Alex, and with Len Sutton and me lugging all the expensive, intimidating, but, thankfully, unused equipment, we headed back in through the hospital's rear entrance, down the corridor, up the elevator, and, without incident, back to the safe but suddenly boring confines of the pediatric ICU. The nurse placed Alex back in his crib and hooked the ventilator tubing back up to his trach. Within minutes, the little boy fell into a deep, sound sleep,

•   •   •

A couple of years ago, while doing a consultation at University Hospital, I ran into Ron Angelman, a private practitioner, as he did his daily hospital rounds. Ron and I were old friends: we had been residents together at Jonas Bronck. Upon seeing me now, he immediately put down the chart in which he had been writing and reached into his briefcase. "You're never going to believe this, Bob," he said excitedly as he pulled out and handed me a small book made of construction paper.

The cover of the book had crude crayon drawings that apparently represented birds. The book's title, written out with the same crayon in somewhat shaky handwriting, bore this out: it was called *Birds*, and the author and illustrator was listed as Alex Holmes. "What do you think of that?" Ron asked as I was taking it in.

The book was eight pages long. As I slowly turned the homemade leaves, I found myself looking at page after page of brightly colored, painstakingly drawn pictures of baby birds and their mothers; at the bottom of each page was a short caption, typed, I assumed by a teacher, explaining what the picture was about. One page showed a small and a large bird, each with a red breast; the smaller bird had a gray squiggly line extending from its face. The caption read, "Baby Robin likes to eat worms, so its mommy flies far away from home to catch them." On another page, a baby bluebird sat in its nest, while the mother flew through the air above it. "I don't know," I answered finally in response to Ron's question. "It looks like maybe a six- or seven-year-old."

"Seven years old is correct," he replied. "Is that all? Don't you recognize the author's name?" I shook my head, and Ron, a little disappointed, suggested I turn back to the first page again.

I did, and found the book's typewritten dedication. It read: "Dedicated to my mother, Maryanne Holmes." And then it hit me. This document was the work of Alex Hernandez Holmes.

What had happened to Alex was a phenomenal story. After our excursion to the backyard of Jonas Bronck Hospital on that warm spring day, Maryanne had taken Alex on many other trips. At first tentatively, for short periods of time and always accompanied by Len Sutton, Maryanne and Alex ventured off the hospital grounds, going on trips to the Botanical Garden, to the Bronx Zoo, to an afternoon game between the Yankees and the Cleveland Indians at the Stadium, and finally, to a barbecue at Maryanne's house in New Rochelle. From the very beginning, Alex did wonderfully. As that summer and fall passed, he became better and better at breathing on his own, and was able to perform small tasks like feeding himself and brushing his teeth without having to be reminded to move his chest wall. Once he'd demonstrated that he could breathe without prompting, Maryanne began the next step: she started to plug off Alex's tracheostomy for short periods of time. Suddenly, the boy could talk. His voice was soft and squeaky at first, and he was somewhat embarrassed to use it, but that changed very quickly; pretty soon, the ICU nurses had to beg him to pipe down, so they could have some peace and quiet. By the time of the first snowfall that winter, breathing and talking had become almost second nature to the boy.

Then Maryanne had taken the final step. She instituted the plan that had been in the back of her mind since the boy had first learned how to breathe on his own: she began the process of adopting Alex.

She and her husband did everything necessary: they hired a lawyer; got documentation from Len Sutton and many of the other doctors who had cared for Alex during his years at Jonas Bronck; produced contracts with surgical supply companies that would provide them with the equipment necessary to care for Alex as he had been cared for in the ICU. Within six months, a relatively short time for an adoption case as complex as this, the Holmeses were awarded custody of Alex. And after a gala party in the ICU almost a year to the day after he had stepped out through the back door of Jonas Bronck Hospital for the first time, Alex left by the front door for good.

I had not seen him since his discharge from the hospital over two years before. Ron explained that he had met Alex and Maryanne, who had given up her job, on the street a few days before. "How does he look?" I asked.

"He's a normal kid," Ron replied. "He's still got the trach, of course, but if you didn't know what was wrong with him, you'd pass him by as if he were any other kid."

"And he goes to school?" I asked.

"Yup," Ron replied, "he's in a regular second-grade class. Mary-anne told me he's doing pretty well. It's amazing, isn't it?"

It truly was amazing. That a boy who didn't know how to breathe could learn to do so, that he could live in an intensive care unit for five years, without a family, a voice, or an apparent chance of ever escaping, and finally escape, that he could watch hundreds of children die over the course of those five years and less than two years later still be able to produce a work as simple and innocent as _Birds_, was truly remarkable.